The DeMilles

AN AMERICAN FAMILY

The DeMilles

AN AMERICAN FAMILY

BY
Anne Edwards

PHOTOGRAPHIC EDITOR
Louise Kerz

HARRY N. ABRAMS, INC., *Publishers*, NEW YORK

Frontispiece: One of the walls of Karnak, the city of
Pharaoh Rameses II, built by Cecil B. DeMille for *The
Ten Commandments* (1923)

Editor: Phyllis Freeman
Designer: Dirk Luykx
Abrams Photo Editor: John K. Crowley

Library of Congress Cataloging-in-Publication Data
Edwards, Anne.
    The DeMilles, an American family.
    Bibliography: p. 234
    Includes index.
    1. DeMille family. 2. George family. 3. DeMille,
Cecil B. (Cecil Blount), 1881–1959—Family. 4. DeMille,
Agnes—Family. 5. United States—Biography.
6. Performing arts—United States—Biography.
7. Politicians—United States—Biography. I. Title.
CT274.D46E29 1988   929′. 2′0973   88-3455
ISBN 0-8109-1144-2

A Times Mirror Company

Printed and bound in Japan

CONTENTS

The Lost City of Pharaoh DeMille

1985

*The rocks from those chambers were carted away to the desert and
the laborers were given no opportunity to speak of their work.
I knew what had happened to the workmen. I heard their silence....
Not even the Pharaohs knew the burial place of other Pharaohs....*

—NORMAN MAILER, *Ancient Evenings*

The dig at Guadalupe, California, to retrieve the lost city of Pharaoh DeMille

THE LATE AFTERNOON SUN CAST LONG, UNDULATING SHADOWS
on the pyramidal sand dunes that rimmed Guadalupe to the west, protecting the ancient town from the open sea. Three men knelt and crawled in the sand amidst a pile
of debris—bits of plaster and concrete. For several hours they had feverishly but
cautiously dug below the surface with bare hands and small trowels, hoping for a sign
of their quarry. They had come to the wilderness of the Guadalupe Dunes on the
northern California coastline in the summer of 1985 to locate the lost city of Pharaoh
DeMille. The only sounds were the shifting and falling of the sand and the even,
buzzard-like hum of a car motor. A young woman, a friend of one of the men, sat in
the car waiting. In June, the heat of the desert could be escaped only inside an air-
conditioned vehicle.

After many months of research, the men were certain that this was the exact
site where DeMille's Karnak, the lost city, would be found. Suddenly, one of them
sat back on his haunches, smiling widely and triumphantly. The men exchanged excited words. Then, whatever they had found they worked to rebury. A marker was
put up on the site. When they had finished, they rose to their feet and walked the
distance to their car to return to Los Angeles, their home base. On the trip back, they
passed through the town of Guadalupe, one of the oldest settlements on the Pacific
coastline, its jumbled streets and houses hidden from the eyes of seaborne invaders

The tent city erected
in Guadalupe to house
the cast, crew, and
animals for the
production

by the dunes, and the brooding, dangerous Sierra Madre Mountains bulwarking the residents to the east. The land between now forms the irrigated, fertile Santa Maria Valley, where much of California's lettuce is grown. In 1923, the town had housed most of the field hands for the surrounding beet fields that contributed the raw material for over 50,000,000 pounds of sugar refined in the nearby sprawling, red-brick plant of the Union Sugar Company. That long-ago summer, the great scenes of the Exodus and the crossing of the Red Sea were shot in the Guadalupe Dunes by the famous film director Cecil B. DeMille, for his silent-screen version of *The Ten Commandments*.

A few old-timers could vividly recall the startling arrival on May 21, 1923, of a caravan of four large, open trailer trucks carrying twenty-one majestic concrete sphinxes, weighing five tons each. These mammoth replicas were unloaded and arranged in two great arcs before the massive scaffolding that was to become a reconstruction of the gates of Pharaoh's city. There had been some anxious moments for the DeMille crew, DeMille himself remembered, en route from Hollywood to Guadalupe, when the great plaster sphinxes, twenty-five feet high, "were ignominiously halted by a bridge too low for them to pass under. No one lost his head, though, except the sphinxes, who were decapitated [the sphinxes were made in two parts] long enough to pass under the bridge and then had their heads restored for the remainder of their progress."

In six weeks, local workers hired by DeMille to assist his own staff raised a huge tent city on the sand flats near the dunes; it was to house 2,500 people and 3,000 animals, all brought from Los Angeles to recreate Pharaoh's city. Because of Guadalupe's curious ethnic mix—Japanese, Chinese, Filipinos, Mexicans, a few Swiss, and a sprinkling of native-born whites—only a few of its residents were employed as extras. DeMille demanded realism for his spectacles and for this particular one, 250 of Los Angeles's population of Orthodox Jewry had been imported, because he believed "that, both in appearance and in their deep feeling of the significance of

Cecil B. DeMille
directing some of
the cast of 2,500
people imported
from Los Angeles
for *The Ten
Commandments*

8

the Exodus, they would give the best possible performance as the Children of Israel." However, on their first day, the commissary department served ham (forbidden to Orthodox Jews) for dinner. DeMille "sent posthaste to Los Angeles [164 miles southeast of Guadalupe] for people competent to set up a strictly kosher kitchen."

Not only did DeMille bring in Orthodox Jews, he built Karnak, the city of Rameses II (from which Moses led the Children of Israel out of bondage), to meet the configurations written by scholars of the scriptures. The city gate and side walls were 750 feet in length and 109 feet high, with the walls decorated in bas-reliefs showing the huge figures of chariot drivers and rearing horses. Jet black colossi of the Pharaoh, thirty-five feet high, composed of clay and plaster on metal frames, and weighing nearly thirty tons each, guarded the gate, two on either side. DeMille called the film "the mightiest of all Spectacles." Certainly the people of Guadalupe had never seen anything like it.

Ernie Righetti was one of the few locals DeMille used as an extra. "They gave us these A-Rab costumes to put on," he recalled. "Next day, they gave us these Hebrew costumes, and told us to run out into the Dunes. Who knows why we were running? The A-Rabs was after us.... I got $18 a day for being out there, plus $2 a day for each of the five horses I let them use in the movie. That was the biggest pay I ever got." DeMille had Hellman Bank's famous Armored Money Car ("It gives bandit-proof protection to funds in transit...") drive up from Los Angeles once a week to pay his people, as the local bank could not handle the cashing of 2,500 payroll checks.

DeMille had contracted to make *The Ten Commandments*, his first Bible film, for Paramount Pictures. As the bills from Guadalupe arrived and piled up, the studio's executives began to panic. By the time the film was only half finished, the studio had spent over $1,000,000. On the start of the fifth week of shooting, one of Paramount's top executives, Elek J. Ludvigh, arrived in Guadalupe and stormed into DeMille's office waving a piece of paper, "an invoice for a pair of stallions we had obtained to draw Pharaoh's chariot. They were magnificent, shining black creatures bought in Kansas City for $2,500.

"'Are you trying to ruin us?' Ludvigh shouted. '...Your contract is canceled! You're finished!'

"That was it," DeMille admitted. "He exercised the 30-day notice clause. I was fired. I went out and in the next 24 hours managed to raise $1,000,000. I was able to have $500,000 pledged to me personally [from A. P. Giannini, President of the Bank of America], two friends...[Joseph M. Schenk and Jules Brulatour] each pledged $250,000. I placed the check for $1,000,000 on the desk of the Paramount executive.

"'There's your money,' I said. 'The picture is mine.'"

Ludvigh hurriedly called Adolph Zukor, Paramount's president, in New York. "Take the money," Zukor advised. But just then Frank Garbutt, a Paramount board member, interposed quietly: "Don't sell what you haven't seen."

DeMille's money was refused, and Paramount agreed to add another $400,000 ("not a penny more") to the budget. By the time the last location shot was made, that figure had been reached.*[1] DeMille felt sure that this—his forty-fifth film—was the greatest he had ever made. But until he had the footage cut and edited, he knew convincing Zukor of the picture's worth would not be easy. What then was he to do about the cost of a full exodus of staff and sets and equipment from Guadalupe? Roy Pomeroy, head of DeMille's special-effects department and the man who had "parted" the Red Sea for the second time in history (actually a visual effect created by superimposing two scenes), suggested that rather than transport the massive set pieces back to Hollywood, where they would have difficulty and additional expense in storing them, the crew could bury everything—the walls, the gates, the colossuses, the sphinxes—beneath the sands of the Guadalupe Dunes. The idea greatly appealed to DeMille's sense of humor.

"If, a thousand years from now, archaeologists happen to dig beneath the sands of Guadalupe," he wrote, "I hope that they will not rush into print with the amazing news that Egyptian civilization, far from being confined to the valley of the Nile, extended all the way to the Pacific Coast of North America."

The outdoor work on *The Ten Commandments* had bronzed and hardened DeMille. He was forty-two years old and in the prime of his life. Women of every age fell under his spell. In Los Angeles, his wife, Constance, waited dutifully for his return. His fourteen-year-old daughter, Cecilia, had come to Guadalupe at his command to watch the father she idolized preside over his city of the Pharaoh. Working with him on the film was his current passion, his scriptwriter, Jeanie Macpherson, and his past love, actress Julia Faye, who portrayed Pharaoh's wife.

He rose at dawn on the last day. The tents had been dismantled, the performers and animals had made a mass exodus. Cecil B. DeMille was left with his immediate staff and the crew who were to bury his city. The winds had risen the night before, and the sand had shifted and covered the wounds made by the tent stakes. DeMille stood at the gates between the giant black statues of the Pharaoh, dressed in the leather puttees that were his standard garb, and directed the demolition and burial. The sphinxes were once again decapitated, the wall broken in large pieces. All the parts were buried as bandits had been years before, in graves dug a few feet from where they stood.

It took almost a full day to complete the task. By nightfall, C. B. (as he was often called) and his company were gone and the city of the Pharaoh was covered with sand. No one in Guadalupe took much notice of this incident. Most of the residents (population 1,130 in 1923) assumed that the city had disappeared the way it had arrived, by trucks that would transport it in pieces back to Hollywood via State Highway 1.

In sixty years, nothing much had changed in Guadalupe (population now 3,629). Folks farmed in the valley. Hard times came and never really went away. Sycamores with mottled gray trunks grew along creek beds that dried up in the summer. And the wind whistled around the dunes, constantly shifting the sand.

Then early one morning in June 1983, three film historians, Peter L. Brosnan, Bruce Cardozo, and Richard Eberhardt, in search of some signs of the buried city of the Pharaoh arrived in Guadalupe. With local rancher Joe Gray as their pessimistic guide, they found their way to the original site. "I don't think you boys will find anything," he warned. "Forty years ago there was still a lot of statues and stuff out

[1] An asterisk (*) indicates that further information may be found in the notes, starting on p. 227.

there. Now it's just scraps of concrete and plaster." Finally he announced, "Well, this is it."

"We stood atop a large mound," Brosnan recalled, "what archaeologists call a 'tell,' about ten feet high and sprawling across several acres of the windblown landscape. The ground around us was littered with shattered pieces of plaster and concrete, and tantalizing pieces of buried statuary protruded from the sand every few feet.... After a few hours of excited poking around... with whisk brooms and nervous hands, we uncovered the sculpted head of a horse six feet wide and in the bas-relief style of ancient Egypt. It was the chariot-drawn horse we had seen in old photos [on the city wall, of the set of the 1923 version of *The Ten Commandments*]. Old C. B. *had* buried the *whole set!*"

The three men did not take the head but reburied it in the sand. Their plan was to return to Los Angeles and raise $50,000 to excavate DeMille's entire set.* They were as obsessed with the DeMille legend as they would have been with Pharaoh's city. C. B. after all had been the King of Kings of Hollywood. They were not sure what they expected of Karnak—perhaps a link to the Godly One, a chance to walk His way once, holding in their hands the glories that His astonishing talents and imagination had created. And it was not difficult to come to believe that in reconstructing Karnak, the city of Pharaoh Rameses II, C. B. began to think of himself in such holy terms. For *The Ten Commandments* was a turning point in his life, vaulting him in a few years' time into a position as pharaoh of the Hollywood epic.

Film audiences, film buffs, the men and women who worked with C. B., his family, his women—all regarded him with awe. He represented a powerful America, undauntable, secure in a belief that what he did was right and sound. He was the monarch of American films, the de facto head of his family—and what a family the DeMilles were. As an American royal dynasty, they ranked with such regal names as Roosevelt and Kennedy, despite the fact that none of their members had ever occupied, or hoped to occupy, the White House.

"August 12 my little boy Cecil was born," the well-known playwright and actor Henry C. DeMille starkly recorded in his diary on the day of his second son's birth.

"But I cannot feel slighted," C. B. later wrote. "Eight words, after all, are a longer history than most of the world's population has had or will have. It is good for the soul to try to imagine how many human beings have lived on this world, and then to subtract one from that number, and see how much difference it makes. Very little; and yet very much, for each one is a link in a chain. If any one who has ever lived had not lived, the whole history of the world might be different, for who knows where the chain may go, what others it may cross, or where a broken link might have led?"

This was probably true either of a pharaoh or an ordinary man. Certainly it is difficult to imagine the American film without Cecil B. DeMille or the American dance minus Agnes deMille, his niece.[2] Let us then go on to the story of a family that became a dynasty and of one member who might not have been perceived as a pharaoh, had one link in the chain of DeMilles been broken.

[2]Cecil and his brother, William, diverged on the spelling of their surname, William preferring the lowercase form "deMille," and Cecil choosing the uppercase "DeMille." Their children retained the respective forms. In quoted material the authors' own preferences have been followed.

DeMille Family Tree

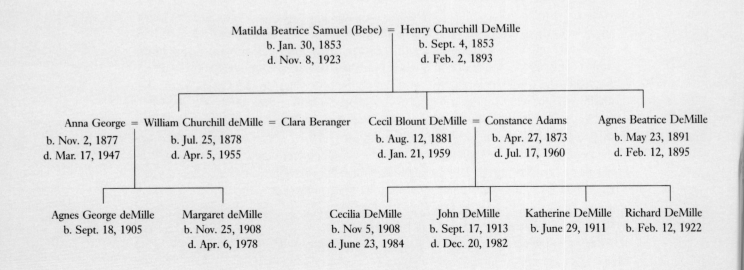

Matilda Beatrice Samuel (Bebe) = Henry Churchill DeMille
b. Jan. 30, 1853   b. Sept. 4, 1853
d. Nov. 8, 1923   d. Feb. 2, 1893

Anna George = William Churchill deMille = Clara Beranger   Cecil Blount DeMille = Constance Adams   Agnes Beatrice DeMille

b. Nov. 2, 1877   b. Jul. 25, 1878   b. Aug. 12, 1881   b. Apr. 27, 1873   b. May 23, 1891
d. Mar. 17, 1947   d. Apr. 5, 1955   d. Jan. 21, 1959   d. Jul. 17, 1960   d. Feb. 12, 1895

Agnes George deMille   Margaret deMille   Cecilia DeMille   John DeMille   Katherine DeMille   Richard DeMille
b. Sept. 18, 1905   b. Nov. 25, 1908   b. Nov 5, 1908   b. Sept. 17, 1913   b. June 29, 1911   b. Feb. 12, 1922
   d. Apr. 6, 1978   d. June 23, 1984   d. Dec. 20, 1982

A Dynasty Begins

1853–1893

If they had not been what they were, I would not be what I am.

—*The Autobiography of Cecil B. DeMille*

AGNES DeMILLE WILL TURN HER PATRICIAN PROFILE TOWARDS you and comment disdainfully, "I was the only one of the DeMilles to inherit the Samuel nose." Her uncle, Cecil, whenever a question of his ancestry was raised, would stress his paternal roots, not the Jewish genes that came to him via his maternal side. In his autobiography, he devoted nine pages to various DeMilles, and two lines—"A hundred and fifty years ago, one of my great-great-grandfathers [Ralph Samuel] was a small merchant in Liverpool, England"—to the ancestry of his mother, Matilda Samuel.

Ralph Samuel was born in Strelitz (now a part of West Germany) in 1738 and settled in 1779 in Liverpool, where he became a successful jewelry merchant. There, on January 30, 1853, Ralph's great-granddaughter, Matilda, was born to Cecilia Wolff and Sylvester Samuel, of 16 Bedford Street North.* In 1856, the Samuels moved to Birkenhead, in the county of Chester. Sylvester had decided to strike out on his own as a manufacturer of watches.

The Samuel family was marked by its aristocratic bearing, intelligence, and ambition, and Matilda was no exception. Tillie, as she was called as a young woman, came to New York from Birkenhead with her parents, her sister, Jennie, and their younger brother (Mark Wolff, born 1858) in 1871, immediately following the latter's *bar mitzvah.* Sylvester's watch business had not proved successful, and he was now a buyer for his family's retail stores in England. The Samuels were comfortably off and

13

settled in an affluent and mostly Jewish section of Brooklyn, where their English accents gave them added social distinction. Tillie possessed an exotic beauty, "slim, bewitching...dark-eyed, vivacious, different somehow from all the American girls...." This uniqueness had been produced by the Sephardic Jewish background of Tillie's maternal heritage. Olive-skinned, almond-eyed, her thick raven hair drawn tightly back from her high forehead to straighten its curl, her full bosom accented by her wasp-waisted frocks (she was always in high style), and with her mellifluous voice, the teen-aged English girl was a bit of a sensation in Brooklyn. Intent that her older daughter would not marry too young, Cecilia Samuel encouraged the girl in her cultural interests. Tillie joined the Philokalia Musical and Literary Association of Brooklyn and quickly displayed a distinct talent for recitation and acting.

On the evening of November 4, 1872, the association presented an "entertainment" which included her reading of the poem "The Vital Spark" and an Irish comedy in which she played the flirtatious and frolicsome heroine, complete with Irish dialect. In the audience that evening was a young, fair-skinned, effete-looking, wire-thin Southerner with burnished red hair, myopic hazel eyes, and an aristocratic and aquiline nose—perhaps not handsome, but a man with a most distinctive appearance. In the social hour that followed the performance, he introduced himself to "Miss Tillie" as Henry Churchill DeMille, a student at nearby Columbia College. After he asked her for her full name, he informed her he would instead call her "Beatrice" because, like Dante's Beatrice, she represented his vision of the ideal woman.

Henry possessed a gentle smile and the cultivated speech of a Southern gentleman—as mesmerizing to the newly christened Beatrice as her accent was to him. He had a penchant for quoting poetry and he sent her some of his own romantic verses. He asked to call on her, but the Samuels had strong objections to their daughter's associating with a young man not of her religion. To circumvent this, Henry joined the Philokalia Musical and Literary Association, appropriately named, as "philokalia" means "love of beauty." From the start, the young couple knew her family would never approve, but with their growing fondness for each other this only added to the romantic aura of their relationship.

When Henry's family heard about his Beatrice, they shared the Samuels' lack of enthusiasm about the match. However, Mrs. DeMill (her son added an *e* to the family name) felt her son's desire to go on the stage a greater threat to his future than marriage to a Jewess. They, therefore, accepted Beatrice with the proviso that Henry did agree to put aside his theatrical aspirations and to wait a year before he and Beatrice married. That same year, 1875, he graduated from Columbia and accepted a teaching position at Brooklyn's Lockwood Academy, a boys' college-preparatory school, which he had himself attended. There was reason behind this compromise: Beatrice had recently been hired by Lockwood as an elocution teacher. Every day they would meet and together walk the two miles back and forth from the academy to Beatrice's home.

Against her parents' objections and without their attendance, Matilda Beatrice Samuel was married to Henry C. DeMille on July 1, 1876, at St. Luke's Church, Brooklyn. The Samuels' refusal to reconcile themselves to their daughter's new religious affiliation only succeeded in driving Beatrice further away from them and Judaism. (Her son Cecil always spoke of "my English mother who is an Episcopalian.") The newlyweds traveled south to Washington, North Carolina, to spend their honeymoon with Henry's family.

When they returned, New York, along with the rest of the country, was taken with presidential election fever. Rutherford Hayes barely won. The hundredth anniversary of American independence was being celebrated with a Centennial Exposition in Philadelphia. Out West, Custer had made his "last stand" at Little Big Horn. The New York press played up the most horrifying crimes in their unrestrained newspaper coverage. Stories such as "The Human Fiend...A Thirst for Blood" related a lurid tale of murder and dismemberment. Central Park was described as "a ruffians' refuge where ladies, children and the unprotected generally are at the mercy of villains." Broadway between Madison Square and Forty-second Street (called the Rialto) was lined with theatres, and there was a roof-garden casino for light opera. Cars were still horse-drawn, but an elevated railway line was being built on Third Avenue.

Beatrice would have preferred to have lived in Manhattan, but instead the DeMilles rented two rooms on Madison Street, near Tompkins Avenue, in Brooklyn, and lived cautiously on their modest salaries as teachers at Lockwood. For Beatrice, the most exciting event of fall 1876 was the visit of Lord Randolph and Lady Churchill. She was the former Jeanette Jerome from Brooklyn, and the Samuels had known the family—and Jennie and Beatrice were approximately the same age. The two young women, whose lives had taken dramatic turns from their roots, appear to have met once during the Churchills' stay in New York, although exactly where or when is unknown. However, Beatrice would refer from time to time to such an encounter. Jennie Jerome's new stature as Lady Churchill greatly impressed her. Just how much, we will soon see.

Some considered C. B. to be "positively Chinese" in his ancestral worship of his DeMille antecedents. He called it "a decent respect for those who begat me." He liked to talk about the genealogy of the DeMilles,* and collect information, relics, and mementos that came down from them. He had even had the tombstone of one Connecticut forebear—Joseph DeMill, who had died in 1800—shipped to California and placed at the foot of a tree on his ranch retreat. Above it he hung a bronze crucifix. He came often to sit before it "in the late afternoon, when the sun [was] slanting through the leaves, falling upon the cross and stone, and think about what they represent[ed], mortality and immortality."

The family can trace its roots back to around the year 1280, when one Gillis deMil was born in Flanders. Numbered among DeMille ancestors is the fifteenth-century Abbot of Euckhout, Anthony deMil; his seventeenth-century cousin Adam, who killed his drunken stepfather with two chops of an ax;* and another Anthony deMil, a baker and member of the Dutch Reformed Church, who set sail in 1658 from Amsterdam to New Amsterdam in the vessel *The Gilded Beaver* along with his wife, Elisabeth (née von der Liphorst), and their two small daughters.* Anthony prospered as a baker and was vitally involved in the political life of the Dutch colony. In 1673, he became the chief law enforcement officer but was removed two years later by the English, who were then in power, and imprisoned for a number of years for refusing to pledge allegiance to the English crown.

Anthony's son Peter was the first of the family to have been born in America.

He moved to Stamford, Connecticut, after his father's death, became a miller and flour merchant and an Episcopalian, the last time a DeMille was to change his religion.

C. B.'s father, Henry Churchill DeMille, was born on September 4, 1853, the oldest child of William Edward DeMill and Margaret Mutter Blount Hoyt.* Washington, North Carolina, where William was mayor and a pillar of St. Peter's Episcopal Church, was situated just off the Atlantic seacoast at the mouth of Pamlico Sound in the northeast corner of the state.

Like most people in Beaufort County, William, a successful merchant, owned no slaves. He could not exactly be said to be an abolitionist, but he had strong reservations about one man's right to own another and was known to have harbored more than one runaway slave.

Henry's antebellum youth was made memorable by his "visits to his father's steamer, *Pamlico*, when it was in port; family dinners at Aunt Betsy Blount's, a mile from town; gathering hickory nuts on a hill opposite their house; and Sunday school, always preceded by Sunday morning breakfast, with plenty of fresh butter, down at [his maternal] Grandmother Hoyt's." He was a dreamer with a fanciful mind. He would sit by the water and watch the boats load and unload, and curl up by a tree and make up romantic stories about seafaring men and the women they had loved and left behind.

Politically, the people of North Carolina were loyal to Southern institutions, but they were more eminently conservative and more attached to the Union of the States than were other citizens below the Mason-Dixon Line. North Carolina was the last state to secede from the Union, and "went out at last more from a sense of duty to her sisters and the sympathies of neighborhood and blood than from a deliberate conviction that it was a good policy to do so." Men in some counties bordering Tennessee went off to the Union side. Others hid out and bushwhacked for a living. But Beaufort County was prepared to fight with the South, and William with it, joining the First North Carolina Confederate Regiment under General Daniel Harvey Hill, on May 27, 1861, just one week after North Carolina took her stand with the Confederacy.

Suddenly, the DeMill family was jolted from its "placid round of safe, happy home life." Fearing that Washington's position on a waterway left it open to attack, William moved his wife and three children with him to Greenville, North Carolina, where he was made Post Commissary in General Hill's division. Shortly thereafter, he followed General Hill into the Battle of Bethel. The burden of caring for her family in the midst of a war fell on his wife, Margaret, still in her early twenties. In October 1863, William was transferred to Kinston, North Carolina, as commissary to General James Green Martin's brigade, General R. F. Hoke's division.* Mrs. DeMill, pregnant at the time, was left alone with her children in Greenville,* as Washington, North Carolina, had been taken by the Union Army.

Henry learned "to knit his own socks and plait the straw for his hats." According to the diary he kept, "the only available meat" was unpalatable pork fat. Mrs. DeMill, desperate to keep her children nourished, offered them "one cent for every slice they would eat." By the spring of 1864, when the Confederates had recaptured Washington, North Carolina, Henry had earned eleven dollars in this fashion.

A Dynasty Begins

William DeMill was captured by a detachment of Federal Cavalry when he returned to Greenville on command in February 1865. General Joseph E. ("Old Joe") Johnston surrendered to General Sherman at Durham Station on April 14, but William remained a prisoner of war until August. When he returned to Washington, his home had been half-burned by Union soldiers and his family was living with the Blounts. With no money, he set to work rebuilding his house as best he could. That year his children "went barefoot to save socks and shoe leather."

Yet for Henry, this was "a very happy year of my life." Henry had appeared in an amateur production of a farce called *Nan the Good for Nothing* and had decided that he would not only act in the theatre, he would one day write his own plays. He was sent to Brooklyn, New York, to attend the Adelphi Academy, conducted by a family friend, John Lockwood (who eventually called it Lockwood Academy), in 1867. Lockwood encouraged the youngster's literary aspirations, and a year later, at fifteen, Henry wrote his first play, *Alone in the Pirate's Lair* (subtitled *The Effects of a Friday's Sail*), and a story, "The Land of Aclen." Henry could not be said to display great talent. He had a certain narrative drive and a predilection for overwrought melodrama that would stigmatize all his future commercial work.

Having refused to take advantage of the bankruptcy law, William determined to repay his creditors, which made Henry's chances of ever attending college slim. However, the Adelphi Academy stressed "thorough welding of religion and learning" and John Lockwood helped the young man obtain a grant or $175 to attend Columbia College from the Society of New York for the Promotion of Religion through Learning.* Acting remained his first love, but when he asked his mother how she felt about his pursuing a career in the theatre, she had replied, "It would break my heart." Nonetheless, he joined the drama society in his freshman year at Columbia. The love of theatre—that would shortly bind him and his Beatrice forever—had solidly taken root.

Her honeymoon stay with her in-laws had prepared Beatrice for the difficult times before her. The DeMills had accepted her, but not exactly with open arms. She had seen how attached Mrs. DeMill and Henry were, and how eager her husband was to please his mother. Beatrice believed that Henry had great writing talent, and that at least a comfortable living could be made for them if he persevered. Mrs. DeMill, on the other hand, thought her son would have a more rewarding life if he became a priest of the Episcopal Church. For the next nine years of his life, Henry was to be torn between two women—his mother and his wife—and two dreams—to become a successful playwright and to be ordained. His wife turned out to have the greater influence.

The kind of poverty that the DeMills had suffered during and directly after the war was foreign to Beatrice. Her family had always believed in buying the best and living in a good environment, and she had been taught from childhood that the primary motivation in life should be the desire to better oneself—intellectually and financially. The idea of living humbly as a cleric's wife simply held no attraction for her. So while Henry, as a layman, read sermons by his favorite clergyman, Charles Kingsley, on Sundays at St. Stephen's Church, Brooklyn, and diligently studied theology and church history, Beatrice encouraged and prodded him to continue writing.

Henry C. DeMille with his class at Columbia Grammar School, where he taught between 1878 and 1881

William Churchill DeMille, their first son, named after Henry's father, was born on July 25, 1878, in Washington, North Carolina, at the home of his paternal grandparents. Churchill was a remote DeMill family name and at the same time an unacknowledged tribute to Jennie Jerome Churchill, perhaps even a bit of wishful fantasizing on Beatrice's part. Shortly after mother and child returned to Brooklyn, Henry left Lockwood and at Beatrice's insistence, they moved to Manhattan, where he found a position as an English teacher at Columbia Grammar School with an increase in salary from $600 to $900 a year. This was supplemented by a welcome fee of $400 for the purchase by *Leslie's Weekly* of an eighteen-part serial story which he had written and Beatrice had submitted. She saw its sale as a favorable omen.

The summer of 1881 was the last that Henry was to be a schoolteacher. As the steaming heat of a New York July and Beatrice's time to deliver her second child approached, Henry took his small family to Ashfield, Massachusetts, in the Berkshire Mountains, where the affluent families of four of his private pupils from Columbia Grammar had summer homes. The DeMilles boarded in a commodious house belonging to a Mrs. Bronson. One room downstairs was given over to Henry as a classroom, where he taught Latin, Greek, and mathematics. Beatrice gave birth to her second son, Cecil Blount DeMille, on August 12, 1881, in the upstairs front bedroom while her husband was conducting his lessons. In the Jewish faith, a child is named for a dead relative, generally one who had a long life. Believing Cecil was a shortening of her own name, Cecilia Samuel was outraged that her daughter had defied this tradition.* A rift that could have been easily mended was prolonged.

When the DeMilles returned to New York for the school term, Beatrice, who had lofty ideas as to Henry's abilities and future, kept the baby and three-year-old William as much out of her husband's way as possible so that he could work without interruption on adapting his old story "The Land of Aclen" into a play. By Christmas, the work, renamed *Robert Aclen*, was complete and the decision of what to do with it had to be made.

Henry remained deeply immersed in his theological study, and though *Robert*

The producer and playwright David Belasco, with whom Henry DeMille collaborated as actor and writer, in his New York office, 1909

Aclen was a comedy-drama in four acts, its plot hinged on Episcopalian principles. Through John Lockwood, he secured an introduction to the Rev. Dr. George S. Mallory, who was not only an Episcopalian clergyman and editor of the monthly magazine *The Churchman*, but most uniquely, co-owner, with his brother, Marshall Mallory, of the Madison Square Theatre. *Robert Aclen* was never produced because the Mallorys did not think the church a suitable background for comedy, but they were impressed with Henry's dialogue talents, his sense of construction, and his intelligence. The Madison Square Theatre aimed to encourage American playwrights and received in excess of 200 play manuscripts each year, of which only eight to ten would be produced. Henry was hired "as play reader at $1,500 a year, plus an additional $1,000 for any original play he wrote, provided it ran 200 nights." The contract was negotiated for him by Beatrice. Henry's job included not only the reading of all submissions, but the selection of those best suited for commercial production. Almost immediately upon acquiring his new post, he began writing his second play, *John Delmer's Daughters*, and met David Belasco, a bombastic, domineering young man from San Francisco who had just signed with the Madison Square Theatre as stage manager, a job he did not plan to remain in long, and had taken only to gain a toehold in New York.

Everything about Belasco displayed spectacular showmanship. Money, fame, and power were his goals, and he pursued them with a zeal that was awesome. Twenty-seven when he joined the Madison Square, discomforted that real success was taking longer than he had planned, Belasco was desperate to find a play that he could transform into his golden chariot. His own work, *Hearts of Oak*, had been produced in Chicago several seasons back but had not made it into New York. He was convinced that all he needed was the germ of a good commercial idea and he could take it from there. His choice of Henry as an ally was predictable. After all, over 200 play scripts passed yearly through Henry's hands.

Beatrice recognized in Belasco a kindred spirit. Both were Jewish and yet did not practice their religion. Belasco at times even affected the habit of a Catholic priest and wore a clerical collar, a preciosity that caused one contemporary to com-

19

The DeMilles

Above, left and center: Henry
and Beatrice DeMille in *Young
Mrs. Winthrop*, by Bronson
Howard, probably fall 1885.
Right: Henry DeMille
as Jim Blakely in his own play
The Main Line, directed by
David Belasco, on tour in
Chicago, 1887

Left: Cecil B. DeMille at five,
1886

ment, "the only vow he's ever taken is a vow of cheap theatrics." They shared a penchant for the romantic and the exotic, enjoyed a sense of elegance and style, and in no way found the desire to become rich a vulgar ambition. In this last attitude, they were also in step with America's materialistic scramble in the decades that followed the heroic years of the Civil War.

Henry was attracted to Belasco much as he had been to Beatrice: by the vastly differing background, the flamboyant personality and somewhat foreign appearance, and the quick intelligence that recognized opportunity and how to grasp it. Henry found a play—a sentimental melodrama, *Elsie Deane* by John Marsden—which nonetheless had a strong story line and some good characters. Belasco suggested that they collaborate on a rewrite.* Henry, meanwhile, completed *John Delmer's Daughters*. It lasted exactly six nights, and had the distinction of being not only Henry DeMille's first produced play but the Madison Square Theatre's first failure.

Not long after this disappointment, Beatrice's father died and left her a small legacy with which the DeMilles bought as a summer retreat "an old pre-Revolutionary house still held together by its original wooden pegs" in Echo Lake, New Jersey. Henry's contract with the Madison Square ran out in June 1885 and was not renewed. He wrote of that summer, "I had to get along by borrowing and other doglike means of living." He meant by that having to accept a minor acting role (which he played for three weeks) in *Sealed Instructions*, under the banner of Albert M. Palmer, one of the great American theatre producers of that era. By the fall of 1885, the DeMilles were fairly desperate, but one thing was now certain. Henry had finally given up any thought of the priesthood. Earlier in the year, he had been listed for the eighth time in the *Long Island Diocesan Journals* as a candidate for ordination. But as before, he did not present himself to the Board of Examining Chaplains to qualify. He never again applied. The theatre had won its battle with the church.

With introductions from Belasco and the former business director of the Madison Square, Daniel Frohman—both of whom had left that summer to join the staff of the Lyceum Theatre—Henry and Beatrice were engaged in supporting roles in the touring company of *Young Mrs. Winthrop*, written by Bronson Howard.* (Beatrice appeared in a small role billed as Miss Agnes Graham.) The children were left at Echo Lake with the mother of Etta Hawkins, the company's ingenue. Belasco had stronger motivation than friendship in helping the DeMilles. Henry was reworking a play by Charles Bernard, an editor of *The Century Magazine*, which Belasco wanted to direct.

The Main Line, or Rawson's Y: An Idyl Of The Railroad by Henry C. DeMille and Chas. Barnard opened on September 16, 1886. Henry played Lawrence Hatton, an artist, opposite Etta Hawkins as Possy, a Western Union operator in Rawson's Y, a way station. Before he can propose marriage to Possy, Hatton believes he must first seek his fortune. He therefore stows away in the last car of a freight train heading west. Moments later, Possy discovers that the car has broken loose and has plunged back down the steep grade of the branch road. Belasco not only brought a freight car onto the stage for Hatton's first-act departure, he recreated a railroad switch room with equipment furnished by the Union Switch and Signal Co. of Pittsburgh.

Belasco's realistic staging* riveted *The Main Line* audiences as the heroine threw the switch that would send her lover's car safely past a siding and then manipulated another lever which would "transfer the car to the main line where it [would] run out on the level and stop unharmed."* Belasco's brilliant stagecraft prompted *The New York Times* critic to laud the play's "almost perfect illusion." The same critic incorrectly promised "*The Main Line* will pay big dividends." It closed in a month. Four years later, it recouped its investment, when Belasco sent the show, with the original cast, on the road to Boston, Chicago, and St. Louis, returning it to New York at the Brooklyn Academy of Music in time for Christmas 1890. "*The Main Line* is a triumph of originality and of stage mechanism," wrote the *New York World* critic. But as Christmas 1886 approached, the DeMilles were nearly $7,000 in debt. This did not dampen their spirits. With *The Main Line*, Belasco's career had taken off. Henry now had a powerful and loyal collaborator, and he had become a talked-about playwright, a "star" of the stage and a member of the regular stock company of the Lyceum Theatre.

Belasco's flamboyance may have shocked others, but it only served to intrigue Henry. He and Belasco became an ongoing writing team directly after *The Main Line*. As collaborators, they were an odd couple: Belasco with his affected dress, his tantrums, his short, dark, electric appearance, the quick gestures and staccato speech, and Henry, tall and frail, his red hair thinning, his narrow nose twitching beneath his pince-nez glasses, the careful cadence of his melodious voice, and the slow, almost balletic grace with which he moved. Belasco believed his stock company could be stirred into better performances if he had a tantrum in rehearsal: "striding up and down the stage, shouting, clapping his hand to his forehead," he would rip off his watch and slam it to the floor, "smashing it to bits." After a few of these startling performances, the cast realized that Belasco had worn a prop watch and had been planning his outburst. Henry, meanwhile, stood silently in the wings.

Shortly after *The Main Line* closed, Belasco joined the DeMilles at Echo Lake to work with Henry on a new play, *The Wife*, tailored directly for his vision of literal theatre. Belasco did not actually write. Henry did that as his collaborator paced back and forth throwing out suggestions in a rat-a-tat voice. Belasco was to say of their collaboration: "Henry excelled in narrative and had a quick wit. The emotional or dramatic scenes were more to my liking. I acted while he took down my speeches. When a play was finished, it was impossible to say where his work left off and my work began."

Henry's mild manner and pliability were perfect foils for Belasco's volatile nature, and Beatrice's ambition assured him that Henry would remain complaisant. The duo aimed to produce a play about high society, something stylish that would call for lavish sets and costumes. At Echo Lake, they came up with a story about a United States senator jealous of his young wife's former fiancé and his need to have her prove her passion for him. A subplot involving young members of the senator's household dealt with "the uneven course of young love." With this sparse outline, the collaborators returned to New York, using the stage of the Lyceum for their work together. Henry "set up a table in the front row of the orchestra and wrote dialogue as Belasco enacted the scenes of the play on the empty stage. 'Now Henry,' he would say, 'give me a speech that begins here and takes me over there. Then I turn suddenly, like this, and see the woman I love.' " (Henry's version of their method of working is at definite odds with Belasco's description in that Henry claimed he wrote the dialogue and his collaborator takes credit for it as well.)

Belasco had inveigled Tiffany and Company into decorating the theatre with its finest chandeliers and appointments to the tune of $50,000 to be paid after the play opened. *The Wife* debuted on September 29, 1887, to harsh reviews, although the critics were in unison about the outstandingly beautiful theatre decor. While Tiffany waited to be paid, Daniel Frohman, the theatre's manager ("a tall, grave man who wore high starched collars and looked forbiddingly formal . . . [and] had a sense of responsibility about the theatre as a profession"), instructed Belasco to place another play in rehearsal. Belasco refused, insisting that *The Wife* was simply overlong. Finally, he got Frohman to wait until he and Henry could cut an hour from the running time. The new version was presented in the fourth week of the run. By Christmas, *The Wife* was an established hit (to Mr. Tiffany's delight) and continued its run for 239 performances.

The collaborators were now an established and successful team and went on to write *Lord Chumley* (premiere August 1888),* which was a great success and made a star of E. H. Sothern.

Belasco had become known as a starmaker and a tyrant. "I coax and cajole or bulldoze and torment, according to the temperament with which I have to deal," he asserted. His methods were sometimes painful or humiliating, but the hopefuls who came to him—and then gave him their unconditional obedience (he was often called "The Master") because they knew in Belasco's hands they could become famous— endured the insults. Not until he met Mrs. Leslie Carter did he become absolutely obsessive about one of his performers.

Mrs. Carter had come to Belasco in "a blaze of notoriety," twenty-seven, a slim woman with green eyes and a mass of fiery hair. Socially prominent and the wife of a Chicago millionaire, more a personality than a beauty, Mrs. Carter had just been sued for divorce on grounds of adultery with five men, and found guilty. She announced her intention of going on the stage. Carter countered by forbidding her to use his name. Mrs. Carter arranged a meeting with Belasco. He was taken with her the moment she entered his office dressed in riding attire. "Do you wish to act in tragedy or comedy?" he asked, not without some humor. "I am a horsewoman," she replied, "and I wish to make my first entrance on a horse, leaping over a hurdle."* That same week, Belasco had secluded himself with Henry in Echo Lake to work on the script of *The Charity Ball*.

Agnes de Mille recalls the story that was told to her by Elizabeth deMille, her Aunt Bettie, of the first meeting between the deMilles and Mrs. Leslie Carter: "One sunny July afternoon in the cottage at Echo Lake, Henry and Belasco were working, with Bebe [Beatrice] keeping watch lest they be disturbed. I was in the front hammock lolling about, eating a peach, when up to the front gate drove a very handsome little surrey and out stepped a vision: a tall, slender lady in an elegant summer dress with a lace parasol. She tripped up the garden path and addressed me. 'You must be Henry's little sister, Bettie. Would you tell your brother that Mrs. Leslie Carter has called to see him?' I did not know how to answer but simply stared. I had heard about Mrs. Leslie Carter, I had heard the men discussing her. She became known to me as the type of woman whom Henry would never allow his little sister to meet.... Mrs. Leslie Carter continued softly, 'Please tell him I'm here.'"

"So Bettie fell out of the hammock," Agnes remembers, "and went into the house and tapped on the study door. Beatrice opened it a crack. 'Mrs. Leslie Carter is out there,' Bettie whispered fearfully.

"'All right,' said Beatrice quietly, 'offer her some lemonade. Ask her to sit down.' And then she ... turned to the men announcing portentously, 'She has come.'

"Henry said, 'Send her away.'

"But David Belasco said, 'Well, since she's come all this long way out in this heat, we might as well see her.'

"And Bettie heard her brother say, 'Oh, Davey, Davey, this is the beginning of the end.'"

Belasco recalled, "I was almost worn out the afternoon she arrived [at Echo Lake]—not having any sleep to speak of in two days—and she was almost hysterical and frantic with fatigue, trouble, and anxiety. She told me much of the story of her domestic tragedy ... and as she told it, I began to see the possibilities in her.... If only she could *act* like that on the stage, I caught myself thinking. The upshot was that I promised to give her a trial."

Henry's prescience proved correct. Belasco intended to make Mrs. Carter the greatest star the stage had known. Mrs. Carter, it seems, did not think that Henry could write the kind of role she needed to achieve this aim. Belasco apparently agreed.

During the period from April 1890 to about June 1891, Belasco worked feverishly to transform Mrs. Carter into an actress. On the stage of Palmer's Theatre and in private rooms under his direction and tutelage, Mrs. Carter rehearsed and memorized thirty roles ranging from Nancy Sikes in *Oliver Twist* to *Camille.* "The magnetism of her highly keyed temperamental nature convinced me then and there that she would go far, if only her natural abilities could be developed and controlled," he later wrote.

With Belasco dedicating all his time to Mrs. Carter, Henry was without a collaborator. The two DeMille boys especially missed Belasco's volatile presence. Belasco had the rare gift of treating children as equals. At Echo Lake, he and Henry had talked and written at desks facing each other for about four hours a day. Then Beatrice had copied their scrawled, heavily marked work in her graceful, even hand, and the boys were called into the living room late in the afternoon to hear their mother and the two men read the day's writing aloud and then were asked their opinions.

The prolific Belasco years had enabled the DeMilles to maintain a comfortable New York apartment at 119 Waverly Place and the Echo Lake house, had paid for an education at Horace Mann School for Bill and Cecil and for Henry (whose father had recently died) to bring his mother, his brother, John, and his sisters Bettie (Elizabeth) and Stannie (Anne) to live in New York. Maintaining all of these responsibilities was a severe financial drain on Henry, and he set to work to write a play on his own. *Das verlorene Paradies* (*The Lost Paradise*) by Ludwig Fulda was being presented at Amberg's, a German theatre in New York. Daniel Frohman's younger brother Charles* (who had a great deal more panache than his older brother) was now a major theatre producer. He suggested that Henry might set to work on an

English adaptation. The play was a strong naturalistic drama that dealt with the rights of labor.

For the first time, Henry was able to apply his considerable knowledge to a creative work. Beatrice was pregnant as he began writing with a young protégé, Mildred Dowling. ("We soon found that an adaptation was not sufficient. We drew out a scenario of a new play, using whatever we found good in the German," Henry later commented.)

Belasco suddenly reappeared, and Henry temporarily had to put *The Lost Paradise* aside. Belasco was a married man with three children and an extravagant lifestyle to support, and for over a year he had not worked except in his coaching of the dynamic Mrs. Carter. But his debts were piling up. A new theatre, The Proctor, was to open, and Charles Frohman had come to him and asked if he could write a play for it. The opportunity was exactly what Belasco needed to pull himself back into the mainstream and away from his financially debilitating relationship with Mrs. Carter.

"I was strongly tempted to write the opening play alone," he later confessed, "but when I saw how much depended upon it I had a touch of stage fright.... It was five o'clock in the morning when I was seized with the idea of asking DeMille to assist me and I hastened to his house [actually the Waverly Place apartment]. I knocked on his door with the vigor of a watchman sounding a fire alarm, and when DeMille at last appeared he was armed with a cane, ready to defend hearth and home.

"About this time the newspapers were full of a bank scandal. A young man employed in a bank had speculated with [bank] funds.... His father...a stockholder, had the sympathy of the entire public in his misfortune. Owing to the young man's speculations, the bank was on the verge of closing, and the newsapers were full of harrowing details. As I read the accounts I came to this sentence in a statement made by the father: 'I'll save the bank if it costs me a million a day!' 'Henry,' I said, 'there's our play!'... Our greatest difficulty was to find a title. Our play was to have a universal appeal. One of our characters was a liberal *Jew*, another a conservative churchman...we selected the name of *Men and Women*."

"A deplorable lack of brilliant invention has marked most of the previous labors of Mr. DeMille and Mr. Belasco," wrote the *Herald* critic in his review, "and even in this play it is difficult to discover evidence of conspicuous originality." The *New York Dramatic Mirror* declared that the play "is cheap enough, its characters false enough to meet the requirements of a class that does not know good art from bad art."

Despite the critics' jabs, *Men and Women* was a box office success. Henry and Beatrice had every reason to believe that they were back again on the road to great affluence if not acclaim. With a third child nearly due, the Samuel family became reconciled. Bill and Cecil were two handsome youngsters, both possessing acting talents, and their parents were not opposed to their training for the stage. Life was good, indeed. And then, to the DeMilles' dismay, Belasco once again decided to break up the collaboration and devote his time to presenting Mrs. Carter in a stage production.

Beatrice's pregnancy was difficult, and twice she came close to death. Finally, Henry's desk had to be cleared so that the doctor could perform an emergency Cae-

Henry George, the political economist whose advocacy of the Single Tax made him world famous; his daughter Anna married William deMille

sarean. Agnes Beatrice DeMille* was born on April 12, 1891, a healthy child, and her mother quickly regained her strength. Henry, back to work on *The Lost Paradise*, and with *Men and Women* a success, presented Beatrice as a gift a site of seventy-six acres on a hill above Pompton Lakes, New Jersey, to build the country estate she had always dreamed of owning.

The Lost Paradise opened at the Columbia Theatre, Chicago, on August 17, 1891, to reviews—("one of the most talented of contemporary playwrights")—that proved Henry could get along without Belasco (but obviously not without a collaborator, although somehow Miss Dowling never received credit). He took his royalties and began construction on the DeMilles' future estate, to be called Pamlico after the boat and river of his North Carolina childhood. While it was being built, the De-Milles lived nearby in an old house that belonged to the Ryersons, a mining family. On Easter 1892, the family took possession of the "large white frame three-story house, handsome by Victorian standards, with turrets and wide porch, surrounded by lawn, overlooking the lake."

Beatrice had never been happier. With *The Lost Paradise* she felt Henry had finally entered the world of the intellectuals. He began work, this time alone, on a new play, *The Promised Land*, which was to be about workers' struggle for a good life. Henry, meanwhile, had joined the local Episcopal parish of Christ Church, which consisted mostly of families of steelworkers, and became a senior warden and delegate to the diocesan convention. The congregation of the church was so poor that it could not support a resident clergyman, and Henry helped out by conducting services as a lay reader. Beatrice instantly became involved in helping the families of the poorly paid workers and was instrumental in the development of a school. She rented space for it in a local store near the Susquehanna Railroad and later moved it to a space over a grocery store. With the help of a Miss Acker, whom she hired as a teacher and whose salary she paid out of her own pocket, Beatrice canvassed the area for pupils.

A Dynasty Begins

The DeMilles had recently read Henry George's *Progress and Poverty* (originally published in 1879) and were now disciples. George was one of the most controversial figures of the time. Born into a poor family in Philadelphia in 1839, he had been forced to stop school at fourteen, and had experienced desperate poverty while trying to support his family. His work as a newspaperman gave impetus to his reformist tendencies. He believed that a Single Tax on land, paid by the landowner, would meet all the costs of government and unburden labor and capital of taxes on their earnings.

Agnes deMille, Henry George's granddaughter, is a spokesman for Georgism and the Single-Tax theory. As she defines them:

> Henry George advocated a Single Tax to be levied on the site value of land. Land was the only thing that was to be taxed, but according to its value. That is, a lot in Wall Street would be worth more than vast farms in Iowa, or if the land contained uranium, gold, or oil, it would then be valuable. Two pieces of adjacent land would be taxed alike irrespective of use. He believed that what the individual makes is his own by rights, and should be untaxed, but what the community makes as a community is theirs. One of the things people jointly make is position or site value, the result of aggregation, commerce, and living needs. This no individual can achieve; it is the product of the community. Men have a right, he felt, to the earth, to natural resources, to air, to water, to land, and no individual should abrogate any part of this for private profit. If you own the land from which a man must draw his sustenance or wealth, you own the man.
>
> He also thought that by taking the annual rental of land according to its site value, the income to the government would be sufficient for all its needs, which today is problematic. George did not foresee Star Wars or welfare, but I know that he believed there would be no need for welfare if everyone had access to what he needed in order to earn an honest living.
>
> It is a complicated theory, and *Progress and Poverty*, which first voiced it, runs to nearly 800 pages. But in essence this is what he and his followers advocate. Father believed in these ideas; Cecil did not. He believed in free enterprise, free grabbing, with any tricks or profits that were possible for the wily individual. There is a fundamental difference between the two points of view.

Progress and Poverty sold millions of copies worldwide, but George was defeated for the mayoralty of New York City in 1886 by the combined forces of conservatives and Catholics (although he won more votes than Theodore Roosevelt, one of his opponents).

Henry George possessed great wit and was a sparkling storyteller. His wife, Annie Fox George, presided over their New York townhouse (bought with the royalties from his book) with considerable charm, and an invitation to the George ménage was most sought after among Manhattan's intellectual set.

On July 20, 1892, Beatrice wrote Henry George:

My dear Mr. George,

My dear husband has read aloud to me your grand book "Progress and Poverty". The solution is now ready for all those who are ready for it. Its perfect success in the future is undoubted. I pray that it may be a near future. I can do but little to aid in the good cause, but I can instill into the growing minds of our two boys the great solution so clearly proved and leave them to do their share. We all thank you with deep heart-felt gratitude, for every line of your Christian "Progress and Poverty". With kindest regards to Mrs. George. Yours truly,

Beatrice DeMille

Henry George answered Beatrice, who continued the correspondence until one day there came an invitation to tea. Within a short time, Bill and Cecil were asked to meet the George children—Anna, the younger, and Jennie (who died a short time later of typhoid)—and the children became good friends. Henry George had a great fondness for young people and always had time to answer questions and manage small surprises. Anna was to recall how her father took them for long walks explaining his theories on various things along the way. And she remembered "so well how he used to buy little boxes of chocolate ice cream drops."

The DeMilles spent Christmas at their new country home. C. B. remembered best "the evenings, I think, when [Father] read to us a chapter from the *Old Testament*, a chapter from the *New* . . . or from Thackeray or Victor Hugo or some other classic. He liked to have his head rubbed while he read, and Bill and I used to take advantage of that to prolong the evening's reading. Father had a beautifully modulated voice. . . . He made everything real. . . . *The King of Kings* and *The Ten Commandments* were born in those evenings [at Pamlico] when father sat under the big lamp and read and a small boy sat near his chair and listened."

On January 25, 1893, Henry went into New York for the opening of the first production in Charles Frohman's new theatre, The Empire, just south of Fortieth Street on Broadway. The play was *The Girl I Left Behind Me*, by Belasco and Franklin Fyles (a reviewer for *The Sun*), and starred "the sizzling" Mrs. Leslie Carter. As Henry was alone, he decided not to open the apartment on Waverly Place but to stay at the Ashland House, a well-appointed club. The establishment was having some sewerage problems, and he returned to Pamlico complaining that the fumes had upset his digestion. Two weeks later—on the morning of February 10, 1893—Henry C. DeMille died of typhoid after issuing a deathbed wish that his sons not pursue careers in the theatre. His casket stood in the center of the living room at Pamlico. "Mother brought Bill and me in," C. B. wrote, "to stand beside [it], just the three of us. She put her arms around us and spoke, not to us but to him: 'May your sons be as fine and noble and good and honest as you were. May they follow in your steps. . . .'"

But it was their mother whom they followed out of the room and into the land of the living; Beatrice who set the standards, Beatrice who, despite Henry's death wish, was determined the name of DeMille would not be obliterated on theatre marquees, Beatrice who, without realizing quite what she was doing, set out to establish the DeMille theatre dynasty.

Beatrice

1893–1906

DAILY FOR SIX WEEKS AFTER HENRY'S DEATH, BEATRICE SAT fourteen-year-old Bill down at his father's desk while the two attempted to complete Henry's play *The Promised Land.* When she read the final manuscript, she knew they had failed. She took an immediate inventory of her assets. Pamlico was free and clear, but she had almost no savings. There were Henry's plays, unperformed at the moment, which meant no current royalties were due. Desperate measures would have to be taken. She had always negotiated Henry's contracts. If she persevered, she believed, she could sell touring and amateur rights. But she needed Belasco's agreement that she could represent him as coauthor.

    The two met in Belasco's offices at the Lyceum Theatre. Whether motivated by guilt or true confidence, Belasco gave her authorization to represent his interests in his collaborative efforts with her husband. Within a matter of days, the name of Mrs. H. C. DeMille, Authors' Representative, went up outside a small office in the Knickerbocker Theatre Building on Broadway.

    At a time of determined puritanism among American women, Beatrice's business venture was a bold move. The crass work of an authors' representative,

The family home at Pompton, New Jersey, after Beatrice DeMille had converted it into a day and boarding school for girls and boys, 1893

Cecil (eleven), his sister, Agnes (about one and a half), and brother, William DeMille (fourteen) in Pompton, c. 1892

which was a euphemism for agent-saleswoman, would not be looked upon as a socially acceptable way for a woman to earn a living. It was a totally unfeminine pursuit which Henry's mother or his sisters—the conditions once wrought by the war now long forgotten—could not have imagined.

Nor did Beatrice's energy and resourcefulness end with a single project. Within weeks after Henry's death, she had begun construction on a building across the road from Pamlico and also added a wing to the main house to accommodate paying boarding pupils in the coeducational Henry C. DeMille School. Eight weeks to the day after his death, the school was ready to receive its first students.

An advertisement in the *Pasquannock Valley Argus* on March 8, 1893, announced that the Henry DeMille Preparatory Boarding and Day School for boys and girls offered "full classical and scientific courses, modern languages, theory of music, drawing, painting and physical culture." Also offered in this location, "ideal for health and beauty," were "tennis, baseball, rowing, skating and coasting."

A carriage was bought to carry day students to and from school. Beatrice's heart might have been in the plight of the steelworkers, but her widowed situation had impelled her to turn her school into a viable business venture. That she managed all these enterprises—the writing done on *The Promised Land*, her arrangements with Belasco, the conversion of Pamlico into a school, and the care of her fatherless brood—is nothing short of amazing. Beatrice was a formidable force. She even managed to affiliate herself with Christ Church in Pompton and raise money for it by putting on entertainments at the school (a clever device that gave her students a chance to perform before an audience). The DeMilles—Bill, then fourteen, Cecil, aged twelve, and little Agnes, two—though fatherless, would never be in want as long as Beatrice was at the helm. But their sad times were not over.

Pompton was struck by one of the worst blizzards of the century on February 7 and 8, 1895. "Roads were blocked and trains derailed. Pompton...was snowed

Beatrice

under, its inhabitants isolated with snow drifts . . . 15 feet deep. Gale winds [blew]," the Pompton press reported. On February 11, Agnes took sick with what Beatrice thought was the common grippe. The school was still isolated, the corridors and rooms frigid. By the morning of the twelfth, Agnes grew worse, and Beatrice sent Bill on horseback over and through the high snowbanks to fetch the doctor. They arrived back too late.

Agnes had died, not of grippe, but of spinal meningitis. She was laid out in an open coffin in the parlor, dressed in white, flowers woven in her hair, a gold crucifix about her neck. Beatrice led her sons down to the side of the "pathetic small white coffin" the night that Agnes died, and as her namesake Agnes deMille related, "forced them to look at the dead child lit by tapers. She then commanded them to kiss the little cold face in the coffin." Then, Cecil recalled, she "made each of us boys put our hand over the dead child's heart and pledge that we would never treat any woman other than we would have wanted Agnes treated, if she had lived."*

Her daughter's death brought Beatrice ever closer to her adopted religion. She became president of the Women's Guild of Christ Church, and the boys were expected to make the church a daily part of their lives, even if they had to attend before classes in the morning. C. B. recalled finding himself the only person to attend an early service.

> I . . . took my place in one of the pews, and waited. When the hour struck for the service to begin, the red-bearded minister came out, in his surplice, went to the altar, and conducted the entire service exactly as if he had had a congregation of a thousand people. I felt some awkwardness when the time for the collection came. I had a nickel for the purpose, but my problem was how to get it on the plate. The minister rose to the occasion. Before time for the offertory, he gravely came down out of the chancel and put the collection plate on the first pew, then as gravely returned to the altar. I went up and deposited my nickel. The minister returned at the proper time, carried the plate to the altar, and offered my gift as solemnly as if it had been gold. . . .
>
> I saw that morning . . . a man's faith. . . . Young as I was [twelve], that minister's conduct gave me a deep sense of the reality of God; and it has never left me since that day.

The youthful Cecil's bond with Christ Church was to grow even stronger and perhaps in this one area created a minor schism between his brother Bill and himself. Bill also followed Christ Church, but he had a more tolerant and sympathetic feeling towards his maternal Jewish roots and was closer to his grandmother Samuel.*

Beatrice just managed to keep her business as an authors' representative afloat. Belasco's name helped in selling Henry's plays to touring and stock companies, but without the school the family could not have lived as well as they did.*

The theatre remained Beatrice's first love. The competition she was up against as a play broker was both solidly male and most formidable. If she wanted to be a success, it was imperative for her to specialize in some branch of playwrighting that had been ignored. She decided to champion the woman dramatist. "Most managers believe that no woman can write a great play," she told a reporter for the *New*

31

York Dramatic Mirror, "and for proof they assert that no woman has written one."

With Harriet Ford, a young author she represented, she proceeded to write a drama, *The Greatest Thing in the World* (the tag line of the play reveals, "Love is the greatest thing in the world"), about a woman's desire to pursue a career versus her natural instincts. The story was strongly autobiographical. A widow with two sons (one named Cecil) decides to go out into the business world to support them herself, but is condemned by her young sons' guardian for such forward action. She is faced with the alternative of giving up her career or her sons. She fights back and in the end retains both. The play opened with Sarah LaMoyne in the lead at The Columbia Theatre in Washington, D.C., the week of February 12, 1900.* The *Washington Evening Star* reported: "The play is a unique offering of a woman; therefore any surprise at its lacking virility would be unreasonable."

The Greatest Thing in the World failed commercially, but it brought Beatrice an enormous amount of publicity—and a great number of women hoping to become playwrights, as well as many young, untried dramatists who were drawn to her "radical" views and her outspoken attitudes. "This is the woman's age," she told one reporter. "Every relation between the sexes has changed because woman has changed. Hereafter, no woman is going to be married without feeling that she is getting as much as she gives. That may sound like a crude statement of the matter, but expresses pretty clearly what I mean.... This theme—woman's intrinsic equality—lies very close to my heart, consequently any play dealing with any phase of this subject makes a special appeal to me. I am indifferent as to the angle from which the author attacks this problem, as long as he states it convincingly." Beatrice had been aroused by the stirrings in the women's movement and she saw the value of the theatre as a means of propaganda.

She now spent less time at the school at Pamlico and devoted more of her energy to her theatre work in her new office in the Hudson Theatre, filled with "great bunches of mountain laurel in the enormous vases on her desk and the growing ferns and the rubber trees about the room...not inappropriate symbols of the person who sympathizes with all that is growing." She became part of a theatre and intellectual world in which her husband had never quite been accepted.

Despite the aura of intellectualism about Henry George, he had been a simple self-educated man. But when he died, except for Mark Twain, he was probably one of the best known Americans and, with Twain, one of the best speakers of his time. The year he died he had run, against his doctor's advice, for mayor of New York City as "Incorruptible Henry George." He seemed certain to win. Four nights before the election, in a hotel on Union Square, his wife, Annie, woke to see him standing alone in the center of the room, head bent back, looking up—almost as though skyward. "Yes, yes, yes," he said, and fell unconscious, dying within hours.

His funeral was a state occasion; "the catafalque was borne through the streets to torchlight and followed by a crowd of fifty thousand. It passed all the borough City Halls and as the procession approached the bells were set tolling." Critic Henry Thurston Peck, a contemporary, added: "Poor people filed past the body for hours. He lay in state...with several Catholic priests and ministers always there, standing close to the body. His obituaries have surprised me in their omissions.

Beatrice

George was a humorist. He told a story splendidly and...was not one of the sour 'intense' radical brethren, but in all ways a genial open-minded little man."

The widow was an intelligent, witty woman, "a Catholic, an Australian, an exotic" with a streak of unrepressible high spirits. ("She was also a remarkable waltzer [and could indulge] in two-hour heats with the orchestra hired to play through supper...."). Annie's in-laws, the Georges, were "upright and staunch," but with the one notable exception, "were not all of them very bright."

Beatrice was at once solicitous to Annie Fox George, who found her "worldliness and zest" refreshing. Beatrice also lost no time in offering her and her fatherless daughter the services of her son, Bill, who was in New York City at Columbia College, after having attended a *Gymnasium* in Freiburg, Germany.

The previous fall (1896), Beatrice had bicycled with Cecil from Pompton, New Jersey, to Chester, Pennsylvania, "to save train fare and for the adventure," in order to enroll him in the elite Pennsylvania Military College. Unable to resist her talent for striking deals, Beatrice did not pay any tuition, but in exchange for Cecil's place at the college, took the daughter of the headmaster, Colonel Hyatt, as a boarding student at Pamlico. With her younger son settled for a time, Beatrice concentrated her energy on Bill, seeing in him the social and material success his father did not live to achieve.

Bill, like all the DeMilles, was "quick, flashing, adroit, and, on a superficial level, intensely mental." With his long narrow face, brilliant eyes, and "the nose of a Spanish grandee," he made a marvelous first impression. Women were instantly drawn to him. He was, indeed, "very sexy. Sex...meant a great deal to him." Anna Angela George, Henry George's daughter, was "completely smitten" with him. (She had, in fact, proposed to him several years earlier, at age eleven, and he had refused.) Not only was he handsome, tall, and lean, "he excelled in track and got medals for running, jumping, hammer-throwing, shot-putting. He fenced and boxed, but above all he played tennis, with passion and skill." Most important he showed considerable literary talent. In his senior year, he made up his mind with the encouragement of his mother that he would switch his major from engineering to drama and that he would become a playwright.

Beatrice set aside an attic room at Pamlico as "Bill's inviolable sanctuary," which he used for writing on weekends and holidays. The girls at the school called it "the Dreamery" and many of them were drawn romantically to him as he taught them fencing or helped them with their tennis strokes. His mother, her hopes set on an alliance with the George family (both Anna and Bill were still considered too young to become engaged), kept a restraining eye on his flirtations. Cecil was graduated from the American Academy of Dramatic Arts in 1900, having transferred from the Pennsylvania Military College two years earlier. During his attendance, he had lived at Pamlico, traveling daily into New York and occasionally staying with Bill overnight at his rooms near Columbia.

The custom of the senior class at Columbia College was to model a comic opera after the style of Gilbert and Sullivan. Bill's class produced *The Governor's Vrouw.** A fellow senior recalled, "When we started rehearsing...we knew [Bill] already had considerable knowledge of the theatre. What was our surprise, then, when he announced he wouldn't ask for a speaking part; he would be content to play Filching Fox, a mute Indian. . . . Bribed by the Governor, [he kidnapped his wife], seized her by the throat so she couldn't yell—that is, not much—and vanished with her into the trackless forest." When Bill's appearance was imminent, he "came out [of the shallow wings] doing cartwheels around the fascinated Governor's wife, who kept twisting her head to see what was happening. The magnificent gymnastics brought Filching Fox nearer and nearer his victim until, having prolonged the exhibition to a good minute and a half, he closed in on her—fell on her, in fact—like a circling plate which has lost its momentum; then amidst thunderous applause he heaved her up and shouldered her off . . . treading deliberately, lifting his feet high, as though carrying a log through tall wet grass." As a performance, it owed more to youthful memories of David Belasco than to any theatre training.

Flamboyance was not to remain Bill's style. After graduating from Columbia, he enrolled in the American Academy of Dramatic Arts, as William *de*Mille. That one lowercase letter soon would epitomize the contrast that was developing between himself and Cecil and Beatrice. As he studied about theatre and wrote in his Pompton garret, he became convinced that the best stories were told simply and humanly. His knowledge of German drama led him to a new approach inspired by Arthur Schnitzler, who was content to take as his theme only a few scenes from life.* Schnitzler's quiet cynicism and reminiscent moodiness appealed to Bill, and he set to work to adapt it to his own style. Whenever he could he attended the Sunday night salon at the home of Brander Matthews (his famous former professor of dramatic literature), where he met and socialized with some of the theatre's most important contributors.

While Bill was writing his first plays, Cecil made his debut as an actor in a small supporting role in Charles Frohman's production of Cecil Raleigh's *Hearts Are Trumps*, which opened at the Garden Theatre on February 21, 1900, ran for nineteen performances, and then toured.

In Washington, D.C., Constance Adams, the daughter of a New Jersey judge, Frederic Adams, joined the company. By the time the play reached Boston, Cecil and the lovely Constance were in love. C. B. recorded that "on the 31st of December, 1900, at midnight, sitting together on the steps of a theatrical boarding house at No. 9 Beacon Street, Boston, completely oblivious of the cold, we celebrated the beginning of a new year and a new century by becoming engaged." He was nineteen and Constance twenty-seven.

It took nearly two years before the couple could get Judge Adams and Beatrice to consent to their marriage. During this time, Cecil's acting career flourished. From *Hearts Are Trumps* he went into *To Have and to Hold*, *Are You a Mason?*, and *Alice of Old Vincennes*, playing an assortment of stock characters in a style that Bill had once attempted and that might be called "Belasco-inspired." Unlike Bill, Cecil would cling to Belasco's stagy methods, scenes often played more for effect than content, and to a commitment to entertain rather than to educate his audiences.

Constance Adams was a dark-eyed beauty with generous features, full brows, and glossy brown hair that she wore in a stylish pompadour that added extra inches to her tall frame.* With her full bosom and small waist, and smoldering, somewhat Latin looks, Constance might have been suspected of possessing a sensuous nature. She was, instead, a cool-headed woman, brought up with strict values, deeply religious

and, as C. B. later commented, "In the whole history of the world, no one has ever been more fittingly named." She carried herself with great dignity and had a certain aloofness that discouraged others from referring to her as "Connie."

Cecil and Constance were married August 16, 1902, in an Episcopal ceremony at the bride's home at 77 Washington Street, East Orange, New Jersey. The Adamses had never approved of their daughter's decision to go on the stage, but Judge Adams found it difficult to deny his daughter her wishes. He had hoped that one season in the theatre would have been sufficient to send her back to East Orange. He blamed her meeting with Cecil for her decision to remain with the company. He had also been wrong in assuming that Constance would give up her young man (or the reverse) with time. The wedding reflected the Adamses' misgivings about their new son-in-law and his theatre family. The guest list was kept down to family members and very old friends. Except for Beatrice, the Samuel family was overlooked (Cecil, of course, must have agreed to their exclusion), nor were any of the couple's theatre colleagues included. Bill served as his brother's best man. Directly after the reception, the newlyweds joined the E. H. Sothern touring company, with which Cecil had recently signed to play Osric in *Hamlet*, Colin des Cayeux in *If I Were King*, and a supporting role in his father's play *Lord Chumley*.*

Judge Adams could well have been right in his disapproval of the theatrical, prematurely balding, willful Cecil DeMille as a son-in-law. On the surface, Constance and Cecil seemed mismatched, destined for an unhappy marriage. C. B. recalled an incident during their touring honeymoon which gives validity to Judge Adams's skepticism:

One night...[in] a little town in Idaho. I was downstairs in the hotel playing poker; Mrs. deMille was up in our room, with a bulldog that we had picked

35

up somewhere along the way.... Suddenly a bell boy appeared at my shoulder with the urgent news that Mrs. deMille was terrified because someone had tried to get into her room. She had the door locked, but she wanted me to come up right away in case the intruder came back. I said to the boy, "Well, ask Mrs. deMille if she can't depend on the bulldog for a while. Tell her I'm winning and if it keeps up, we can pay our bill."

C. B. was later to claim that what he knew about directing a crowd he had learned from Sothern during this tour. "Sothern gave every single extra an appropriate distinct, individual line to say. The audience could not hear the lines, but they saw and heard a crowd of real people talking and acting like real people."*

That same year, 1902, through Belasco, Beatrice met the illustrious architect Stanford White, known for his love of young women, his moodiness, and his addiction to white mint liqueur and brandy almost as well as for his designs of the first Madison Square Garden, the Washington Square Arch, and the Century Club. A man in his middle years, he had fallen desperately in love with a beautiful teen-aged showgirl, Evelyn Nesbit, then appearing in *Floradora*, and declared himself her guardian. Though only sixteen, Nesbit was hardly a naïf and was at the time enjoying the attentions of John Barrymore. When the show closed in May 1902, after 500 performances, White—to remove Nesbit from Barrymore's influence—placed his youthful charge in Beatrice's care at Pamlico, where Bill became her fencing instructor. Nesbit appears to have been attracted to Bill, but he was not so inclined (or else Beatrice warned him of the danger). Nesbit turned to another young man, Harry Thaw, who had seen her in *Floradora* and followed her to Pamlico. Beatrice at first discouraged Thaw's overtures. Nesbit kept a diary that contained numerous references such as, "Bill deMille, that pie-faced mut," and to Beatrice, "who is in cahoots with Stanford to keep me prisoner." Further passages revealed how the lascivious Barrymore had found Nesbit at Pamlico, how Beatrice refused to allow him to see her, how he left passionate "notes addressed to her on the tennis court and at various places around the property."*

Beatrice seemed more inclined toward Thaw as time went on. "Mother had told Evelyn that she should study the drama," C. B. later wrote, and "that, while her beauty would give her a start in the theater, as it had done in *Floradora*, only study and hard work would bring her real success.... Evelyn ... did not really want theatrical success.... Mother took another tack." Why not marry the rich Pittsburgher, Harry Thaw, who was also madly in love with her and had come to Pamlico to see her, bearing expensive gifts? Thaw had wealth, youth, and position.

"But I don't like Harry Thaw," Evelyn said. "There's something wrong with him." Nesbit's diary revealed her suspicion of his homosexuality, and her fear of violence on his behalf.* Nesbit, nonetheless, married Thaw. White remained her guardian and their illicit relationship continued until Thaw discovered the truth. In 1906, when the lovers were attending the opening night performance of *Mamzelle Champagne* in the roof theater of the Madison Square Garden, Thaw shot and killed White.

On March 30, 1903, after a year's engagement, Bill and Anna Angela George were married in an intimate family ceremony at the George home. Cecil and Con-

Cecil, then the director of the Standard Opera Company, playing the role of Florestein in its production of Michael Balfe's *The Bohemian Girl*, 1906

stance were on the road, and so Uncle John DeMille (Henry's younger brother) was Bill's best man. Anna's cousin, the Reverend George H. Latimer of Philadelphia, performed the ceremony. The newlyweds spent their honeymoon in Washington, North Carolina, with the Blounts. Beatrice had redone Bill's attic studio and two adjoining rooms into a small apartment, and the couple moved in upon their return. With the marriage, Beatrice had achieved two goals. The DeMilles and the Georges were now related, and Bill (so she thought) was saved from the lures of young and unconnected actresses.

"There were some pre-nuptial confessions that shook Mother," Agnes deMille wrote. "Mother liked Father to be admired, but she kept a pretty stiff rein on [his] flirting.... But Father could not refrain from flirting with all females, and they in turn adored him and spoiled him." Anna had difficulty coping with her husband's roving eye. "She, the beautiful baby of a world-famous man, had been raised as a little princess. She was small, five feet, wore a size one shoe... and child's gloves; she had showers of red hair that hung to her waist.... Her skin was milky, her eyes blue and of an intensity to stop speech, and when she grew angry she looked as if she had holes in her head and you could see through her to the sky beyond."

Anna's belief in Bill as an unquestioned genius created a great bond between herself and Beatrice (she called her "Bebe"). His first success was in writing one-act

A magazine article, c. 1904, showing Cecil (left) and William, describes them as "The sons of the late Henry C. de Mille [who] have inherited their father's talent for playwriting"

vaudeville sketches. Then in 1905 he wrote *Strongheart*, a drama about an Indian who fights intolerance to compete in college football. The play was a success and Anna and Bill moved from Pamlico into Manhattan. Beatrice felt the shock. Anna, after all, was to enjoy her older son's success, not she.

Though closely knit by ties of affection and respect, Bill and Cecil were a study in contrasts. Cecil greatly admired Bill's intellect, and he accepted the fact that his ability was not as cerebral, that he was more an entertainer than an artist, more a showman than a philosopher.

As she had done for Bill, Beatrice had converted several rooms into an apartment for Cecil and Constance when they were off the road. This meant that the brothers had been able to spend whatever free time they had together at Pamlico. Cecil's intention had never been to make acting his lifetime career. Writing, directing, and producing for the theatre were his real aim. At Pamlico, with Bill's guidance, he began to write plays. Beatrice did her best to interest the New York producers, but in the end was unsuccessful.

This was the time of the Stanford White murder trial, and the daily newspapers printed excerpts from Evelyn Nesbit's diary with their mention of Beatrice and Pamlico, an association that caused some moments of social awkwardness. Beatrice threw herself even more ardently into her work, founded the Women Dramatists' Society, and built up her list of clients to include Mary Roberts Rinehart, James Montgomery Flagg, Wilson Mizner, Zoë Akins, and of course, the brothers—William C. and Cecil B. DeMille.

In Search of Adventure

1906–1913

*Playing on the road was not easy, but it gave one a feeling
of and for America—the America between the coasts....*

—*The Autobiography of Cecil B. DeMille*

TO PLAYGOERS, BROADWAY REFERS NOT TO THE THOROUGH-
fare that cuts through Manhattan Island from Bowling Green near its tip and eventually leads to Albany, but to the midtown theatre section. In 1905, it extended for a
mile and a half on Broadway, where fifteen of the major theatres were situated. From
1900 to World War I, the New York stage "was provincial and parochial; it bore no
serious relation to life," according to Brooks Atkinson of *The New York Times*. Nonetheless, he added, Broadway in the early years of the twentieth century possessed
"charm and a kind of disarming simplicity." From 1900 to 1910, the city had more
than doubled its population of 1,500,000 to 3,500,000 as European immigrants
streamed into Ellis Island. Life in New York suddenly became crowded and pressured and Broadway audiences, who paid two dollars for the best seats, were seeking
entertainment and escape.

The plays Broadway produced had little or no relationship to the exciting new
ideas taking form in all other areas of the arts worldwide. In France, Henri Matisse
and his group of Fauvists had shaken the art world in 1905. In the same year, Richard Strauss premiered his opera *Salome*, Sigmund Freud published *Three Treatises on
the Theory of Sex*, and Einstein revealed his first theory of relativity. Banking was being regulated, child labor controlled, political corruption exposed, work had started

on the Panama Canal, and a five-cent cinema in Pittsburgh was showing an eleven-minute film, the longest of its time and one of the first to tell a story. The European theatre had emerged fresh from a lackluster century. "Ibsen and Shaw were dramatising ideas. Chekhov, Gorky, Strindberg, Rostand, Schnitzler, Hauptmann and Sudermann were discussing truths of life or were writing with the virtuosity of poets." The big hit of Broadway in 1905 was George M. Cohan's *Little Johnny Jones*, and the two songs he sang in it—"Give My Regards to Broadway" and "I'm a Yankee Doodle Dandy"—with their shameless flag waving and sentimentality were very much in the mood of what Broadway was presenting. In this atmosphere Beatrice found her most successful niche.

With all cultural pretensions left behind in her need to be self-supporting, Beatrice had discovered a talent for telling a simple story in a theatrical way. Writing a play was too time consuming. Instead, she took her clients' work and helped them turn it into a commercial product by doctoring the script herself. Producers now came to her looking for good properties. Since she had a dramatic and inimitable voice, she often could tell a story better than the script read and sold many plays by this method. A vital, attractive woman with an instinct for the theatrical in her dress and a sharp wit, Beatrice attracted many eligible (and she claimed "ineligible") men, but she seemed uninterested in the idea of remarrying. She liked being Mrs. Henry C. DeMille. The name, the respect it engendered, suited her well, and she was intent on helping her sons succeed. She also enjoyed not having to answer to any man for her actions.

She had represented Bill and Cecil on their early collaboration *The Genius.* The play was not good. After she had retitled it *The Genius and the Model*, and helped to rewrite it, she managed to get a production mounted for the 1906 season. But if Cecil thought he might have an overnight success as a playwright and put the rigors of the road behind him, he was sadly mistaken. *The Genius and the Model* had only twenty-one performances. Bill went on to write the successful *Classmates* for the following season while Cecil toured with the Standard Opera Company in *The Bohemian Girl, Martha, The Chimes of Normandy,* and *The Mikado.* He "acted, sang, booked theaters, managed" and even filled in—with no apparent difficulty—for the ailing conductor.

With Bill and Anna living in New York, Cecil had decided it would be more convenient for him and Constance to move to the city. But between road tours, Cecil and Constance had to call on Bill to help pay the rent. The brothers tried another play, *Son of the Winds,* but Beatrice suggested they work on it more before submitting it. Bill's *Classmates* was still running on Broadway when Belasco agreed to produce his *The Warrens of Virginia,* the story of Agatha Warren, a Southern girl during the Civil War who falls in love with Ned Burton, a Northern soldier. Cecil was cast as Agatha's brother, Arthur, and little Gladys Smith portrayed their younger sister, Betty. The winsome Miss Smith shortly after decided to use the more unusual name of Mary Pickford.

"Not long after rehearsals started I had my first taste of David Belasco in action," Pickford recalled. "One night I was brought up sharply to attention by a loud and commanding voice.... 'Hold everything.' Mr. Belasco walked up on the stage. The set was a stately dining room of one of the old Virginia mansions, authentic in

An advertisement for the play *The Warrens of Virginia*, 1907, by William deMille

A production of *The Warrens of Virginia*, with Cecil B. DeMille at left, 1907

every detail from rugs and antiques down to a crystal and silver molasses container. ...Mr. Belasco elaborately stalked that jar. Everyone froze. Mr. Belasco adjusted his glasses [then he] tasted the contents of the jar...and dashed it into a thousand pieces on the floor, and began to jump up and down on the sticky mess, thereby driving it deeper and deeper into the beautiful Oriental rug...[then] he ordered the property man to clean up the stage. 'Never,' he shouted, 'use maple syrup if the script calls for molasses.'...To me David Belasco was like the King of England, Julius Caesar and Napoleon all rolled into one."

Before opening on Broadway, there were four weeks on the road. The first performance of *The Warrens of Virginia* was presented in Boston. From that point, Belasco worked tirelessly on Bill's script, polishing and perfecting the dialogue with him as the company moved from city to city. The play opened in New York on a Monday night in November 1907.

The Warrens of Virginia was a turning point in both Bill's and Cecil's careers. With its fifteen-month run and many touring companies, Bill became an established playwright. Cecil, with a dependable weekly wage during the long New York engagement, was able to remain in the city, to continue writing (with and without Bill) when it went on the road, and perhaps of the greatest advantage, to work with and study Belasco's style. "[Belasco] liked to talk his work, to construct the way he had constructed with my father," Cecil recalled. "He confidently expected actors to work for him for less money than other producers would pay them, and the wisest among them did. ...There was never a rigid Belasco formula, but there were Belasco ingredients that the public came to expect from him always [the literal productions, the stars], and he did not disappoint them."

Although Cecil could recognize the reasons for Belasco's success, he was not yet able to apply what he had learned to himself. Bill was fairly affluent by now, but after the money from *The Warrens of Virginia* ran out, Cecil fell on hard times. He kept writing plays,* but once his checks from Belasco had stopped, he had to borrow on his life insurance to make ends meet. A baby daughter, Cecilia, was born to Cecil and Constance in 1909, and he had helped "the doctor deliver at home because [he] could not afford a hospital or nurse...." He "often walked from Times Square to 110th Street [where they lived] to save the nickel carfare to buy milk." Pride kept him from going to Bill unless desperate, and Beatrice, though doing well, was hopeless with balancing her budget and never seemed able to make expenses and income meet. Cecil hit rock bottom just at the time that he believed his career was finally about to take off.

In the summer of 1910 Cecil (now twenty-nine) came to Belasco to negotiate a business loan (against rights to a play, *The Stampede*, written with Lillian Buckingham, a client of Beatrice's). Belasco turned him down first, then agreed to pay him a weekly stipend for six weeks so that he could go somewhere and write a new play. Belasco was to have the right to produce the play if he liked it. If not, Cecil would owe him the money. The play he wrote (alone in a rustic Maine hut) was about a man who survived the death of his body and was called *The Return of Peter Grimm*. It was a quasi-religious comedy complete with a séance and a returned spirit. Belasco proceeded to use Cecil's story as the basis for another play, with new characters and plot inventions of his own. He did not tell Cecil what he had done until the play was in production with the great actor David Warfield in the title role. *The Return of Peter Grimm* was credited as being "by David Belasco." Buried in the small print of the lesser credits, "among learned references...to authorities on the subject of physical research," was the note "based on an idea by Cecil B. DeMille."

Shortly after its out-of-town premiere at the Hollis Theatre in Boston, and as the show was heading into New York, Cecil went to the newspapers, which deemed his situation important enough for a two-column front-page story with such headlines as these in *The New York Times:* "CECIL DE MILLE CHARGES BELASCO TAKES CREDIT DUE HIM AS AUTHOR OF DAVID WARFIELD'S PLAY"; "Spent Three Years Writing It and Is Barely Mentioned on Program"; "IDEA WAS DE MILLE'S. Author Remains Away from Premiere and May Go to Court."

The Times article went on to say:

Belasco takes the lion's share of the authorship, making it appear that "The Return of Peter Grimm" is really a creation of his own.

Belasco further strengthened that idea in the public mind by his curtain speech at the opening in Boston, when he declared that the play was the result of an experience which he asserted that he had on the night of the death of his mother. He averred that on the night that she departed this life in San Francisco he awakened suddenly in New York and saw his mother standing beside his bed, and that she spoke to him as when in the flesh, bidding him good-bye, and saying she was about to leave for another world....

It is no new thing, of course, for Belasco to be charged with irregularities in the matter of claiming credit as author of plays produced by him....

Cecil did not sue Belasco. In fact, he found it difficult to believe his childhood hero had deliberately cheated him. "Probably he believed in all sincerity that *The Return of Peter Grimm* owed more to his work and less to mine than was actually the case," C. B. wrote. "Perhaps it was like the pony he promised me when I was seven or eight years old. Perhaps he just forgot."

Cecil's lack of success and his financial problems greatly troubled Beatrice, and in 1910 she took larger offices in the Astor Theatre Building and formed the DeMille Play Company. ("I enjoyed the title of general manager...but mother remained the real general," C. B. wrote.) The company produced and financed plays, both for Broadway and the road. All three DeMilles drew a weekly salary along with their participation and the royalties from their own works. William was a successful playwright, and content to spend most of his time in writing, but Cecil was learning all aspects of the theatre, from the business side to casting, directing, and publicity. Beatrice still retained her position as an authors' representative, which meant that when the DeMille Play Company produced one of her authors' plays, she received a double percentage as both producer and agent.*

Vaudeville was at its height in 1910, and Jesse L. Lasky was one of its important impresarios. Lasky, "natty with his high stiff collar and pince-nez, at once charming and businesslike," was the master of the short musical play that was often the substantial filling in a vaudeville production, with acrobats and song and dance teams offered first and after. An idea for one of these musicals that needed a writer to develop it brought him to Beatrice, whom he found "seated behind her desk, in one of her flowing yet for the occasion not over-feminine velvet gowns." Lasky claimed he had been inspired by "a big billboard advertising Mission Coffee.... A plot started brewing in my mind around the billboard figures [a group of Indians, several padres and a beautiful Spanish girl]... the beautiful girl in the mission had been found by the Indians, taken to the padres and brought up by them. The hero would be a surveyor laying out a railroad line. He would fall in love with the girl and be obliged to tell her that [the mission was to be destroyed].... I'd bring the billboard alive in an operetta called *California*.... I went to see Mrs. H. C. DeMille." Lasky asked Beatrice if Bill was available to write *California* for him. Bill was not, but Beatrice suggested Cecil. Lasky did not jump at the idea. "I had no intention of entrusting my great idea to a lesser luminary than William, and certainly not to an actor who had made a couple of stabs at playwriting, so I tried to make a strategic withdrawal. But Mrs. DeMille's motherly instinct made a powerful alliance with her business interests, and there was no escape for me.... she insisted I step into a rear office and meet Cecil. [We] surveyed each other suspiciously.... I hemmed and hawed through the story thread of my operetta.... Cecil's eyes were taking on a glint of insight.... When I finished, he leaned forward and exclaimed, 'Say, I like that!'"*

Lasky engaged him for a one-hundred-dollar advance and a twenty-five-dollar-a-week guarantee. With *California*, Cecil had his first success, and went on to write the book for two other musical divertissements, *In the Barracks* and *The Antique Girl*, all three written with the collaboration of Robert Hood Bowers (music) and co-directed by Cecil and Lasky. The two men became good friends, vacationing together summers without their families in the Maine woods and for three years lunched almost daily at the Claridge Grill. Lasky recalled, "We used to daydream about exploring the South Seas someday, and started to save money for a yacht by consecrating a box to that worthy cause and dropping small change in it whenever we met. One Saturday night, discovering the yacht fund had swollen to $100, we cruised down to...Greenwich Village and turned our mythical yacht in on more tangible schooners."

Cecil and his family were surviving, but not much more. He directed a play called *The Marriage-Not*; produced another, *Cheer Up*; wrote two unproduced plays and some dialogue for Mary Roberts Rinehart's *The Water Cure*, and collaborated on *After Five* with Bill. To date, Bill's only unsuccessful plays had been those written with his brother. Cecil's contributions were always an attempt to lighten and theatricalize Bill's more serious and reflective themes, and the two elements never emulsified. Bill's play *The Woman* teamed him a second time with Belasco in the summer of 1911. It opened in Washington. ("We all missed you," Bill wrote Belasco. "President Taft was in a box, occupying a special chair big enough to accommodate his dignity, and I got the thrill of my young life when he sent for me after the final curtain and told me how much he liked the play.") *The Woman* had originated two years before with another title (*The Machine*) and quite a different set of characters. In his usual style, Belasco had put his own imprint on the play. However, Bill fared better than Cecil and retained his authorship.

He now had two daughters, Agnes George (born September 18, 1905, and

Sheet music for a song from *In the Barracks*, a vaudeville operetta for which Cecil B. DeMille wrote the book, 1912. The producer was Jesse L. Lasky

named for his dead sister) and Margaret George (born November 25, 1908). A year after Anna and Bill had married, Annie George had died and Anna received a small inheritance with which in 1909 she and Bill bought a modest rustic house at a place in Sullivan County, New York, called Merriewold Park. The house had been built by playwright Charles Klein (a client of Beatrice DeMille's). The family summered there and Bill wrote in a small lean-to in the woods. ("Men with intellects thought in separate, reserved places, guarded from family disturbance, like shrines," Agnes commented.) Merriewold Park was "a lovely stretch of wild woodland," where Henry George in the 1890s had bought "a little cabin-like" home.* Many of his single-tax followers had joined in the purchase of a large tract which they bought cheaply, and they formed a congenial community.

Life at Merriewold remained as informal as in Henry George's time. Anna recalled that when the family's clothes were too worn to give away, they used to save

Merriewold, the house in Upstate New York bought by Anna and William deMille in 1909 where they spent summers with their daughters, Agnes and Margaret

them to wear at Merriewold. In New York, in their apartment on 118th Street, the deMille family lived with the accoutrements of affluence: fine clothes, sufficient household staff, and a more formal ambience. Bill was photographed in his book-lined study and written about in *The Theatre* magazine. He was successful and Anna was tremendously proud of him.

"That Mother and Father were in love," Agnes wrote about a summer in Merriewold, circa 1912, when she was about six years old, "I knew as I knew that the woods were green and budding. They walked hand in hand; I remember them picking lilies of the valley . . . and the look he bent upon her, and the blue dazzle of her return gaze."

On Saturdays, "Aunt Bettie de Mille Pitman, Father's young Southern aunt, played the [upright] piano . . . between two pendant oil lamps. . . . The grown-ups danced the fox trot. . . . Mother wore a home-made and enchanting dress of Japanese silk and real lace which revealed her milky bosom. Her masses of red hair were caught up by gold combs."

Agnes deMille's assessment of her father's playwriting ability fell considerably short of her mother's view of him as "an unquestioned genius." Anna claimed Bill "had the wit of George Bernard Shaw and the tenderness of James Matthew Barrie. [To Agnes] he had nothing of the sort. He was a journeyman craftsman, who could tailor a well-made plot (usually with help) and turn out dialogue which acted very well and which was sometimes extremely funny. His work possessed, however, no real distinction or style. He knew his rules: he could hold attention, build suspense, and make a point. That's a lot, but it doesn't last. . . .

Agnes deMille in
1906

"He was sufficiently vain to bury his shortcomings under his singing, tennis-playing, and after-dinner speaking, which was brilliant. If he could not be one he acted the part of a great playwright and his minor skills made him able to bear better the fact that he wasn't a first-class writer."

Beatrice refused to believe any such thing. She treated Bill with a kind of reverence that she did not bestow on Cecil. And, yet, she was closer to her younger son, more frank with him, more relaxed. In fact, she and Cecil both treated Bill as the patriarch of the family, and he did his best to live up to the title. In these years, the family always gathered at Bill and Anna's homes. Cecil preferred to meet his friends and collaborators away from his modest apartment. But a constant flow of guests came and went at Bill's. "There were, of course, Father's collaborators, all kinds and sexes," Agnes remembered. "There were relatives. The distinguished Jewish relatives from England, quite superior, with marvelous, refined accents; the American relatives...and...Cecil, who was a young and brilliant and adorable man, with a very handsome wife and a small, uncontrollable daughter....Cecil...had an open touring car...[and] was interesting because he was full of ideas, such as the hunting trips...and the new ventures for the theater."

A strong bond existed between the brothers. Yet a sense of rivalry was apparent. Bill thought Cecil was too undisciplined and extravagant. He also did not have high regard for his theatre ability. (Cecil "had produced a succession of plays, ranging from cheap melodrama to high-class comedy, all of which had one element in common: a complete lack of power to please the public," Bill wrote.)

To Bill's "disgust, [Cecil] took little interest in politics," but Cecil admitted he had voted in 1912 for Woodrow Wilson, "and his orderly vision of a New Freedom; perhaps...[because he] unconsciously saw something of [his] father in that scholarly, intense southerner who had also left his quiet academic life to preach to a larger student body from the political rostrum, as [Henry] had gone from the schoolroom and pulpit to the stage."

Cecil was getting restless, and despite his own and all of his mother's attempts to send his theatre career into orbit, it remained earthbound. The world was in ferment and so was Cecil. One day when having lunch with Lasky at the Hotel Claridge on Forty-fourth Street, he announced, "I'm pulling out. Broadway's all right for you—you're doing well. But I can't live on the royalties I'm getting, my debts are piling up, and I want to chuck the whole thing. Besides there's a revolution going on in Mexico and I'm going down and get in on it—maybe write about it. That's what I need—a stimulating and colorful change of scene."

Lasky had another good friend, his brother-in-law, Sam Goldfish, a successful glove salesman. Goldfish had been talking to Lasky about the idea of going into the film business. Several companies were making short-reelers which were shown in continuous vaudeville houses as a means to empty the theatres between acts so that new customers could be seated. "I told Sam I would have nothing to do with a busi-

Great-grandmother
Samuel with Agnes,
left, and Margaret,
Morningside Drive
near the deMille
apartment on 118th
Street

ness that chased people out of the theatres, even though I might be grateful it did," Lasky recalled.

As he sat across from Cecil, an idea formed: "To keep Cecil from doing something foolish alone, I proposed we do something foolish together.... All I could think of at the moment was Sam's harping topic of conversation.... I said, 'If you want adventure, I've got an even better idea—let's make some movies!'

"His eyes gleamed, and before I was over the shock of hearing my own unconsidered suggestion, Cecil put out his hand, grabbed mine, and said, 'Let's!'"*

Bill was at Merriewold when he received word of Cecil's plans to enter into the picture business and sat down in ill-humor to write him:

> Merriewold Park, N.Y.
> September 3d 1913
>
> Mr. Cecil B. DeMille.
> 220 West 42d St. New York City
>
> My Dear C.,
>
> I was quite disturbed to get your letter of last week telling me that you, Jesse Lasky, Sam Goldfish and Arthur Friend have formed a company to go into the moving-picture business. I knew, of course, that your last two productions in the theater had divested you of everything except your ambition and personal charm, but I did not suspect that you had reached the point of utter desperation. After all you do come of a cultured family, two of whose members have made honorable names in the field of drama, and I cannot understand how you are willing to identify yourself with a cheap form of amusement and which no one will ever allude to as an art.
>
> I do not blame Jesse so much, as his years in vaudeville have probably made anything else seem attractive; nor do I censure Sam, whose experiences as a high-pressure glove-salesman might easily stimulate a wild desire to bite the thousands of hands which have fed him. Arthur's work as a lawyer has naturally made him familiar with the depths to which human beings can sink in their desire to acquire wealth, so to his legal mind, teasing nickels and dimes out of the mentally immature by making photographs leap and prance is no doubt a vast improvement on murder or highway robbery.
>
> But you—who were born and raised in the finest traditions of the theater—You who have undoubted dramatic ability and stand more than an even chance of making your name known in all the big cities of the United States—to throw away your future; end your career before it is well started and doom yourself to obscurity if not, indeed, to oblivion, seems to me a step which calls for protest from those who really care what happens to you....
>
> You say that you believe this strange medium can be used to tell a story dramatically, and that you propose to use what you know of dramatic art to develope [sic] a new technic [sic] for the screen; but how can you develope a drama without words, and with characters who all seem to be afflicted with St. Vitus' dance?
>
> Before committing yourself to Lasky and Goldfish I do wish you had

waited until after the opening of "After Five" [which he and Cecil had rewritten and Beatrice was producing]. I'm leaving here for New York next week to start rehearsing it with Colin Kemper [as director]. Who knows?—it may turn out to be another "Seven Days" in which case you as one of its authors will not have to sell your pure white body to the films....

When you get stranded out there in the West I will send you your railroad fare—as usual.

I suppose Mother is heartbroken. This must be a terrible blow to her for I know what hopes she had for you and what faith in you—

However—you were always a determined little cuss and I guess you'll just have to learn from bitter experience what a mistake you are making.

Well, I've said my say, so good luck and may the God of all the Zanies have you in his care.

With love—(which is akin to pity).

Your brother.

William.

Within three weeks, the Jesse L. Lasky Feature Play Company was organized with a total cash capital of approximately $20,000; Jesse was president; Goldfish, vice-president and business manager; Arthur Friend, secretary and legal adviser; and Cecil, director general. The new company announced that it would make feature pictures with a running time of one hour or more, a daring innovation, for films at this early stage were mostly five- to ten-minute one- and two-reelers. Because costs—land, labor, and materials—were cheaper, and climate and sunlight superior, in the West, the Jesse L. Lasky Feature Play Company decided to establish itself in Flagstaff, Arizona. With Beatrice's help, it secured the rights to *The Squaw Man*, a play by Edwin Milton Royal that had been a Broadway hit some seasons before. Next, the company managed to convince stage star Dustin Farnum to play the lead.

A week before he was to depart on his Western adventure, Cecil went to see Bill. "He...suggest[ed] that I part with five thousand dollars and acquire a quarter interest in the company," Bill recalled.

" 'Oh, no,' I said, with all the wisdom of an elder brother. 'Up to now, I've kept out of your various ventures with the result that every time you got stranded, I was able to lend you enough to get you and the company back to New York.'

"He smiled his singularly disarming smile. 'Quite sure you don't want to come in with us, Bill?'

" 'Boy,' I replied. 'There have been times when I wasn't sure of my name; times when I didn't know whether I was awake or asleep...but this one time I am sure with the deepest certainty a human being can feel. I do *not* want to go in with you.' "

In "one of the two most fateful conversations" Cecil and Constance had ever had (the other being his proposal of marriage), she agreed to follow him with five-year-old Cecilia if the venture was successful. Meanwhile, "she bundled up the family silver and gave it to [him] to take to Simpson's pawn shop" so that he would not have to travel with empty pockets.

A Strange New Medium

1913–1915

Cecil is "De" Mille.
William is "de" Mille.
Cecil is a showman...
William is a student...
Cecil is daring, and dynamic.
William is subtle and gentle...
Cecil is from Balzac.
William is from Barrie.

—ADELA ROGERS ST. JOHN, *Photoplay*, 1923

CECIL HAD SET OFF BY TRAIN FOR FLAGSTAFF, ARIZONA ("AN Indian picture ought to be made in real Indian country"), in mid-November 1913 with his star, Dustin Farnum; Oscar Apfel, a director who had some experience in making one- and two-reelers; Alfred Gandolfi, a cameraman who owned a crank-handled movie camera, and $5,000 to make *The Squaw Man*. Two weeks later, Lasky and Goldfish had not heard from him and were beginning to get worried.

> Cecil seemed to have disappeared [Lasky recalled]. Finally a telegram arrived—but it wasn't from Flagstaff. It said, "FLAGSTAFF NO GOOD FOR OUR PURPOSE. HAVE PROCEEDED TO CALIFORNIA WANT AUTHORITY TO RENT BARN IN PLACE CALLED HOLLYWOOD FOR $75 A MONTH. REGARDS TO SAM. CECIL."
> Sam hit the ceiling....when you're [vice-] president of a company you assume is located in Flagstaff, Arizona, it's very disconcerting to have it turn up in a place you've never even heard of. Sam was all for calling the company back where we could keep an eye on it. We argued for hours. At last we agreed to let them stay and wired Cecil: "AUTHORIZE YOU TO RENT BARN BUT ON MONTH-TO-MONTH BASIS. DON'T MAKE ANY LONG COMMITMENT. REGARDS. JESSE AND SAM."

Lasky assumed Cecil had continued westward to follow the sun. Rain and snow when the group arrived in Flagstaff have both been cited for the change in Cecil's plans. "We should have been a sorry lot if a little rain discouraged us," C. B. countered. When he stepped off the train at Flagstaff, he had been shocked to see a landscape that looked more like North Africa than Wyoming, the locale of *The Squaw Man*. Filming in Flagstaff would have required a complete rewrite. "The train was beginning to practice puffing its lungs and pulling itself together, the way trains used to do, before continuing its westward journey. There was time only for a very quick decision...."

"At the end of the railroad line was Los Angeles...[where] other picture makers had been working...on and off for some years. The California climate was good, there was a great variety of scenery." They would also be farther away and perhaps safe from the watchdogs in the Motion Picture Patents Company (called the Trust), which controlled production through monopoly of the Edison patents. The Trust fought with weapons and violence to hold the fledgling industry in its iron clasp, and to keep independents from pirating Edison's patented designs. The major cause of the dispute was Edison's patented Latham Loop, a mechanism incorporated in the motion picture camera. Gandolfi's camera was approved by the Trust, but the company was daring to make a six-reel picture, which would run sixty minutes, and the Trust only sanctioned one- and two-reelers, which it made with little money and great profits, and it did not want to be forced to compete with a longer picture.

Hollywood then was a parcel of land separated from Los Angeles by eight miles of country road and so named by Mrs. Horace Henderson Wilcox, the wife of a prohibitionist who had bought the acreage in 1894 for a country home. The first motion picture studio had been established there in 1906.* Henry DeMille's old friend Hobart Bosworth played the lead in *The Power of the Sultan*, believed to be the first dramatic film made entirely in California. Within a few years, D. W. Griffith traveled there to make use of the authentic Western background, and Mack Sennett with two former bookies, Charles O. Bauman and Adam Kessell, started a new production company they named Keystone.

The L-shaped barn that C. B. turned into a studio was fairly undistinguished though large enough to accommodate all his picture-making needs. One of its "yellowish heat-beaten wings ran along Vine Street and the other stretched back, parallel with Selma Avenue," where the Jesse L. Lasky Feature Play Company sign was posted.* "Stalls were turned into offices, dressing rooms, and a projection room. One end of the barn was used as a storeroom. In a clearing made among the acres of orange and lemon trees that went with the barn, a small wooden platform was built on an open stage." Production started on *The Squaw Man* on December 29, 1913.*

Finding a studio location was one thing, a home another. Hollywood landlords did not want to rent to film people, whom they called "movies" (a "word... vaguely suggestive of irritating insects"), unaware that the term referred to the product.* "For rent" signs stated: "No 'movies,' no Negroes, no Jews."

The local banks even refused to open accounts for "movies." Cecil found a place at 6136 Lexington, a short distance from the studio, and then, affirming to his neighbors that "those 'movies' are crazy," he moved in with Sheba, a tame, gray prairie wolf he bought through a newspaper advertisement. At nights, "the wolf would

Cecil B. DeMille with some of the cast of *The Squaw Man*, the feature-length movie he directed in 1913–14; he made two later versions of the film

pace the four sides of the [living] room, silently, intently, hour after hour.... I suppose she slept sometimes," C. B. speculated, "but never while I was wakeful." Daytime, he put the animal on a leash and brought her to the studio, where he let her roam untethered about the set to the constant terror of cast and crew, who did not have the same faith in Sheba's domesticity.*

Once *The Squaw Man* was in production, Cecil felt secure enough to bring Constance and Cecilia to Hollywood. His leading lady, Winifred Kingston, found a more suitable place for the DeMilles to live, a small cottage in the Cahuenga Pass, between Hollywood and the San Fernando Valley, with open country surrounding it. He sent Constance enough money for a train compartment. She chose instead to travel by Pullman berth and to retrieve their silver from the pawnshop and bring it with her. Cecil met his family at the railroad station in a hired open touring car, the back filled with violets—"fresh flowers in January to symbolize [his] welcome."

Considerable violence and sabotage were perpetrated by the Trust during the making and editing of *The Squaw Man*. Several days after shooting had begun, C. B. found the film "unwound, thrown in a heap on the floor...scraped, pitted, disfigured, as if someone had...dragged it between heel and floor....It was completely ruined. So would our company have been, if I had not had [an] extra negative at home." The cutting room was now never left deserted, with C. B. and Mamie Wagner, the cutter, alternating night shifts. Cecil carried a gun in a hip holster at all times and was twice at the point of using it.

A car was useless on the rough, dirt road that led from the DeMille cottage to the studio and so Cecil bought a horse. With lunch and the negative slung over his shoulder in a leather pouch and his gun at the ready, he traveled by horseback to the studio. One day, as he rode "homeward in the dusk...zing! a sharp whizzing sound passed by [his] head, followed soon by the crack of a shot." Cecil drew his gun, "ready to shoot," but the sniper had silently withdrawn. A few days later, in the same spot, another bullet was fired in his direction—and missed aim (or perhaps the shot was a warning) and the assailant was nowhere to be seen.

Lasky followed Constance and Cecilia to Hollywood. He had come to see how pictures were made in California and what C. B. was doing with the money he had raised.

> We carried [our lunch] to the studio, and at noon we had our sandwiches with coffee made on a little kerosene stove...work stopped on the open stage as soon as the sun went behind a cloud....On a very cloudy day the cast didn't even show up....But we took full advantage of the sunshine when we had it—there were no unions to frown on sixteen hour days. If it looked like rain, the set was quickly covered with huge tarpaulins to protect the props.
>
> Cold weather...caused tiny flashes of static electricity inside the cameras which ruined the film. We never knew until a batch had been developed whether it would have to be shot over....When we wanted to find [a location to shoot in] the whole company set out in search of it. Cecil and I...rode ahead on horseback, with the crew and cast following in two cars. When we found what we wanted, we stopped and shot a scene, then went on to the next setting we needed....
>
> We reveled in the outdoor life of picture-pioneering and dressed the part in boots, jeans and lumberjack shirts, not to mention Cecil's pistol....[He] wore a cap turned backward, and adopted leather leggings for the convenience of location scouting on horseback and as protection against cactus and rattlesnakes in the desert regions.

Lasky was still in Hollywood when shooting was completed and the film assembled. Cecil gathered together about fifty people to view the finished product. "Cecil gave a signal, the lights went off, and '*Jesse L. Lasky Presents*' flashed on the screen. Then the words immediately went into convulsions, dancing and crawling right up over the edge of the screen, and then magically appeared at the bottom and started working [their] way up again."

The preview had to be called off and the audience sent home. Something was wrong with the film, and the projectionist could not discover the cause. Cecil and Lasky were in despair. They had used up all their capital, "spent all Sam [Goldfish] could collect as advances [from theatre owners in each state], and there remained unpaid bills." While Goldfish sent a stream of telegrams to Hollywood asking for release dates and getting no replies, Cecil and Lasky took the film to "Pop" Lubin in Philadelphia, the owner of the best film laboratory in the country. "Cecil went into the lab [with the technicians]," Lasky recalled, "and left me pacing back and forth outside, sweating in an agony of suspense, knowing that if the film couldn't be saved we were ruined....[It took] Lubin's men [the most harrowing half-hour] to spot the trouble." As an economy measure, Cecil had used unperforated film and a hand-operated punch, which had altered the speed when the film was projected.

A Strange New Medium

The Squaw Man was shown to the trade at the Longacre Theatre in New York on February 17, 1914, less than two months from the first day of shooting—a miracle of sorts considering the obstacles it had encountered. Bill, Anna, and Beatrice were in the audience. The film broke several times, but despite this, "and a musical accompaniment which paid little attention to what was happening on the screen, the story held; it was essentially *drama*, the acting restrained and realistic, the emotional climaxes poignant," Bill remembered. "As the picture ended, a buzz of excitement and applause told us that...the film was a smash hit and the Lasky Company was a successful, important force in the new world of the cinema...

"'I tell you, Bill,' said C.B., 'you'd love it out there [Hollywood]. How about it—will you come?'

"'I might get away for three months,'" Bill replied.

The brothers shook hands. Beatrice looked from one to the other and then turned away. She claimed that at that moment she had felt certain the DeMilles were not only riding into the sunset, but hell-bent for disaster.

About six months after Cecil had gone to Hollywood, Beatrice decided she would at least like to see what was involved in making movies.

On July 7, 1914, she wrote Cecil:

Dearest Boy:

I have just come from a pretty strenuous meeting between Messrs. Roeder, Bookbinder, J. W. Rumsey [lawyers] and your very humble servant—& Mother. Result....If I had been of the male gender, or any other female than Beatrice, there would have been a law-suit of the largest dimensions [Beatrice was withholding all film rights on her properties]....I am a total wreck after the strain...Don't you think it is about time I had a letter from you direct? I won't be responsible if I don't get one pretty soon. Your wobbly—Pal B deM.

On July 13, she seemed relieved to reply to Cecil's answer to the above:

Dearest Boy:—

Your telegram just to hand telling me you had purchased my railroad ticket to California. Well that settles it. I am coming. BUT—...I have one big thing on hand which I must get to a certain stage before I depart....So if it is O.K. for you I shall leave about July 31st or August 1st. Won't it be jolly hav[ing] you all on your birthday. I am aching to see you all. The railroad company say[s] if I give them one week's time to get me a good lower berth, that will be O.K. I am glad you want me.

Your perked-up
Beatrice

Beatrice obviously had no idea that Cecil was not yet setting the world on fire. On September 11, 1914, a few days after Beatrice's return to New York, Jesse Lasky wrote Cecil:

It seems that some of your creditors are beginning to bother Mr. Friend [the lawyer] so I wish you would let us know if, after three or four weeks [to allow time to make up the cost of Beatrice's trip] you could let us deduct, say $30 per week out of your salary [$200] as Mr. Friend thinks he probably can make some arrangement to pay them small sums until the debts are settled.... We will continue to pay Mrs. H.C. [Beatrice] $50 per week which [will also be deducted].

The accounts that are particularly troublesome are Martin [a banker] who has a judgement and has examined us in supplementary proceedings; John Wanamaker [a department store] and Brett.

No other claimants are bothering now.

Regards,

Jesse

After her visit to Hollywood, Beatrice reported to Bill that one might as well live in the Sahara Desert. "The hills were burned brown as a dog's back, and no brooks...and very little rain." Despite her dislike of the terrain or the climate in Southern California, the businesswoman in Beatrice had quickly recognized the potential of moving pictures and spoke to Bill about it. Bill had just suffered a severe blow. The comedy he and Cecil had written before Cecil had gone to Hollywood (*After Five*) closed after scathing reviews. "Perhaps," Anna told him, "Hollywood *would* be a good change. Tell Cecil 'yes.'" On September 26, 1914, Bill arrived in Hollywood.

Constance met him at the station. "After a chaste family salute" she told him that Cecil was filming *The Rose of the Rancho* out at the newly acquired three-hundred-acre Lasky Ranch in the San Fernando Valley. With the success of *The Squaw Man*, the Jesse L. Lasky Feature Play Company had made and released another popular film, *The Call of the North*, and had three more pictures—*The Virginian*, *What's His Name*, and *The Man from Home*—in various stages of post-production. Within a few hours, Bill had changed at Cecil's request into old clothes and had joined him at the ranch. As he drove up to the location where the filming was taking place, he sighted "a solidly-built person, dressed in corduroy pants and puttees, a flannel shirt open at the neck, with dark sun-glasses, and a slouch hat pulled well down over his eyes. His clothes were wet with sweat [it was September and the temperature over 100°] and his face and arms caked with dust.... [It was C. B.] He...rushed over to me."

In "his nine months in the West...he had bronzed and hardened, he was about twenty pounds heavier with not an ounce of fat."

"'Hello, Bill,' he said.... 'How's Mother? Here, put on one of those cowboy rigs and get on a horse—you're one of the attacking Gringos. The boys will show you what to do.'"

"Costumed, booted and spurred," Bill mounted a great steed and on C. B.'s command emerged from behind some underbrush with two rugged-looking cowpunchers on each side of him riding hell-bent and shouting and shooting as they approached the camera. "Because my attention had been devoted to staying on my horse," Bill admitted, "all my cartridges were intact. Guided by my infallible sense of

showmanship, I held my fire until I felt I was ... close enough [to the camera] to be important. Then I began emitting lusty yells and firing my gun. When I had given what I considered an excellent performance, I noticed that I was alone; the others had checked their horses some distance back; I had put on my show just after the camera had stopped turning."*

In the following two weeks, Cecil exposed Bill to every facet of filmmaking. Finally he was given the script of *The Rose of the Rancho*, which Cecil had adapted from a play by David Belasco and Richard Walton Tully. When he had finished, he told Cecil that he now understood what had to be done to write for the camera. C. B. handed him a script of the play *Cameo Kirby*. "We're in a hurry for it," he said, "but because you're new at the game ... you can have two weeks to do the job."

Bill wrestled frantically with this new form of story construction. He now had "to write entirely for the eye and disregard the ear. ... Robbed of language, [he] felt like a fish trying to swim without fins." But he succeeded, and within a month, *Cameo Kirby* was before the cameras and Bill was not only working on a film adaptation of his play *The Warrens of Virginia*, and several other projects as well, he was organizing a scenario department to deal with the deluge of submissions and to develop screenplays. He was being paid $200 a week and felt he could not bring his family west on that amount. On February 10, 1915, he wrote Sam Goldfish a second request for a raise:

> Sam, I'm only asking a raise from two hundred to two fifty per week as head of the [scenario] department and I might add that in my first three months on the job, during which I was working at a reduced salary "to learn the business" I completed, alone and unaided, the full, feature length scenarios of *Cameo Kirby, The Goose Girl, Young Romance, After Five, The Gentleman*

always ended." It took several more letters and Beatrice delayed her departure. "I was unshakable," Cecil confessed. "Mother stood firm." Not until late autumn 1915 did Beatrice finally board the train for California and "on her own terms."

Cecil bought her a house on Argyle Avenue in Hollywood. "She liked it; but she promptly rented in addition an apartment away off in Long Beach.... She started writing scenarios and, surprisingly, our company bought some of them...not very good scenarios," Cecil confessed. "I provided her with a respectable little vehicle. It was soon traded in on a huge and ancient Packard....

"Life with mother was always adventurous. She was a prime prospect for any scheme for making a fortune overnight."

Beatrice later wrote, "Mother and Brother had been coaxed into the game [movies] by Cecil"—a statement a long way from the truth. However great their first reservations might have been about Cecil's "wild destructive venture," both Bill and Beatrice had followed him to Hollywood as soon as they saw that there was money to be made in moving pictures. Bill was to do well, but his relationship with his brother was reversed forever. Cecil's one-fourth interest in the Jesse L. Lasky Feature Play Company had made him over $2,000,000 by 1915, and the success of his films brought him power and fame. In his first two years in Hollywood, Bill became a well-known scenario writer. But pictures were a director's, not an author's, medium, and so he, too, turned to directing. From that moment, there was no way back. Despite his ability as a director, he would always stand in his younger brother's shadow. And Cecil never gave Bill a second chance to invest in the company. Bill was the boss's brother, but he was only a salaried employee. True, by 1917 his salary was $4,000 a week, but Cecil was a multimillionaire.

"Hollywood [in 1915] was different from what I thought [it would be]," Ag-

A lobby card for the first film William deMille directed, *Anton, the Terrible*, 1915

An early picture of Cecil directing, with his Pathé camera riding on an improvised mount

nes commented. They stayed the first few nights with Cecil, but Anna quickly found them "a dear little ugly house of our own, snuggling at the foot of a hill and boasting a banana tree and a rose garden." Hollywood was not unlike a country town in the East. Maples and chestnuts were replaced by palm trees. The main street, Hollywood Boulevard, "was a shambling, drowsy street of box stores and shingled houses under the dusty crackling palms and pepper trees." The only public conveyance was a trolley that clanged down the eight miles from Laurel Canyon to the heart of Los Angeles. On it every morning rode the entire working staff of the studio, carrying their lunch boxes. But Cecil, the director-general, and Jesse Lasky, the producer, rode to work in cars. Bill traveled by trolley. When Cecil "came home to dinner with Pop, they walked," Agnes recalled. "I used to see them, crossing the vacant lot in the red sunset, their putteed legs scratching through the dried yellow grass. They carried briefcases and talked with heads lowered.

" 'Anne' [his private name for Anna], called Father, 'I've brought Cecil home.'

" 'Cecil?' said Mother in a fluster. His effect on the womenfolk was always that of a cock in a barnyard, and Mother, like all his female relatives, looked upon every chance to serve him as an indulgence on his part."

No co-worker or family member dared to contradict Cecil, whose conviction was "total and unassailable," but, Agnes wrote, "before his mother [her grandmother], Bebe, his spirit sometimes quailed. She talked to him about all his work. She would sit opposite him at dinner decked in the extraordinary collection of laces and beads and flowers with which she covered her beautiful gray curls and talk to him sometimes very sternly. He always listened...more to her than to the critics."*

Cecil "seldom came home to dinner before ten or eleven at night. His table

Margaret deMille at left, Agnes in the center, and their cousin Cecilia, Cecil's daughter, at right. Hollywood, Christmas 1915

stood ready before the living room fireplace set with Italian lace and crystal; the double boilers waited on the stove. Aunt Constance gave him his dinner every night herself, prepared it and served it no matter what hour he came in," Agnes remembered. Soon, however, his wealth became so great that he bought a magnificent home in Laughlin Park neighboring Charlie Chaplin's house and on a hill overlooking Los Feliz Boulevard, about five minutes from the studio. Then came the purchase of a large ranch, Paradise, in the foothills of the Sierra Madres off Little Tajunga Canyon, a yacht, a Rubens, a fine library, swimming pool, tennis court, show horses for young Cecilia, and inevitably adoring mistresses. He went to bed every night armed with a gun. On Christmas, with the entire family gathered, Cecil sat "like a Pasha at the head of [his] table carving the roast pig. All the females lined the sides murmuring and attentive," Agnes recalled, "with Father, the older brother, somewhat sardonic, tucked away among them."

One day in 1923, Beatrice came to Cecil "and asked for a few hundred dollars for what she described rather vaguely as medical expenses." Cecil thought "it was the game again, and made the answering gambit." Beatrice did not respond "as usual. Tears came into her eyes." She told Cecil the truth. "She was not playing our game. She had learned she had cancer." During the summer of her grave illness, Cecil was filming his silent version of *The Ten Commandments* and commuting between Guadalupe and Los Angeles. As Beatrice refused to go into the hospital, she was cared for at home by a private nursing staff. As long as she was conscious, she insisted on her hair being coifed and her face made up when her sons or others came to see her. Despite severe pain that even the large doses of morphine could not allay, she would discuss with Cecil the progress of his film, adding her comments on the biblical issues in the script. The picture's Moses—Theodore Roberts—came to see her, a bit of irony she was able to find amusing. "I knew they [the Jews] would send an emissary in the end," she told one caller. She died on October 8, at the age of seventy, with the knowledge that the dynasty she had spawned, due to the "movies," was now known worldwide.

The Early Silent Years

1915–1918

*As far as directors are concerned, Cecil B. DeMille
mounted the greatest show on earth. Commanding
absolute loyalty from his staff, he directed as though
chosen by God for this one task. . . . Lost in the clamor
is Cecil's elder brother, William. He cared more for
psychological reality than melodramatic action, and his
style was as different from Cecil's as a miniaturist from
an epic painter.*

—Kevin Brownlow, *The Parade's Gone By*

MANY YEARS AFTER BEATRICE'S DEATH, CECIL ACKNOWLEDGED, "She remains the dominant figure, the strongest force, the greatest, the clearest and best experience. . . . It was she who taught her sons what it was to fight." Beatrice had also instilled in him "enormous ambition, competitiveness, and a desire to dominate." But her strength of character and her fierce independence caused Cecil great confusion in his view toward women and sex. Drawn invariably to strong women, he instantly set a course to dominate them. Unlike most men, he was able to realize some of his sexual fantasies through his direction of the actresses in his films and the characters they portrayed.

Quite certainly, the stage of his film career that took him through to the end of World War I was Cecil's best period as a director. Virtually all of these pictures were based on popular plays, but transposed to the screen with a larger-than-life vitality and a theatrical bravura achieved partially through dynamic lighting and partially through clever treatment of shocking material. During this time his themes were at their most experimental.* From the start, he had been a powerful force in the film industry. A few of his early efforts proved he could also be an exceptional director, most specifically when he dealt with bizarre stories that leaned heavily on sex, sadism, sacrifice, and spectacle, and ended with a moral message. The moralistic aspects harkened back to his father's religiosity and views and Cecil's desire to please

Henry. The greater influence, however, was Belasco, who served up "spectacle as the backdrop if not centerpiece for theatrical productions which had a significant moral dimension." *The Cheat*, filmed in 1915 (one of C. B.'s few early films from an original story), was not only the embodiment of these influences, but a genuine masterpiece, as visually powerful today as when Cecil made it.*

An extravagant socialite (Fannie Ward) gambles and loses $10,000 she has collected as treasurer of a Red Cross charity event. Too terrified to tell her husband what she has done, she goes to a wealthy Burmese dealer in ivory (Sessue Hayakawa*) who is part of her social circle and agrees to enter into an affair with him in exchange for the money which she must return.* The enormity of what she has done forces the woman to confront her husband (Jack Dean) with her desperate need for the money. He gives her a check, which she presents to the Burmese, presuming it will settle her debt to him. But he refuses to accept it. A struggle ensues in which he overpowers her, rips her clothes from her shoulder, and with a hot iron brands his logo (used to mark all his possessions) into her bare flesh. She then shoots and wounds him as her husband enters. The husband takes the gun from his wife and subsequently stands trial for the shooting. In the courtroom, the wife steps forward to accept the blame and humiliation, by baring the brand on her shoulder.*

The Cheat set standards of acting, decor, frame composition, and lighting which were not surpassed for years, not even by C. B. "DeMille avoids all . . . black and white stereotypes," wrote one film historian. "Even the Burmese 'villain' is shaded gray so that his sexual passion for the rich woman who cheats him is viewed as a more honest motive than the husband's desire to cover up the scandal. There is genuine pathos . . . conveyed by the near stylized (but not theatrical) acting by Fannie Ward and Sessue Hayakawa. In some shots they play like dancers before a white abstract background [actually brightly lit Chinese paneled screens]. There is one staggering shot in which DeMille focuses on nothing until the actors gesture into the frame from the side [the camera remains stationary]."

A middle-aged former beauty, still dainty and petite, with a laughing face framed in auburn curls, Fannie Ward, an English actress, had appeared on the stage in Europe and the United States. Cecil signed her for the role of the young society woman against Lasky's and Goldfish's instincts. Theatre people called her the "Wonder Girl" because of the amazing way she had of looking perennially young. It appears she was forty-three when she starred in *The Cheat*, which was her second film.* Cecil had been right. The vanity and the beauty of the baby face that "took hours to fix up" was perfect for the woman in *The Cheat*. Fannie (Mrs. Jack Dean at the time) was not easy to work with. Stubborn as well as vain, she crossed swords with her director almost on a daily basis. Additionally, Cecil had been forced to cast Jack Dean, a weak performer, as her husband in the film. "You have made Fannie Ward a great star," Sam Goldfish wrote Cecil after seeing the final cut.

The Cheat was made the same year that D. W. Griffith released *The Birth of a Nation*. Griffith's picture certainly has received more attention, but *The Cheat*'s influence on films and filmmakers, nonetheless, was profound. Above all, its "sexually charged content" was a first in the industry. Cecil was less impressed with his reviews than he should have been. *The Cheat* was initially banned in several states* and was not particularly successful in the United States (though it was in France), and

Cecil, like his idol Belasco, did not consider a work well done without the public's approval and a comfortable profit to bank.

Cecil had made *The Cheat* under the worst possible conditions. Added to the problems of working with Fannie Ward and Jack Dean, six days into production, another Lasky picture, *The Golden Chance*, ran into trouble and Cecil was forced to direct both films simultaneously. From 9:00 A.M. until 5:00 P.M., he was on the set of *The Cheat.* His secretary served him dinner at his desk. He rested until 8:00 P.M. and then shot *The Golden Chance* until 2:00 A.M. The few remaining hours he slept in his office. He claimed that when he went home (whenever that could have been), Constance was waiting for him, "as always." Both pictures were completed on schedule. Perhaps the pressured atmosphere on the sets, the unique situation which ruled out time for many retakes, contributed to the artistry of the direction, performances, and camera work. Ironically, *The Golden Chance*, a mediocre melodrama at best, also benefited from the most obvious problem of a nighttime-only production: the loss of natural light.

The critic of *The Moving Picture World* wrote on January 8, 1916:

> There is a new force in this [screen] play. I speak of the wonderful lighting effects which seem to lend an indescribable charm and lustre to numerous scenes....Never before has...the skillful play with light and shade, been used to such marvelous advantage....If paintings in a Rembrandt gallery or a set of Titians and Tintorettos were to come to life suddenly and were then mysteriously transferred to the moving picture screen the effect could not have been more startling than it was.

Only in one other picture, *The Whispering Chorus*, also made during Cecil's more experimental years, would he direct a film with truly innovative camera techniques. Cecil invested a large sum of his own money "as well as his heart" in this film. Its photographer was Alvin Wyckoff and its art director Wilfred Buckland, the same team that had worked with Cecil on *The Cheat* and *The Golden Chance*, and the effects they went for were equally innovative and startling. For the scenes of the hero fighting his conscience, a chorus was visible behind his own image. The light was eerie, dark and shadowy, and the mood of the film almost that of Greek tragedy. The public protested against the picture's "abnormal morbidity," and the exhibitors pulled it from their theatres. "It lost a great deal of money," Agnes recalled.

Film historian Kevin Brownlow claimed in 1968 that after *The Whispering Chorus*, "DeMille changed his attitude toward his audiences. As he lowered his sights to meet the lowest common denominator, so the standard of his films plummeted." However, twenty years later that assessment does not reflect the complete truth. Cecil did end his experimentation after the box office failure of *The Whispering Chorus*, but he directed some delightful—if more commercial—comedies during the next decade. His spectacles, which the more elite of the contemporary critics took great relish in lambasting as superficial and C. B. as pandering to the public, still grip the attention of the viewer. They also look surprisingly fresh and compare well with and often surpass contemporary spectacles costing twenty times more, many of which received critical acclaim.

Cecil scored many more successes than failures, and the Lasky Company rode especially high during the World War I years. Before the war, "Europe really had the jump on us," Lasky wrote. In France, Sarah Bernhardt had appeared in the title roles of *Camille* and *Queen Elizabeth*. Italy had produced *Cabiria* and an eight-reel spectacle, *Quo Vadis*. In 1914, England had already developed Kinecolor, a successful color process. "These countries might have seized a far greater portion of the world trade," Lasky continued, "had not the war stopped their movie activities just when they were getting well under way . . . by the end of the war we were so far ahead technically and had such a grip on foreign audiences that our gross revenues put us in an impregnable, commanding position."

The four original partners of the Lasky Company were millionaires. Cecil's life-style was more flamboyant perhaps than the others. Though thirty-three when the war began, over draft age and with dependents, Cecil still talked about joining up as a pilot. Since he could not fly, he took lessons and then bought his own plane *and* flying field in Santa Monica. Lasky accompanied him on his first solo flight and recalled:

> There were two places in the flimsy little bi-plane. I sat in the forward one, gripping the sides of the cockpit as though I were trying to hold [it] together. . . . We took off and I was just getting fairly well adjusted to the idea of still being alive when Cecil shouted something to me. I looked back but you couldn't hear a thing over the roar of the motor, and the goggles gave him a terrified expression. Suddenly the motor cut out and so did my heart. All I knew was that when the motor conks out you're a dead pigeon. . . . But Cecil had just shut off the motor for a moment to warn me that he was going to demonstrate some fancy turns. . . . [The experience was so terrifying] I couldn't bring myself to go up in a plane again for years.

When America finally entered the war in 1917, Cecil organized and captained a home-guard unit made up of studio personnel and drilled his men "with real Springfield rifles up and down Vine Street [accompanied by a full brass band] with as much relish as though he were showing General Pershing how to do a scene."

Above, left: A scene from *The Whispering Chorus*, directed and produced by Cecil B. DeMille, in 1918. The gloomy sets by Wilfred Buckland and cinematography by Alvin Wyckoff, featuring multiple exposures, created an aura of "abnormal morbidity" that translated into box-office disaster—despite the excellent performance by Raymond Hatton

Above, right: DeMille started to fly in 1917 and in 1919 set up the first commercial airline to offer regular passenger flights in the United States. Here he prepares to take Jeanie Macpherson, a screenwriter, for a flight, c. 1919

The Lasky Company produced thirty-six films in 1915, and Cecil was responsible for over half of them. His *Carmen* (adapted by Bill from the Mérimée novel), starred one of the Metropolitan Opera's greatest contemporary divas, Geraldine Farrar, the first great star lured to Hollywood.*

Farrar's decision was influenced by the fact that she had "recently overtaxed her voice to the point of despairing she might ever sing again and the chance to give her throat a rest in silent pictures couldn't have come at a more opportune time." Other inducements were a salary of $20,000 for each film, Cecil as her director, "a private railroad car to take her and her family to Hollywood, a house completely furnished and staffed with servants for her stay, a car and chauffeur at her complete disposal, a private dressing room...built right next to the stage [another first] and equipped with a grand piano for her practicing." *Carmen* had always been one of her favorite roles, and she was pleased to recreate it on film.

She departed New York with great fanfare. Banner headlines followed her train journey across the country. The Santa Fe Railway depot in Los Angeles, as well as the path she would take through the station to her waiting limousine, was carpeted in red. Schoolchildren lined the way, showering her with rose petals. Every room except the staff quarters in the estate that had been rented for her stay had been banked with flowers.

She insisted on meeting with Cecil the day of her arrival (Lasky had met her at the depot as C. B. was filming). To her surprise he told her they would shoot *Maria Rosa*, a less strenuous picture, first, then *Carmen*, but release the two films in reverse order. That way Cecil felt she could "cut her teeth without biting off the more difficult role." Bill had written the scenario of *Maria Rosa*, based on a hit Broadway play of the previous season. Farrar agreed the plan was sensible. Within a week she was before the camera. "[Cecil] outlined briefly the scenes, their intended length, the climax," she recalled of their first of six films together.* "[He] set his cameras at all angles to catch the first enthusiasm of a scene.... We were cautioned to beware of undue emotion, disarranged locks, torn clothing, etc. We were allowed free action as we felt it, so we acted our parts as if we were engaged in a theatre performance."

Both films had the same cast—Farrar, Wallace Reid, and Pedro de Cordoba. By the time *Carmen* was put in production, they played extraordinarily well with each

other. "I asked [Cecil] if we might have music during our scenes, as I was so accustomed to orchestral accompaniment for certain tempi and phrasings," Farrar remembered. "I believe this started the habit for music 'off stage' for all, later aspirants to emotional appeal." Farrar had played *Carmen* opposite Enrico Caruso's Don José, under the baton of Arturo Toscanini, the previous season at the Metropolitan Opera, and although Bill's adaptation was of the novel not the libretto, she fell into the character quite easily.* "My biggest fighting moment," she said, "was not where [Micaela and Carmen] claim the bewildered Don José, but a vigorous quarrel in the tobacco factory where the amiable Jeanie Macpherson, [Cecil's] right hand scenarist and an actress of no mean ability, loaned herself to my assault in a battle that made screen history."*

The Rose of the Rancho, filmed the previous year, when Bill had arrived in California, had marked Cecil's first association with Jeanie Macpherson. Her dynamic entrance into his life occurred at a time when Constance had moved out of the bedroom they had previously shared and into a room of her own. Various speculations have been made as to the cause. At age forty-one, Constance had suffered a miscarriage. She might have feared an unwanted change-of-life pregnancy. Or sex may always have been distasteful to her, and she had just now decided to take a stand. Cecil does not appear to have had a serious affair until this time—if he had even philandered at all. Neither Lasky nor Bill thought that was the case and they were in a close enough position and sensitive enough to observe the truth. No argument had transpired. Cecil and Constance were as loving as always; Constance was just as dedicated to him. In public and within the intimate circle of their family, they treated each other with the greatest respect—almost a kind of reverence. Constance filled her time with work for orphanages and a four-year-old boy named John, whom the DeMilles adopted. But Cecil was a young (thirty-three), vital man at the time.

Above, left: A party the night Geraldine Farrar became engaged to Lou Tellegen, a Dutch movie actor, in Hollywood. Among the guests, left rear: Reine Belasco and Cecil B. DeMille (in tuxedo), Anna deMille (wearing dark necklace); middle row, beginning second from left: Lou Tellegen, Constance DeMille, Geraldine Farrar, William deMille; front row, beginning third from left: Wilfrid Buckland, Veda Buckland, two unidentified men, Jeanie Macpherson

Above, right: Jesse L. Lasky, Jr.'s, birthday party in Hollywood, c. 1915. Front, far left: the birthday boy; standing, second from left: Agnes deMille, her mother, and Veda Buckland; standing, second from right: Constance DeMille and Jesse, Sr.; seated in front of him: his wife, Bessie Lasky. Margaret deMille is in the front, right of center. The girls are wearing Red Cross headgear, appropriate for the World War I bandage making they did under the leadership of Anna deMille

Opposite: Cecil B. DeMille directing on the set with musicians, possibly as a result of Farrar's request that she have "mood music" while she did her scenes

The Early Silent Years

Jeanie Macpherson—"a lovely, petite girl, sensitively feminine but with the high spirits of one descended from a clan whose head could use the noble Scottish title"*—was thirty and a thoroughly modern woman, not really the "girl" of Cecil's description. She had marvelous red hair, a saucy upturned nose, and a peppery tongue. Born in Boston of well-to-do parents, she had initially planned to become an opera singer. But while she was studying voice in Paris, her parents suffered financial reverses. Jeanie returned home and went on the stage. Griffith had hired her in 1908 for a role in *Mr. Jones at the Ball*. She quickly became one of his "stock company" and made many films with him.

She remained with his company through 1911, making her last appearance under his direction in *Enoch Arden*. Griffith found (as Cecil would) that Jeanie had a good head for story and he liked to discuss scripts with her. They obviously had an affair, how serious it was is impossible to say,* but Jeanie was impressed with this kind of power-driven man. On his part, Cecil was understandably intrigued by Jeanie's association with Griffith, the one man he considered his equal (or perhaps more) as a filmmaker.

There is a story that she secured her first job with Griffith after she sent him a letter which read: "I want a job. If you catch me on a Scotch day I will make money for you, and if you catch me on a French day I will act for you." Griffith telephoned her. "Which day is it now?" he asked. "A French day," she replied. "Put on a pretty dress and come over here," he commanded, and she was hired.

At the time that Cecil was going into production on *The Rose of the Rancho*,

Jeanie had just finished writing and directing a script for Universal called *The Tarantella*. Another story has been circulated that while she was shooting her film on location, Cecil was working close by, and she wrote him tersely: "Kindly vacate at once. J. Macpherson." He sent a note back by the same messenger. "Go chase yourself." She then showed up on his set, demanding he move away, and he angrily refused. She lost the fight but returned to ask him for a job as soon as her assignment ended. They crossed swords again, but Cecil liked her spirit, was intrigued by her background, and recognized that she was talented. He hired her for a small role in *The Rose of the Rancho*, which was still in production, and put her on salary, although her job was somewhat ambiguous.

By the time Jeanie had made her second DeMille film, *The Girl of the Golden West*, in which she appeared as Nina, her affair with Cecil was an open secret. After her role as Frasquita in *Carmen*, she was given an office that adjoined his and put on salary as a scenario writer. Cecil had discovered her great gift for story. Between the years 1915 and 1933, Jeanie was indispensable in Cecil's life and his career. She either authored or coauthored (often with him) his best films—*The Cheat, Joan the Woman, The Whispering Chorus*—most of the successful Gloria Swanson films, including *Male and Female* and *The Affairs of Anatol*, and received solo credit for the scripts of *The Ten Commandments, The King of Kings*, and *Madam Satan*.

Their relationship was volatile. Jeanie enjoyed jousting and confrontation, and she was not unlike Beatrice in her business acumen, story mind, and self-reliance. She and Cecil fought often, but mostly over their work. When she had an opinion that he did not agree with, she seldom backed down. These confrontations heightened their sexual relations. A study of Jeanie Macpherson's scenarios (many originals) reveal her strong sexuality, a streak of sadomasochism, her attraction to strong, dominating men of power and wealth, and her need to best them in the everyday world and to be overpowered by them in sex. She was a truly good writer with a brilliant sense of story construction.

Cecil had either adapted or coadapted from a novel or play every one of his films until Jeanie began writing for the Lasky Company. Together they adapted *The Captive* (1915) from her story—the first original scenario Cecil had produced. The title character was Mahmud Hassan, a Turkish nobleman taken prisoner in the war between Turkey and the Balkan states. Hassan is assigned as a slave laborer to Sonia, a woman who runs a farm in Montenegro singlehanded. In the beginning, she is tyrannical. He stands up to her, and soon they are in love. When Turkish soldiers overtake Montenegro, Hassan aligns himself with Sonia and the Montenegrins against his countrymen during a siege on her farm. The Montenegrins win, but Hassan is forced to leave. Since he is unable to return to his own country, the two, though reduced to the status of refugees, joyously take to the road.

Hector Turnbull wrote the original story of *The Cheat*, but in her adaptation, Jeanie added the memorable invention of the branding iron that marked the film, as it did the picture's heroine. She hit her full stride with *Joan the Woman* (the story of Joan of Arc), which she wrote alone. The final cut of the film ran two hours and fifteen minutes, twice the length of Cecil's former features.* Joan of Arc was more forceful, a little less the victim of her voices, than in previous versions. Despite the intrusion of a jarring modern prologue and epilogue, the film was both impressive

Farrar as Joan of Arc, in the film *Joan the Woman*, 1916, directed and produced by Cecil B. DeMille

and gripping. In it Cecil had his first opportunity at spectacle with marching crowds, prancing horses, massed effects of courtiers and soldiers, cathedral scenes—and, of course, the burning of Joan at the stake. Throughout the entire summer of 1916, Cecil and Jeanie labored day and night together on *Joan the Woman*. Cecil was determined to bring Belasco's realistic theatre to the screen, as the film's Joan, Geraldine Farrar, recalled:

> In the gory fight of the Siege of Orleans moat, and subsequent capture of the towers, we were all immersed in cold water up to our shoulders for hours. The water itself was pleasantly cool.... [but] the August sun blazed down upon us like a furnace.... My task was to rise from the moat, scale the ladder with that accursedly heavy banner held high, and enter a breach in the wall...in a shower of rock. This battle raged for about a week with retakes and close-ups.... For the climax at the stake, my clothing, skin and hair were treated with a fluid to make scorching impossible. I had cotton, saturated with ammonia, placed in my nostrils and mouth.... The flames were truly terrifying and the experience was not without some danger.

Since it was summer vacation time, Agnes, then a youngster of ten, spent every day she could on the set or on location. "The Sunday the battle of Les Tourelles was shot out at the studio ranch every director on the Lasky lot was commandeered as a lieutenant to Cecil. Pop stood in full costume in the line . . . [wearing] an iron hat and the cross of Saint George on his chest.... We [visitors] sat around watching in open cars with picnic baskets. It was something like an English hunt breakfast-.... During the burning [of Joan of Arc] Uncle Cecil stood at the stake for hours trying out smoke.... Farrar stood until she was obliterated by smoke and flame.... When they burned the dummy [for closeups] and its hair caught and flaked off in a single shower of fiery cinders, she turned sick and had to [leave]."*

At this time, Cecil still edited his own films and Jeanie would work side by side with him in the cutting room. Constance appears to have accepted her. The three of them even traveled to New York together for the premiere of *Joan the Wom-*

One of the cabins at Paradise ranch, Cecil B. DeMille's hideaway in the foothills of the Sierra Madres

The living room of the main building at Paradise, with the organ and pool table

an.* The picture did well but more important than its financial return (double its astronomic $300,000 cost), it was the beginning of the DeMille formula "to tell an absorbing personal story against a background of great historical events."

Of the twenty-two films that Cecil produced and directed between the spring of 1915 (*The Captive*) and autumn of 1918 (*Till I Come Back to You*), Jeanie authored fourteen of the scenarios. Between the latter date and 1932, Cecil made only six of his twenty-four films without her. As her power at the studio and in his personal life grew, their private battles at times approached full-scale war. By 1918, Cecil began affairs with other women. At the ranch he had bought in 1916 and named Paradise, he found he "could recharge the batteries of energy" his work required. That was, indeed, part of it. But Paradise also supplied a hideaway for him and Jeanie in the beginning, and later for the other women to whom he was attracted. Jeanie did not accept his sexual adventures as "saintly," as did Constance. Many of their fights were begun on this basis.

When not in production, Cecil would go to Paradise (about twenty-five miles from the studio) on Thursday afternoon and stay until Saturday—either alone or with Jeanie or another woman.* Constance never came to the ranch. "She never chose to," her granddaughter, Cecilia Junior, later said. The main building at Paradise was a giant log cabin with a tree growing "right through it, and Indian and cowboy relics everywhere, with one small bedroom, two giant bedrooms and a very, very large kitchen with help quarters upstairs," she recalled. "Then you went down a long path to [Cecil's] stone house—then a big pool [made by damming a river], then up an incline to three guest cottages, and beyond that, the caretaker's house. [Paradise] was about one thousand acres." Infrequently, when Jeanie could not come, he brought his daughter Cecilia and, in later years, his granddaughter, but essentially he felt Paradise was not a children's place. "When they [the DeMille children] were invited however (usually on a special holiday), they either stayed with him or in the main house. The cottages were for outside guests"—most often Chaplin, Lasky, and other filmmakers.

The living room was over sixty feet square and contained a pool table, many conversation areas, and doubled as a dining room with a table at one end that comfortably sat sixteen. Male guests brought black tie and cummerbund, but in their closets were hanging Russian Cossack silk shirts of various brilliant colors, with big billowing sleeves, that they were expected to wear to dinner (only H. G. Wells appears to have refused to do so). His granddaughter attributes the shirts to the fact that "Cecil was a student of Tolstoy." Agnes remembers that "The colored Cossack shirts were allotted strictly by Cecil's protocol: white satin for producers, purple satin for directors, and red satin for everyone else including five-star generals, presidents of universities, or heads of state. If they were not producers, they were not awarded anything but red."

> After dinner [his granddaughter said], appeared what he called "A Paradise Tray"—several really—one with diamonds on it, and one with rubies or silk scarves. [The trays] were little wicker things—like tea trays, round and about eighteen inches in diameter and stuffed full of things—a ruby bracelet—always one really marvelous thing. The women played pool or whatever game was the moment's rage to see who got to go first and choose from the Paradise Tray. He'd sit back glowing, watching this game going on.

No shooting was allowed with either gun or camera, although Cecil carried an ivory-handled revolver beneath an opera cloak when he walked the distance from his house to dinner in the event that a rattlesnake might cross his path. Cecil loved animals, and there were many deer and fox on the property. He would often bang on an empty can, and they would come up and eat right out of his hand.

The Laughlin Park area in Hollywood, where Cecil chose to live, was described in a 1915 prospectus as "a residential paradise on a noble eminence, a replica of Italy's finest landscape gardening, linked to the city by a perfect auto road [Los Feliz Boulevard]." An architect by the name of Dodd had bought the land for development of estate homes. Only two houses had been built at that time, one somewhat larger than the other. They stood, because of the slope of the property, almost side by side, separated by a sixty-foot strip of land. (Dodd originally occupied the smaller house, later Charlie Chaplin rented it for a year. Then in 1926 Dodd's recent widow sold Cecil the second house, and he commissioned architect Julia Morgan to design a sixty-foot-long conservatory to link the two buildings.)

With the acquisition of a large home, Constance's life took shape. She remained as dedicated to Cecil's needs as ever, accepted Jeanie's presence in her husband's life without complaint, and ran an organized household. Agnes found Constance:

> ready for all eventualities. I remember one April afternoon began for her with a children's hospital committee meeting that was interrupted by a hysterical summons from across Los Feliz Boulevard because of the drowning of a child in a nearby reservoir. She went to the victim's home, cleaned the house, prepared supper for the brothers and sisters, comforted the mother, returned, bathed and dressed, put in a brisk half hour hunting flies and ants for ... [her adopted son, John's] neglected alligator, presided at the dinner table of her own children, sat with them while they studied, and at midnight was found trailing alone around the cellar in a red velvet negligee in search of the special Liebfraumilch which Cecil liked with his late supper.

Bill and his family lived nearby, as did Beatrice, and on Thanksgiving and Christmas, the family all went "up on the hill" to Cecil's to celebrate.

[On Christmas] Cecil took the whole morning to open his presents, [Agnes recalled]. They were piled on five or six tables around him as he sat before the great fireplace.... He always waited until the children opened their presents and the real excitement began. The family sat around watching and gasping with admiration [as he opened gifts from celebrities and every worker in the studio]. The process sometimes lasted three or four hours....

... Likewise, Cecilia, as heir apparent, was favored with a memento from every employee, and was only saved from throwing up with excitement by being marched off to take a nap.

Cecil lived like a prince potentate, and Constance "moved through this luxury and excitement with unruffled poise." She "kept the place ready for the master. Frederik, the beautiful Norwegian butler, and Helja, the Finnish maid, helped." Yet, with all her selflessness, Constance must have felt a void in her life. She was always in the position of waiting for Cecil to come home. She was not a part of his work or his social life. And despite her attention to small household details, she had three other servants besides Frederik and Helja to take care of everything else.

Her work for a children's hospital began in 1914, and John, a "beautiful curly-haired" child, had come to live with them soon after. Cecilia, two years older than John, "put a wicked wedge that was pretty solid" between them. But Cecilia wasn't small John's only problem. "He was very aggressive and difficult—he'd find ways to be difficult," was what another family member said.

Constance often brought home children from hospitals or orphanages for a weekend or a holiday. But not until 1920 did she give her heart away to another orphan, a startlingly beautiful nine-year-old girl named Katherine Lester, whose father had been killed in the war and whose mother had died of tuberculosis "after burning up all the family mementos, except for four books on Buddhism, which she left to Katherine."*

"Katherine's father was an English flier and he came from a very good family," Cecilia Junior later remembered. "He married a girl they did not approve of. He was killed, and she went to them and asked them for help for herself and the child, but they offered none." She thought she had relatives in Canada, and so she made her way there but could not find them. By now she had learned she had tuberculosis and headed down to Southern California in an old car presumably for the warm weather and because she had information that her relatives were there. "She pinned a note to Katherine every night saying, 'If I'm [found] dead, take this child and contact these people [the father's family in England].' She died shortly after reaching Los Angeles and Katherine ended up in an orphanage, the family in England obviously having refused her care."

"Though it was so long ago, I have certain strong memories," Katherine recalled. "I remember children crying themselves to sleep, lonely children that were punished for bed-wetting—nobody really cared [about the children].

"A woman wanted to adopt me but the board didn't approve," Katherine continued. "I was invited to come to the [DeMille] house. I'd grown up with only my mother for company, and here I was with at least fourteen people every night. I just sat there, you know—and they said that they really wondered whether they should

The living room of Cecil's home in Laughlin Park. Over the baronial mantel is a painting by Dan Sayre Groesbeck, a failed artist but a successful designer of sets for many of Cecil's movies

The loggia that was built to link Cecil's house with one that he had bought from Charlie Chaplin. He is standing, in this photograph from the 1940s, with his granddaughter Cecilia (Citsy)

adopt me because I never spoke. They weren't sure. Then, finally one day—they were talking about dogs, and I'm mad about dogs anyway—so I piped up and began to talk, and someone—maybe Cecilia—said, 'By God—she speaks!'"

"Everyone fell in love with Katherine," Cecilia remembered. "She was so beautiful and so nice. 'Would you like to call me Mother?' [Constance] asked. She said she would like that very much. The minute the adoption papers were taken out there was a knock on the front door. The family from England had kept tabs on this little girl, let her go right through the ordeal alone—her mother's death, the orphanage, everything—but they sent a lawyer to see if this Hollywood director and his wife were suitable to adopt this girl! [Constance] kicked him out of the house and that was the last we heard from him and Katherine was adopted."

"I remember the formality of going to court and telling the judge I wanted to be a member of the family," Katherine added. The family in 1920 consisted of Cecilia, eleven; John, ten; and Katherine, nine. "By the grace of God I understood the world [the affluent life of the DeMilles] we lived in," she explained, "because—I don't know—I just had the ability to do it and I loved it. It was exciting. I read feverishly. I was always being told to get my nose out of a book. John—it was hard for him. I think he may have been a little jealous of my coming in. Interestingly enough, it didn't seem to trouble Cecilia at all. It may have, but she didn't show it. She was very bright—excellent in anything she did. She was an A student and headed the student body at school. Then I came along and went to the same school and got A's and was elected president of my class. Since John couldn't compete, he sometimes was very aggressive—very difficult."

Prodded into recalling life in the DeMille household, she remembered: "When I first came we were all young children, and we ate first at a little table and then we were allowed to sit up till Father came home, talk to him, ask him questions—but he was usually pretty late 'cause he worked late and then he would go see the rushes, and he would come home very tired—park the car down in the garage and walk up the long hill. We always said, 'This is ridiculous. Why don't you drive up here and one of the servants will park the car.' But, 'No,' he said, 'it's refreshing. I like it.'"

A smile flickered across her face. "That was an occasion, when he came in that front door and we went to see him. We'd kiss his cheek and it was cold from the

75

Daughter Cecilia DeMille, C. B., Katherine, and Mrs. DeMille on the grounds of their home overlooking the Hollywood Hills, in the early 1920s

night air. You remember these little things. He brought a surge of excitement into the house. We'd [Cecilia, John, Constance, and Katherine] sit around—if it was very late he'd eat off a tray in the living room. We'd have a fire going or something, and we would sit on the sofas and ask him questions—'What did you shoot today? What does so-and-so—one of his stars—look like?' Mother would say, 'Don't ask too many questions. Father is tired. Let's let him eat in peace.' He would just tell a little bit about his day and then he'd ask about ours.

"Mother was a very nice lady—very undemonstrative"—she said, the last with a hardened edge to her voice—"but you knew she loved you—she cared—but she could be *cold*. These are things as a child I didn't ponder. I was an adopted child. It was great fun, it was exciting to live there. I could play wonderful records on the Victrola. There was a swimming pool and a tennis court, there was everything you could possibly want. But I kept the name Lester as a middle name—Katherine Lester DeMille—and pictures of my parents [displayed], and I kept up with other relatives in England. I remember orphanage children who didn't remember their parents and how it troubled them. I remember mine very clearly. I'm deeply grateful for that.

"We rarely went to Paradise Ranch," she replied when asked about Cecil's private life. "That was Father's estate. He did take me on his boat—the *Seaward*. It was a lovely boat, about ninety-five feet or so. I was the only one who loved to go sailing. Everyone else got seasick. We'd go to the Channel Islands—Santa Cruz, San Clemente, Santa Barbara—they were practically wild country then. Father let me bring a friend. He usually would be working—most times Jeanie would come along. She was a very bright woman. Now Julia [Faye], his other lady friend, was not too bright. We children used to do a rather mean imitation of her."

Katherine's memories of Beatrice ("Bebe," she called her) are sketchier: "I just have a childhood impression of her. Father held her in great respect—a kind of awe—and we all were expected to cater to her as he did. She had a great elegance about her. I don't think she particularly liked children and was not demonstrative to us—but she adored Father, you could tell that. And Uncle Billy. In the early years he and his first wife [Anna George deMille] and the girls came over with Bebe a lot. He

76

was a very vital personality. Father admired him very much and considered him more intelligent than himself—an intellectual."

The family circle, however, was not yet complete. One chilly morning in November 1922, Cecil's lawyer, Neil McCarthy, found a nine-month-old baby boy in a basket on his doorstep. It seemed like the opening of some penny-dreadful novel, and that was apparently what the brothers DeMille had purposefully planned. For the boy was William's child, born to a woman with whom he was deeply in love, although he remained married to Anna. The mother, Lorna Moon, a beautiful, brilliant author and playwright, was ill with tuberculosis, and though not incapacitated, did not feel able to care for the baby. After consulting with Cecil, and obtaining McCarthy's agreement to help, William had the tot placed on his doorstep. McCarthy gave a public statement of this discovery. Constance and Cecil then stepped forward and said they would happily take the boy as a third adopted child.

The baby was named Richard DeMille. Although Bill fully acknowledged the child to Cecil and McCarthy, "he couldn't very well bring him home to Anna, not to that Victorian lady," Cecilia Junior explained. "Once he was seen with another woman, and he was asked if he was being faithful. They meant to his wife. He said, 'I am faithful in my infidelity.' The brothers made a pact. Cecil would adopt Richard. But he would not be told his true father was his 'Uncle Billy.' The one who died last was to tell him." And so Richard joined Cecilia, John, and Katherine, believing as he grew up that he was of unknown heritage and yet confused why he so resembled the men of his adoptive family.

In 1915, Bill had been refused admittance into the Los Angeles Country Club because of his association with "movies." He had been more interested in the use of their tennis courts than to align himself with men of prestige. Nonetheless, the rejection drew him closer to his peers and associates. While in New York his social life had centered around the George coterie and the good folk of Merriewold; in Hollywood he stuck close to the "movies."

As the daughter of "a great man," Anna was not able to make this "compromise." Born late in her parents' life, she knew her father only after he had attained world renown. She had been raised in a family preoccupied with "the problems of mankind, dedication and high-mindedness." A priest had been excommunicated on her father's behalf. The Irish revolutionary leaders conferred with him. Sun Yat-sen and Tolstoy paid homage, and one hundred thousand people walked in Henry George's funeral cortege. The move to Hollywood did not change his daughter's view of her proper role in life, nor others' in regard to her. Tolstoy's son Ilya came to pay his respects. Karl Marx's granddaughter came to tea. And Margaret and Agnes "grew accustomed to standing with aching knees in the crowds while [their] Mother laid wreaths on public monuments, [to] watching her enter parliaments and banquet halls which rose in tribute."

Unable to accept her husband's transition from respected playwright to being a "movie," she turned to making a career of being Henry George's daughter, her veneration of him bordering on the religious. She had encouraged Bill to follow Cecil to Hollywood to ease their temporary financial problems, but had never expected him to remain. Agnes said of her mother: "Having known one authentic genius, she took for granted that anyone in whom she placed her faith and love must stand head and shoulders above the surrounding multitude. This was a bit tough on her husband and daughters." (Of her sister, Margaret, Agnes commented: "My relation varied. She wasn't intimate and she was my baby charge and I felt protective, but not always. I couldn't stand her being pretty and helpless and cuddly and meddling. I was jealous of her beauty. We must have had an intense sibling rivalry because I took a terrible revenge. I have forgotten her as a child.")

Anna's household was a rigid one. The girls dined apart from their parents until they were well in their teens, went to bed at eight until they celebrated their sixteenth birthdays, and then were only allowed an extra hour. They were dressed exactly alike to prevent jealousy, were not permitted to read the newspapers. "Resting [Anna] considered a waste unless it was done strenuously, that is, on a bed, on one's back, with one's eyes closed....'Don't just sit there, dearie,' she would say coming into a room. 'Do something!'" The girls were put on dress allowances from the time they were eight, and all their spendings were drawn from this; it was never enough. "I lived in debt to Mother forever," Agnes wrote. "Nothing was ever counted by Mother as having any value unless it had a moral purpose....She had neither understanding nor patience. With extravagance or luxury of any sort she grew downright intolerant....she could not permit herself to do anything pleasant unless she felt she was doing it for someone else's sake. I have known her to eat a bunch of grapes over a period of days and never have a sound one, keeping exact pace with the mold....She was a rock...a fortress. It was as though the shadow of her father stood behind her and quietly laid his hand on her shoulder."

Few "movies" were invited to her home, nor did Anna accept many invitations from them. The family's frequent visits "up on the hill" to Cecil's had little to do with the brothers' careers. Constance was never herself involved in Cecil's work,

Opposite, left: Count Ilya Tolstoy, son of the great novelist, visited Anna deMille in Hollywood in 1917 to pay his respects to the daughter of Henry George—a man he and his father considered one of the great thinkers of our time

Opposite, right: At eleven Agnes deMille played a role in *The Ragamuffin*, 1916, written and directed by her father, William

Below: Margaret deMille being terrorized by Agnes in the Wild West town of Hollywood, 1915

but she took a keen interest and a great pride in it and she welcomed his friends and associates (and mistresses) whenever they came. She, however, set the family gatherings as sacrosanct; few outsiders were ever included. But for Agnes and Margaret, their visits to their uncle's home were always exciting, for Cecil ran pictures for them after dinner, and the brothers shared amusing stories about their current or past projects. Bill had tremendous wit, and at Cecil's it had a chance to dazzle.

Anna's frugality seemed to gain Bill's approval in the early Hollywood years. He drove a secondhand car and their house was modest. Despite all his original prejudices, he had become completely enthralled with the business of making moving pictures and had shown more than a routine ability. Within a year, he was a director for the Lasky company, and his films—although not anywhere as commercial as Cecil's—did well and more: they received the critical acclaim Cecil's often did not.

William directed his first film based on his own scenario, *The Ragamuffin*, in 1915.* "I wanted to launch my own boat," he wrote. "Much to my relief, C. B. fell in with the idea.... The writing department was in good shape and contained at least two people ready to take executive control [Jeanie Macpherson was one]. I was to write my own story, direct my own picture....

"Probably the most valuable thing I learned from my first production was the close bond which should exist between director and writer. I had discovered that the two functions require a certain amount of adjustment to each other even when combined in one person."

Bill directed his pictures in actual continuity, which would even be unique today (because of the cost of such an approach). He did so, he said, because the films he chose to make depended "considerably for their value on the consistent and progressive development of character, rather than mere physical action ... the method of starting with scene No. 1 and proceeding numerically to the conclusion [allows] the players' characterizations to become well sustained."

Over Anna's original objections, Agnes (at ten) was given a small role in *The Ragamuffin*, which assuaged her envy of Cecilia's appearance in *The Squaw Man*. "Father didn't care how he looked on the set. He directed in his old clothes, an old battered tennis hat which he refused to change or throw away. He gave himself entirely to the business on hand and was extremely bad-tempered if he was interrupted, but he never raised his voice to his actors. With them he had endless patience, coaxing, cajoling, analyzing. He was adored by cast and technicians who usually called him 'Bill' with familiarity and affection. Cecil, on the other hand...appeared for work...in well-cut riding breeches and leather boots. His manner was princely and courteous.... If he lost his temper it was in the grand manner.... He held the belief that he got the best work from people when he had stripped their nerves raw, when they could no longer think, when they acted through an instinct of rage and desperation. If they turned in a fair piece of work and he struck them across the mouth, they'd turn in a better one the next day."

Unfortunately, most of the early silents of William deMille have vanished. *Miss Lulu Bett* (1921), based on a Pulitzer-prizewinning play by Zona Gale, is one that survives.* The film is a gem, brilliantly directed. One film critic said of it: "The sense of observation reaches a standard very seldom excelled and deMille's compassion and his realistic treatment give every scene a truthfulness rare in the cinema."

When screened in the 1960s, it brought this comment: "It retains its magic, and this fragile, delicate little story can still move its audience to tears."

The story centers around a middle-aged spinster in a small town who lives in her authoritarian sister's home and under her domination. The monotony of her life is broken when her brother-in-law's brother comes to visit, flirts with her, and jokingly goes through a mock marriage ceremony with her that turns out to be legal. Lulu goes off with her new husband only to find he has another wife. She returns to her sister's house and is the object of abuse and unrelenting gossip until she stands up to both her family and the town, acts that endear her to the simple and loving village schoolmaster, who marries her.

> This beautiful . . . [film, wrote one critic], evokes the mood and to a remarkable degree, the intimate feelings of an important era for Americans — just after World War I when large numbers of women began to take their first very personal steps toward emancipation . . . deMille gives us a picture of the oppressiveness of life in an American small town in [1920], the narrow lives, the pride and fear of scandal, and the Jazz Age restlessness of the young. He avoids the theatrical and melodramatic. This is the story of ordinary people, and he defines them by suggestive details:—the daily humdrum routine of cooking, eating, washing the dishes. He makes use of the intimacy of the camera. His actors are restrained, his close-ups of them reserved for moments of dramatic tension.

While Cecil's directorial style was beginning to outdo Belasco's, Bill was moving into the area of more intimate theatre. The man who had been a commercial but superficial playwright had found his place as perhaps one of the first directors of *cinéma vérité*. The problem was one of timing. Picture audiences for the early silents came to see larger-than-life stories, with characters played by stars they could idolize but with whom they could not identify. Bill adapted *Carmen* for Cecil, as well as his own larger canvas, *The Warrens of Virginia*,* and slick comedies like *Why Change Your*

Opposite: William deMille and cameraman L. Guy Wilky shooting a scene from *Men and Women*, starring Claire Adams and written by Clara Beranger, 1915

Opposite, below: Lorna Moon, the Scottish-born writer with whom William deMille had an affair—and a son

William sent this autographed photograph to his mother on his thirty-ninth birthday

Wife? But as a director, his choice of material was far more nuanced and far less commercial. This did not appear to disturb him and he did not become snobbish about what he was achieving in film. When Robert Benchley referred in print to Bill as "the subtle and intelligent member of the deMille family," Bill commented to Agnes, "I wish they would not use me as a hammer with which to whack Cecil." She added: "The only thing that made Father lose his temper . . . was criticism against Cecil, artistic, moral or spiritual. . . . He simply would not have his kid brother picked on, no, not even when kid brother sat astride Hollywood . . . and was one of the very rich men in the business."

A good mind attracted Bill as much as a beautiful woman. Anna possessed both, and yet she had never been able to put an end to his roving eye. As it happened, two women entered his life in the teens, both writers—Clara Beranger and Lorna Moon. No one doubted that Clara was in love with him and that he enjoyed her company. She worked on several of his films, including *Miss Lulu Bett.* But it was the more dramatic, intellectual, and exotic Lorna Moon who first mesmerized him.

Lorna Moon had been born and reared in the lowlands of Scotland. She was a red-haired beauty with dark, seductive eyes, a keen intelligence, sharp wit, a natural writing ability, and an enormous lust for life. She married an Englishman who was killed in the war without ever seeing the daughter he had fathered with her. Restless, ambitious, adventurous, she left the child behind with friends and came to New York, where she wrote and published many short stories and became a literary star. In 1919, she was wooed to Hollywood where she wrote three successive successful and sophisticated comedies—*Don't Tell Everything, Her Husband's Trademark,* and *Too Much Wife*—and met and fell in love with Bill deMille, who had never known anyone quite like her. Lorna was part New York sophisticate and part Hollywood good-time girl.

She found out she was pregnant about the same time as the doctors diagnosed her tubercular condition. She hid out in suburban Monrovia, a discreet distance from Los Angeles, to have the child, whom she christened Richard, after Richard Mead deMille, a great-great-uncle of Bill's who had written an enormous work on theology that had taken him almost his entire mature life.* The childbirth had weakened her, and after nine months of attempting to care for the boy, she became convinced she must give him up so that what strength she did have could be expended in writing and in fighting her disease. But Richard was the first boy to be born to the DeMille brothers. John might be carrying the DeMille name, but he could never be expected to continue its heritage. When told of Richard's plight, Cecil was determined to raise the boy as he felt he should be raised—as a DeMille. He took his plan to Constance, who agreed to be a party to it. No one considered the idea of Bill's taking the baby home to Anna ("I think that she simply would have dropped him off the balcony one day—I mean, how can you raise a mistress's child?" a family member commented).

When the DeMilles's lawyer, Neil McCarthy, announced to the press that he had found a baby on his doorstep, he also revealed that the philanthropic Mrs. De-Mille and her husband, the film director Cecil B. DeMille, had been the first people he had called, due to Mrs. DeMille's connection with orphanages. The DeMilles had come over to his house and decided on the spot to save this child as they had saved two other orphans they had adopted. No one questioned the veracity of the story. Richard was brought to this new home, and a small sunroom off the upstairs hall was converted into a nursery; an adjoining room was used by the nurse who cared for him. None of the DeMille children knew about Richard's true parentage, and that included Agnes and Margaret, who were, after all, his real half sisters.* Richard's birth—though undreamed of by Anna—created an unsurmountable barrier between her and Bill. A few years later, they were divorced, and he remarried— not Lorna Moon, however, but the patient, understanding Clara Beranger.

Lorna Moon fought a valiant battle against tuberculosis for the next several years. She married a Canadian, had two more children, left them, and returned to Hollywood. By 1929, still in her early thirties, she was at the height of her fame with stories being published frequently in one of the top literary journals, *The Century Magazine*. Her book of short stories, *Doorways in Drumorty*, had enjoyed tremendous success, and her first novel, *Dark Star*, was a best seller and quickly purchased by Metro-Goldwyn-Mayer as a vehicle for Marie Dressler and Wallace Beery (retitled for films *Min and Bill*). In 1927, the year she had returned from Canada, she had written the scenarios for four M-G-M films. The effort had obviously been too much for her.* For the next three years, she was confined to her bed.

The amazing number of articles written about her at this time reflects her notoriety. Her last interview was given on an April day in 1930 from her bed in her home in the Hollywood Hills. She wore a striking green dressing gown, and her red hair was spread out on the pillow behind her head.

"I don't want people to be sorry for me," she said, smiling. "Haven't I written a book that everyone is reading [*Dark Star*]? Tuberculosis didn't stop John Keats from writing his poetry, or Robert Louis Stevenson from writing his short stories," and she seemed to enjoy suffering "the intellectuals' disease," for after all, "Schiller, Mozart, Raphael, Watteau, Weber and Chopin also had tuberculosis. [Anyway], I find living in a horizontal position for three years after being perpendicular for one year actually interesting. Perhaps because I live so intensely."

A few days later, she insisted a friend drive her to a sanatorium in Phoenix. Near Albuquerque, she took a turn for the worse and entered a hospital, where she died on May 1. Her estate went to her estranged husband and two children in Edmonton, Canada. Richard was never to know his real mother, and he would be a man before he would learn that William deMille was his father. He was reared believing he had been deserted, "one of the sad orphans," as Katherine recalled of her orphanage life, "who did not know their parents." Richard, however, often sat unknowingly opposite his real father at family gatherings. Uncle Billy was his favorite because of his intelligence, the deMille he admired the most, though he loved Cecil.

"I remember sailing boats in his [Cecil's] bathtub while he was taking a bath—I was like four years old or something—he would take his washcloth and put air in it and put it under the boat and let it go and the air would come up and knock the boat over. I would sail boats with little sails all around him in the bathtub. He had a lot of limitations about what sorts of things he was willing to interact about—but he was a warm father figure." Nonetheless, something drew him to Bill. "I was basically an idea person—and everybody else in the family, except William, were action people.... William and I were idea people."

In June 1927, Anna and William deMille agreed to a divorce. His second wife was Clara Beranger, who had written the scripts for several of his movies

Carrying the Torch

1918–1928

During the shooting of [The Ten Commandments,] . . .
*Theodore Roberts and James Neil, in Biblical costume and
make-up, . . . had been waiting patiently for an hour outside
the Director-General's [Cecil's] office. Finally [they] sent in the
message: "Just say that Moses and Aaron are waiting to see God."*

—WILLIAM deMILLE, *Hollywood Saga*

A NEW SEXUAL FREEDOM CAME INTO BEING JUST AFTER THE END
of World War I. Cecil, "not entirely inexperienced and having done much reading,"
recognized that the time was opportune for the smart, sophisticated comedy drama
which "avoided life in the raw and served it *en brochette* with spicy sauces." Over the
next four years, Cecil's films dealt with various forms of feminine lure, set against a
background of visual beauty and luxury. Sex was presented seductively, tantalizingly,
with lurid implications, but never explicitly. He was accused of being a romantic
evangelist. Said one contemporary critic: "Loosened marriage bonds, broken homes,
financial insecurity, and orphaned children were a growing threat as the twentieth
century rolled in. A neurotic frenzy of 'coddled sensibilities' (Henry James's phrase)
struggled to maintain the trap of conjugality by embracing the entrapment." Together Cecil and Jeanie understood how to translate this need into a commercial and pal-
atable product. The recipe was simple: "missionary zeal mixed with generous doses
of attractive hedonism—the right amount of titillating naughtiness and risqué forays
into the world of the delightfully amoral rich." An audience busy censoring its unconscious desires could indulge in the guiltless fulfillment of those desires mainly
because of the religious overtones and the moralistic endings of his films.

"Hit sex hard," Cecil is said to have instructed his performers, and within
two years, he joined Mary Pickford and Charlie Chaplin as one of the three greatest
box office attractions in film. Except for D. W. Griffith, no other director had attained the drawing power of a real star. Cecil had started his long career of "director" pictures where his name, not those of the stars, was above the title.

He made ten pictures between November 1918 and November 1922. Jeanie wrote eight of the screenplays, and Gloria Swanson starred in six and became the ultimate heroine of his jazz age films. *Photoplay* magazine pronounced *Male and Female* "A typical DeMille production.... When Miss Swanson requires a bed... it is such a bed and such a boudoir as we have never seen before." *Variety* described one of her costumes in *Don't Change Your Husband* as a "gold cloth and lace negligee trimmed with metallic fringe... so loud it should have awakened her sleeping husband." After losing her spouse to *femme fatale* Bebe Daniels in *Why Change Your Wife?* Swanson orders new gowns made "sleeveless, backless, transparent, indecent." (Years later film historian Sumiko Higashi commented on these pictures: "DeMille's frivolous attitude towards marriage and divorce may have been titillating but it certainly reinforced the notion that women... were interchangeable commodities.... [Wives] functioned as decorative objects or ornamentation.") Several of these stories had as their theme sexual frigidity or incompatibility, which by the end reel was solved by a wife's transformation into a "seductive, playful, fashion-plate." The majority depicted "the marital misadventures of the [childless] leisured class... for married couples had to be unencumbered to pursue a frivolous, irresponsible, and hedonistic life style."

Gloria Swanson had come to Hollywood in 1916, shortly after she and actor Wallace Beery had married.* Only nineteen at the time, Gloria had no acting experience outside of small walk-on or bit parts in her hometown Chicago's Essanay Studios. Soon after, she was teamed with Bobby Vernon in a series of lightweight romantic comedies for Triangle Films. When that company faced bankruptcy, she signed to appear in DeMille's *Don't Change Your Husband.** Cecil had been watching her growth as a performer and had taken the opportunity to sign her as soon as she was available.

"I first noticed her," Cecil recalled, "simply leaning against a door in a Mack Sennett comedy.

"Gloria was, of course, very young then, but I saw the future that she could have in pictures if her career was properly handled.... I never told her, until after her first few successes under my direction, why I was handling her career in a certain way; but she was intelligent enough to know and patient enough to wait.

"I kept her, so to speak, under wraps. If a pun may be permitted, they were gorgeous wraps... Nothing was spared to bring out all the glamour that was Gloria."

When I drove up to the studio... [Swanson remembered of her first day of work in *Don't Change Your Husband*], one of Mr. De Mille's assistants was waiting to show me to my dressing room... Vases of freshly cut flowers [from Cecil] stood on almost every flat surface....

When my hair was in place, two women brought in my costume, a beautiful white day dress, and helped Hattie [her dresser] get it on over my hair. A few minutes later, Pinkerton detectives arrived with three velvet-lined jewel chests. Everything was real, and I was supposed to pick what I wanted to go with the dress. [Later I learned] Mr. De Mille always had his actresses pick out the jewelry they wore in his films so that they would act as if they owned it. I chose a delicate necklace and earrings, and an assortment of rings and bracelets.* A few minutes before ten I heard a violin start to play nearby, and an assistant director came to lead me to the set.

We stood off to one side as Mr. De Mille entered like Caesar, with a whole retinue of people in his wake.... Everyone stood in rapt silence as [his] eyes swept over the set. Looking at every detail with absolute concentration, he peeled off his field jacket and a Filipino boy behind him caught it as it left his hand. When he was ready to sit down, the Filipino boy deftly shoved a director's chair under him....

When he saw me...he came over, took my hand, and led me toward the set. "This is your home," he explained. "Take all the time you need to get acquainted with it. If anything seems wrong, we'll talk about it."

Cecil never allowed his actors (before talkies) to use a script. Very carefully, he told them what the story was about and what each scene meant, but he never gave specific instructions or directions. Swanson remembered a young actor on the film who asked DeMille if he would explain how he wanted him to play a scene. "'Certainly not!' [C. B.] bellowed. 'This is not an acting school.... When you do something wrong, *that* is when I will talk to you!'"

"Working for Mr. De Mille was like playing house in the world's most expensive department store," Swanson reminisced. "Going home at night to your own house and furniture was always a bit of a letdown. I finally said to him one day, 'Mr. De Mille, you're giving me terribly expensive tastes.' (Other people called him Chief and C. B., but I always called him Mr. De Mille.)

"'There's nothing wrong with wanting the best,' he said. 'I always do.'" He had been paying her only $150 a week. He raised this amount to $200 and agreed she would be making $350 a week in two years. "That seemed an unbelievable figure," she later commented. "I was absolutely thrilled. We signed [a new contract] on December 30, 1918, just Mr. De Mille and I!"

A week or so later an item appeared in a gossip column that Cecil and Swanson were having a torrid love affair. Swanson was stunned as her heart was elsewhere at the time. A few days later a note came from Constance inviting her to a small dinner party. "Hattie [Gloria's dresser] told me that's what Mrs. DeMille did every time stories appeared about her husband and another woman. She invited the other woman right to her home to quash the story. For years, the columnists had gossiped about what they called Mr. DeMille's harem, which included Jeanie Macpherson, Annie Bauchens [his film editor], and Julia Faye." The name of Gladys Rosson, Cecil's loyal secretary, could also have been added to this list.

"There wasn't a woman in his life who wasn't devoted to him," Cecilia Junior said about her grandfather. "I mean to the point that everything else went—everything—there was an incredible relationship he had with women of all kinds. Nonsexual with women in the family, sexual with his mistresses. But the devotion he demanded was total. The ones he was truly serious about he brought home. Julia [Faye] might come for a movie. Jeanie Macpherson came more often because they worked on scripts together. Jeanie was his first major affair and she remained the love in his life for many years. They were working partners and it would never have distressed [Constance] to have [Cecil] have a working partner as a mistress...that

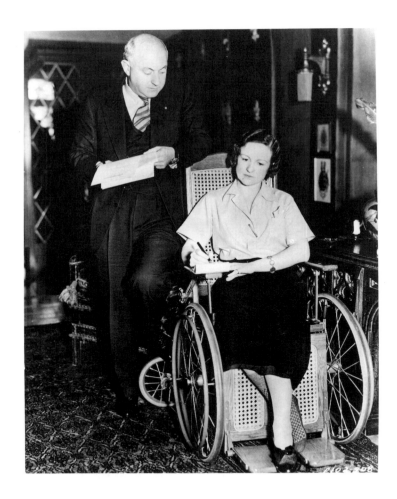

Cecil with the invaluable Glady[s] Rosson, who refused to let a bro[ken] leg in the 1940s interfere with h[er] duties

way it was just done without being flaunted. But he didn't like to involve himself with his leading ladies.

"I'll tell you a story. Gloria [Swanson] and [Cecil] were watching the rushes of *Male and Female* together. Gloria really had a crush on him and she just got up—in the midst of it and in the flickering light from the film sat in his lap and put her arms around him. He said [later to Cecilia Junior], 'I sat there, I never moved. I never put her back in her seat or expressed any emotion. I kept my hands to myself. I think it was the hardest thing I ever did.' And I asked him, 'Why did you do it?' and he said, 'I had a star who was in love with me. I could pull more out of her in a day if we remained friends. If we became lovers I would have lost some of my control.'

"Gladys [Rosson] was another matter. She very early became a fixture in the family. . . . Gladys was always there whatever the hour whenever he needed her. She was right there. He was her life. She adored him."

Cecil had hired Gladys as his secretary in 1914, the summer she was graduated from high school. She quickly became his dedicated right hand. It was Gladys who brought him dinner on a tray when he worked late at the office, although she had begun work even before he had; Gladys who arranged things at Paradise so that when he arrived for the weekend, everything was in order; Gladys who allowed herself to be "burned at the stake"* for Geraldine Farrar in *Joan the Woman*; Gladys who attended him with a mixture of ramrod dignity and maternal tenderness. Small, slim, her brunette hair drawn severely back from her high forehead, her dark eyes flashing behind a pair of gold-rimmed glasses, Gladys was a vital woman, quick on her feet and nimble of wit. "Gladys was patient," Cecil would later write. "Patience is a virtue requisite in those around me." Gladys was to be with Cecil for thirty-nine years. For the first two decades of their association, her patience was as godly as Constance's complacency. The DeMille family and their close associates all appear to have known that Gladys was deeply in love with her boss and had willingly dedicated her life to him. In the early 1930s and for nineteen years thereafter, she was his mistress. "Grandmother was old enough [then] and she was never concerned," Cecilia's daughter would later admit. "Gladys had been a fixture in the family for so long that Grandmother would ask her for lunch, and they would be seated in the dining room together. I used to eat with them often. [The family was all aware that Gladys was his mistress at the time.] It was quite polite. Gladys always referred to Grandmother as Mrs. DeMille, and she called Gladys— 'Gladys.'"

To compensate Gladys for her abject and unfulfilled early devotion, Cecil became a "godfather" to the entire Rosson family, helping her brother Richard to a career as a director, her brother Hal to become one of Hollywood's top cameramen, and giving her brother Arthur steady work as his second unit director,* as well as always being generous to Mrs. Rosson and Gladys's two sisters, Helene and Ethel (known as "Queenie").

Male and Female, filmed in 1919 and based on James Barrie's satirical play about class barriers, *The Admirable Crichton,* was the third film Gloria Swanson made for Cecil.* By changing the title, Cecil had emphasized a more universal subject: the battle of the sexes. He concentrated on another aspect of master-slave domination from *The Captive*—the slave who becomes master. The Barrie play contained only a passing reference to a quotation from a William E. Henley poem—"I was a King in Babylon/And you were a Christian slave/...I bent and broke your pride." This became the main theme of the film and the basis for the flashback sequences, allowing Cecil to concoct his favorite mix: "sex, sadism and religious sacrifice."

Swanson claimed he saved the most dangerous scenes (the flashbacks) "until the very last." These were scenes that took the characters from contemporary England to ancient Babylon.* Swanson played Lady Mary, a rich, spoiled, willful young woman stranded on an uninhabited tropical island during a South Seas cruise with her aristocratic family and friends. Her father's butler, Crichton (Thomas Meighan), is the only person in the party capable of survival in such primitive circumstances and takes command, becoming during the group's two-year stay on the island a monarchial figure, whose fantasies take him back to a Babylonian past where he is the king.* In these scenes Swanson is brought before the king (Crichton), who tells her she must renounce her religion and become his bride or face a den of lions on the other side of a golden door at the foot of the steps to the throne. Lady Mary (now an Early Christian) chooses the lions. In DeMille (and Belasco) tradition, real lions waited behind the door.

"...Mr. De Mille said I should confront them [the lions] in the manner of a very dignified Christian saint," Swanson wrote. "He believed in reincarnation and tried to demonstrate it in...these presentations of people living in different ages simultaneously on the screen. He actually believed that people had to come back to earth and suffer for the sins of their past lives."

The set of the lions' den had been constructed in an enormous swimming pool, painted entirely with black lacquer and converted into an arena. Swanson entered it wearing an all-white costume which transformed her into a frail, virginal moving target.* Around the edge of the arena were arches and a flight of stairs descending into it. Heavy wire mesh enclosed the whole set.

There were two sequences to shoot [Swanson recalled]. In the first I had to descend the steps and approach the . . . gate [to the den]. I was told to remain perfectly calm, for the gate was made of painted wood and therefore easily breakable. If a lion . . . [got] excited or angry and jumped up against it, he could smash right through it. . . . In the second sequence, I had to lie on my stomach [inside the den] and have a lion put his paw on my bare back.

Once I was in costume, Mr. De Mille escorted me into the great enclosed set. When the lights hit me, I walked across the floor of the throne room toward the steps, and at a given moment the trainers cracked their whips and the lions were released. I could see the shapes of the animals beyond the gate. I took a few more steps forward, then froze, petrified, as one lion unexpectedly moved to the side of the gate and bounded up out of the den, landing a few feet away from me.

She was whisked to safety, but when the scene was repeated, again a lion sprang forward. The lion trainers called out instructions to her to stand absolutely

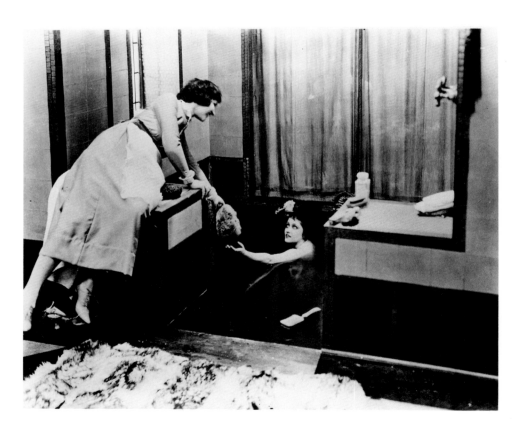

still. Swanson was too terrified to do otherwise. Finally, a trainer stepped in front of her and drove the animal back with a whip and a chair. Pandemonium reigned as C. B. shouted, "That's it! Cut! Fine!" He rushed over to Swanson to see if she was all right and to tell her that the scene "looked marvelous" and that they had "got all of it." Feeling contrite to have put his star through such a grueling ordeal, he suggested they omit the scene with the lion on her back. Swanson had regained her courage and insisted on proceeding.

"All right, young fellow," [DeMille replied,] ... "let's go," and with that he took me by the hand and escorted me back onto the set and down the steps to the lions' arena.

This time, [remembered Swanson,] I had to lie on the floor and remain absolutely still. I would ruin the scene if I couldn't control my breathing. My back was bare to the waist. I could hear a lion's claws scratching the floor as the trainer led him in on a leash. Then I could hear another trainer whisper to Mr. De Mille, who came and knelt beside me.

"I must ask you something for your own safety," he whispered. "You're not menstruating, are you?"

"No," I replied very softly.

He stood up and said to the trainer, "We can proceed. Everything's fine."

Then I could hear the lion breathing near me. They put a piece of canvas on my back to keep the lion's manicured claws from making the slightest scratch. Then they brought the lion up to me and put his paw on the canvas. Ever so slowly they pulled the canvas aside until I could feel his paw on my skin. Every hair on my head was standing on end. I could hear the camera grinding and then the crack of the trainer's whip. Every cell in my body quivered when the animal roared. His hot breath seemed to go up and down my spine.

When the scene was over, Cecil asked her to get into another costume so that he could redo one or two close-ups, which would complete the shooting. Swanson suddenly fell to pieces and admitted through her tears that she just could not continue. The lion, the tension, had been too much.

"How lovely," [Cecil replied.] ... "I was beginning to think that you were the perfect machine, that you could do anything. But now I know you're much more than that. You're a real woman...."*

He sat me on his knee, [Swanson confided], and from one of his desk drawers he pulled out a velvet tray covered with brooches, rings, necklaces, and a whole array of other beautiful jewelry. He told me he had planned to give me something at the finish of the picture, but that he thought I should have it now. He smiled broadly, patted me on the hand, and said, "Take your choice."

Opposite: Julia Faye, as Gloria Swanson's maid (left), hands her a sponge in *Male and Female*, 1919

Above: Faye was reputed to have the most beautiful feet in Hollywood, and in 1959, C. B. wrote: "She has been in nearly every one of my pictures since 1917." After his death, she continued to receive a stipend from the DeMille family

"The matter of product [now having been successfully negotiated, Zukor proceeded to battle to] control the booking offices which stood as middlemen between the manufacturer and exhibitor."

These made "politics look like amateur theatricals," William deMille recalled. "When the carnage finally subsided...the shy Mr. Zukor emerged...holding...complete control of Paramount, the strongest distributing organization in the field. [Ultimately he controlled Paramount Pictures.]...the penniless immigrant of twenty years before was now the strongest single figure in motion-pictures."

Shortly thereafter, the corporation absorbed Artcraft and began acquiring hundreds of motion picture theatres throughout the United States.* It marked the end of the stranglehold the Trust had on the motion picture industry. Sam Goldfish was elected chairman of the board, and Cecil retained his title of director general.

Not long after the merger of Zukor's and Lasky's companies, Zukor demanded that Goldfish be asked to sever his contract with the company because of a growing antagonism between the two men. Zukor insisted that since Lasky had brought Goldfish into the organization he be the one to tell him of the decision—and within the next forty-eight hours. "I had tremendous respect for Zukor's courage and qualities of leadership," Lasky wrote of his emotions at that time. "I felt sure that with him at the helm our company had a glorious future. But Sam was my sister's husband,* and while he lacked Zukor's experience, he also was a brilliant strategist." Lasky and Cecil met and they decided to buy Goldfish out for $900,000, which they estimated as his share of the stock (actually a low accounting) and with this money Goldfish, with Edgar Selwyn, formed Goldwyn Pictures Corporation. (Two years later, in 1918, he merged the first syllable of Goldfish and the last of Selwyn to become "Goldwyn.")

"In the early years, Sam was one of [Cecil's] best friends," a family member said. "They used to lunch together and go to Paradise and spend weekends together. Sam's grammar was terrible, and he used a double negative once while they were conversing. [Cecil] said, 'Sam, do you know what a double negative is?' The moment he spoke, he knew he should not have said it. He looked at Sam's eyes and later said, 'There was a film there that I knew I could never wash away. I have regretted all my life saying that.'"

Goldfish, now Goldwyn, called the end of his relationship with the Jesse L. Lasky Feature Play Company "one of the bitterest chapters" in his life. The acrimony was long—over thirty years—in healing.

When the time came in 1920 for Cecil to renew his contract with Lasky and Zukor, other film companies offered him higher stakes to sign with them. Lasky knew Cecil would not leave the company he had helped to form, and he took advantage of that knowledge. Cecil accepted his offer of $260,000 a year, although United Artists was willing to double that. Cecil also formed a company of his own as he thought "that the day might be coming when an independent company might be a useful entity." Called Cecil B. DeMille Productions, it was a partnership formed with Constance, Neil McCarthy, and Mrs. DeMille's "youthful and brilliant stepmother," Ella King Adams (who also was C. B.'s script reader) as Cecil's partners.* He continued to make some very successful films for Lasky and Zukor: *Something to Think About* and *The Affairs of Anatol*,* starring Gloria Swanson; *Saturday Night* and

Manslaughter (which featured Roman orgies), with the elegant, sophisticated Leatrice Joy (who popularized bobbed hair and man-tailored clothes), and *Adam's Rib* ("a tale of the youngest flapper and the oldest sin," which also included slaves in the Stone Age), with Anna Q. Nilsson, Hollywood's first Swedish star.

"After *Male and Female*, DeMille's work never went beyond the chemise and the boudoir," Cecil's good friend Chaplin harshly commented. After *Adam's Rib*, still another story about a restless wife (this time one attracted to a former king), Cecil began to feel maybe Chaplin was right.

One of Cecil's great gifts was "his intuitive ability to gauge and anticipate public taste." In 1918, *Old Wives for New* had begun an entire cycle of sociosexual comedies that had been big box office. Objectively, these films had been "the wish-dreams of the twenties"; subjectively, they had coincided with Cecil in real life playing out his own sexual fantasies. These emotions did not subside in 1922, but another aspect of his temperament was revealed: a lofty obeisance to religion, which he sincerely believed made up for his depiction of (or predilection for) lavish display and slavish sexuality.

Two sex scandals rocked Hollywood in 1922: the murder of leading director William Desmond Taylor, rumored to have been involved with "dope, blackmail, and indescribable orgies," and the indictment of popular comedian Roscoe (Fatty) Arbuckle for manslaughter following the orgiastic death of Virginia Rappe, a starlet and young beauty. Cecil complained of "a sickness in Hollywood . . . a crumbling of standards." Hollywood had been labeled "a citadel of sin," and Cecil felt "It was necessary for the industry to do something." What that should be he was not sure. But matters in his own life were mounting in tension: fights between Jeanie and Julia (who now appeared in small roles in almost all DeMille's pictures), the hedonistic tone of weekends at Paradise, his dissatisfaction with the content of his films, his resentment of Zukor's power in the company, his guilt toward Constance, his reliance on Gladys, and his many responsibilities.

Cecil became obsessed with the desire to have an audience at the Vatican with Pope Benedict XV to discuss various aspects of his life. Upon receiving a reply that His Holiness would see him, Cecil, his Japanese valet, Yamabe, and his French art director, Paul Iribe, set out for the Eternal City. Upon their arrival in Rome, Cecil and Iribe, dressed in formal clothes, arrived at the bronze doors of the Vatican, only to be told that the Pope had died that very morning.

Cecil returned to Hollywood, spiritually frustrated and physically weak (he had become ill with acute rheumatic fever in Paris). After a short recuperation, he decided on a bold move: to let the public choose the subject of his next film. Barrett Kiesling, a young man in the studio publicity department, arranged with the *Los Angeles Times* to sponsor a contest. A prize of $1,000 was to be given to the entrant with the best idea for a picture. Eight contestants suggested a story dealing with Moses and the Ten Commandments, and Cecil agreed to give each of them the full prize money.

"Here was a theme that stirred and challenged in me the heritage of being Henry DeMille's son," Cecil confessed, recalling his father's habit of reading the

Bible aloud to his sons. Jeanie went immediately to work on the screenplay. As it was finally developed, it was a modern story with a biblical prologue.

Cecil was determined that two time frames—biblical and contemporary—should be used, the first to be shot in Technicolor (extremely innovative in 1922), the second in black and white. It took months for Jeanie to shape "scattered situations" into "the mosaic of a complete, coherent story. My first thought was to interpret the Commandments in episodic form," she wrote in the premiere program. "I worked for several weeks along these lines with growing dissatisfaction. . . . The story didn't have the right 'feel'. It was bumpy. It started and stopped, ran and limped. . . . I started in all over again." She was to try numerous approaches until she hit upon a theme—"namely that if you break the ten immutable laws they will break you!"—applied this to both the ancient story of Moses and Aaron and the modern (1920s) tale of the McTavish family's two brothers, Dan and John, and their stern mother, whose moralistic attitude forces one son into atheism and the brothers against each other.

Jeanie Macpherson described her screenplay thus:

> Egypt. The days of the glory of the Pharaohs. Such majesty and power and corrosive magnificence as exist only in those periods of history when one small class lives upon and is heedless of the blood and tears of tens of thousands of people held in subjection.
>
> The Children of Israel in bondage. Bereft of hope they toil in the desert, building walls and temples and pyramids. Faithful to their God despite the vindictive oppression of a ruler and a people who worship graven images, they finally see hope when Moses is raised up to plead for their liberation from slavery . . . [and finally to lead] the Children of Israel [out of] their captivity. . . .
>
> Then Pharaoh suffers a change of heart, and orders his war chariots to start in pursuit of the Jews. The Children of Israel are at the Red Sea. . . . Death or captivity seem inevitable, but Moses prays, and then the Lord sends a pillar of fire to stop the charge of the Egyptians and at the same time divides the waters of the sea so that His Chosen People pass in safety . . . to the other shore. . . .
>
> The exaltation of the prophet soon passes. . . . [While he is on Mount Sinai receiving the Ten Commandments from the Lord] his people have set up a golden calf and worshiped it. . . . Moses . . . descends from the mountain and crashes his tablets of stone into the scene of idolatrous worship and licentious revelry. The golden calf is destroyed and turned to dust.
>
> As the dust settles figures emerge slowly from a misty background. . . . A primly dressed mother sits at a table in a modern room . . . reading from the Bible to her two sons. It is San Francisco; the time is [the 1920s]. . . .
>
> One son, Dan, is bored and cynical. The other son, John, is tolerant and . . . deferential to his mother.
>
> "That's bunk," says Dan. He intimates that the Ten Commandments may [once] have been all right . . . but that the world has changed. The deeply

religious mother...is affronted. Hugging her Bible to her flat breast, she turns her [disbelieving] son out of her home....

The mother is relentless, [and] she is warned by her good son that she is using the cross for a scourge, but will not relent. Later she does let Dan return, but the next Sunday she starts to leave home, Bible under her arm, because this sceptical son and his sweetheart, Mary, a waif reared by his mother, are dancing on the Lord's Day....Dan and Mary defy the Commandments together....Now it so happens that the good son also loves Mary....

After the intermission, the film takes up the lives of these four people three years later. Climaxes of thrilling power are reached and in the end the Eternal Law is vindicated.*

The modern story bore a strong resemblance to Cecil's *The Return of Peter Grimm* and indicates that he had a great influence on Jeanie's scenario and that, perhaps, he was the prime author of the modern sequences. Both Peter Grimm and the contemporary story of the Ten Commandments open with a righteous mother reading the Bible to her two grown sons.

Cecil began shooting *The Ten Commandments* eight months after Jeanie had begun the screenplay. The New York office had been enthusiastic enough about the project to allot a budget of $1,000,000. Much encouraged by this material show of faith, Cecil sped Moses on to his trek across the Sinai—actually, the sand dunes of Guadalupe, California. He raised his tent city, reconstructed Pharaoh's palace, imported his thousands of Israelites and Egyptians and animals and props. Soon Zukor telegraphed Lasky, who was in charge of production: "I AM VERY MUCH CONCERNED...COST ALREADY...OVER SEVEN HUNDRED THOUSAND...." Cecil took it upon himself to wire back: "...AS AN...EVIDENCE...OF MY FAITH IN THIS PICTURE, I HEREBY WAIVE THE GUARANTEE UNDER MY CONTRACT ON THIS PICTURE, OTHER THAN THE REGULAR WEEKLY PAYMENTS...."*

"Cecil...began pouring money into [the film] with boundless energy. It looked to the business office like an open-ended investment," Lasky commented. When he confronted Cecil, Cecil's eyes blazed. "What do they want me to do?" he snapped. "Stop now and release it as the Five Commandments?"

The heat in Guadalupe was almost intolerable, the work schedule killing, the organization nearly overwhelming. He had cast Julia Faye as Pharaoh's wife, a situation fraught with difficulty when Jeanie was also on location. His relationships with Lasky and Zukor placed an even greater strain on him.

The Ten Commandments opened, appropriately, at Grauman's Egyptian Theatre in Hollywood on December 4, 1923, and at the George M. Cohan Theatre in New York on December 21. The critics were almost unanimous in their admiration and wonderment at his cinematic achievements—the use of color, the spectacle, the ancient tabloid—but faulted the modern story.* Despite this, *The Ten Commandments* was a huge box office success, tripling the company's investment in a matter of only weeks after its release.

With this success, Cecil made a trio of lavish, costly pictures (*Triumph, Feet of Clay*, and *The Golden Bed*). For *Feet of Clay* (with an elaborate sequence in the after-

Overleaf: *The Ten Commandments* was C. B.'s (and Hollywood's) first epic spectacle. The costs ran well over $1,000,000, which was a colossal sum in 1923. Everything about it was outsize: an enormous cast, a tent city built to house them, and publicity to match. In New York City it opened at the George M. Cohan Theatre, in Hollywood at Grauman's Egyptian (a predecessor of the Chinese). Its cast was full of stars: Leatrice Joy, Richard Dix, Nita Naldi, Agnes Ayres, Theodore Roberts, and Julia Faye

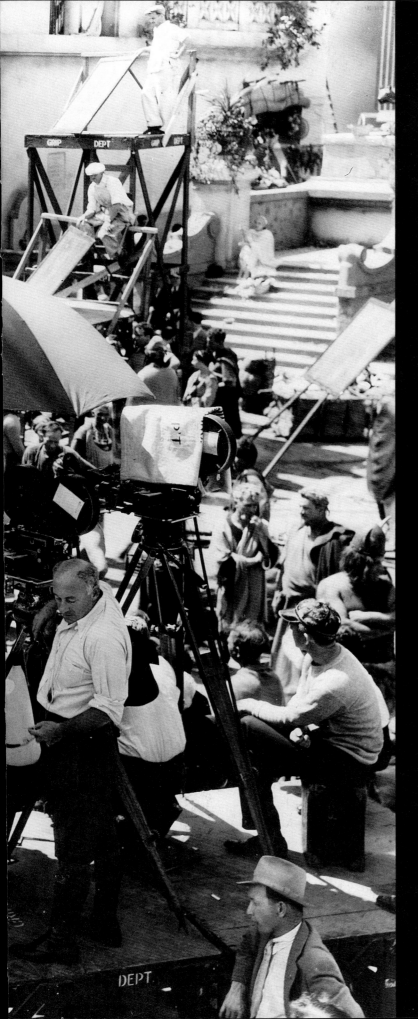

D. W. Griffith with C. B., whose admiration for the creator of *The Birth of a Nation* was enormous. "I, like every other worker in motion pictures, am his debtor," he wrote

world), he hired five yachts and reconstructed a baroque mansion where in a spectacular ballroom scene all the women wore real jewels; for another ball of extraordinary splendor in *The Golden Bed* (in which a man embezzles money so that his wife can squander it by giving extravagant parties), male actors licked chocolate from live female "candy bars."* For the same film, Edith Head designed gold-plated riding boots. "DeMille . . . had horrible taste," she later admitted. "He liked flocky things; he liked things that made people say, 'What the hell is that?' He told me, 'I never want anything shown to me as a design that you could possibly buy or wear. I want something original.' I knew that the average . . . elegant lady [who rode horseback] in Central Park did not wear gold boots. DeMille loved it—no, he liked it. He never said he loved anything."

Only one person outdid DeMille in the spectacular proportion of his productions—Cecil himself. "This rapidly expanding trait got to be more than our Eastern office could stomach," Lasky later confessed, "despite the fact that Cecil's prodigious expenditures invariably paid very handsome dividends. Rental terms had to be jacked up to meet the strain [and the] conservative elements [Zukor's staff] didn't favor risking such sums on a single picture. I was informed that Cecil was going to get the ax unless he allowed his contract to be altered to give the company more control over his pictures."

Cecil recorded that, "In July [1924], D. W. Griffith left United Artists and signed with Paramount for three films. In early November, there was no DeMille picture listed in Paramount's semiannual announcement of forthcoming productions. . . . On December 2, Mr. Zukor asked Jesse to open discussions with me relative to a possible readjustment of my contract."

Two items were under contention—the costs of the sets and costumes of

Carrying the Torch

Cecil's films and the expense of his personal production staff. Most film companies at that time hired people for each film. Cecil, believing he had to keep an efficient staff together between pictures, refused to do this. On December 18, Zukor's assistant, Sidney Kent, wired him an ultimatum: "...WE OBJECT TO...THE ADDED EXPENSE CAUSED BY YOUR SEPARATE UNIT...MR. ZUKOR FEELS THAT THIS MUST BE TAKEN OFF OUR BACKS."

Cecil felt sufficiently sure that this could be worked out to book passage to sail to Europe (incongruously) with Constance, Jeanie and her mother, Julia Faye and her mother, cameraman Peverell Marley, and his new art director, Mitchell Leisen,* to scout locations for Marie Corelli's *The Sorrows of Satan*, which he was negotiating to purchase. They did not sail. Lasky stated simply, "His contract was not renewed and he left the employ of Famous Players–Lasky." Cecil wrote, "We did not sail. After meeting with Mr. Zukor, Jesse Lasky and Sid Kent, [in New York, en route to Europe] I began the year of 1925 as one of the unemployed.... [I have had] few bitterer moments than when one of those gentlemen [Zukor] said to me, and the other two heard it in unprotesting silence: 'Cecil, you have never been one of us.'"

Cecil returned immediately with Constance to California. Jeanie remained but a few days later sent Cecil a telegram:

DEAREST CHIEF—HERE I AM JUST LEAVING CHICAGO [on the] SANTE FE-CALIFORNIA LIMITED CAR THIRTY SIX DRAWING ROOM B AND YOU MIGHT BE A NICE BOY AND SEND YOUR LITTLE BONZO A WIRE AND TELL HER YOU ARE GLAD SHE IS COMING EVEN IF YOU AIN'T   ANYHOW SHE WILL BE GLAD TO SEE HER BIG CHIEF LOTS OF LOVE AND KISSES FROM—SHAMPLE [her code name]

Cecil telegraphed back the same day:

MISS JEANIE MACPHERSON
CAR 36 DRAWING ROOM B WESTBOUND CALIFORNIA LIMITED SANTA FE TRAIN
ARRIVING ALBUQUERQUE, NEW MEXICO, 10:30 A.M. OCTOBER 10TH

GREETINGS   IT IS GOOD TO HAVE YOU SPEEDING TOWARD US   WE HAVE MISSED THE TURNED UP NEB [NOSE] AND THE SASSY DISPOSITION   I HAVE THE CALF PROPERLY FATTED AND WILL KILL ON ARRIVAL   MUCH LOVE   C

Upon his return, Cecil had set right to work activating Cecil B. DeMille Productions and made *The Road to Yesterday* and *The Volga Boatman* in the next year. A disclaimer in the latter's opening title emphasized that it pleaded no political causes. A story of two aristocrats caught in the revolution, the film did manage to stay neutral by having one (Princess Vera) elect to join her lover, a Volga boatman helping to build a new Russia, while the other (Prince Dimitri) chose exile. To Americans in 1925, Prohibition seemed a more vital political issue than Communism. The exotic backgrounds and the eroticism of *The Volga Boatman* contributed to its tremendous success. Mitchell Leisen, who had gained a considerable reputation after designing the sets for Douglas Fairbanks's *Robin Hood* and the inspired palace scenes for *The Thief of Baghdad*, was hired for *The Volga Boatman*, which required a similar set. Lei-

C. B. directing (right) a peacock; (below, left) a dinosaur (for *Adam's Rib*, 1923, starring Anna Q. Nilsson); and (below, right) an alligator

Opposite: Cecil and Willian (aboard Cecil's yacht *Seaward*) were both good seamen—possibly a heritag from their Southern forebears

Cecil liked pleasant workin quarters. In this story conference for *Feet of Clay*, 1924, his ship is off Catalin Island. The set designers fc this film about a return fror Eternity were the French A Deco specialist Paul Iribe and Norman Bel Geddes

sen recalled that "C. B. was very anxious to see the palace set where a banquet takes place, but I pleaded with him not to go down there until it was dark. He thought I was stalling... but he waited. [When the time came] we went down [to the set] and I knocked on the door. A liveried footman opened it and we went in. I had used a highly polished black marble floor, perhaps the first time this had ever been done and there were torches everywhere which reflected in the floor. Best of all the banquet tables were loaded with the most fantastic food I could find. C. B. said, 'I can see why you wanted me to wait.'" He called the whole company down and had a feast.

The *New York Telegram* pointed out "the nice Lubitschean direction of a

naughty scene where faces register the successive stages in a suggested undressing of a princess."* Since the Volga boatman of the title was the dashing William Boyd (one day to become a legend as Hopalong Cassidy), viewers came away from the film believing it was passion not politics that was at the heart of the film. Leisen thought C. B. "had no nuances. Everything was in neon lights six feet tall: *Lust, Revenge, Sex.* You had to learn to think the way he did in capital letters."

William deMille now terminated his contract with Famous Players–Lasky and joined the staff of directors at Cecil's new DeMille Studios in Culver City (formerly the Ince Studio), purchased with $500,000 advanced by Jeremiah Milbank of the New York–based Producers Distributing Corporation. Cecil was "out to challenge the mighty majors"—Famous Players–Lasky, First National, and his Culver City neighbor, Metro-Goldwyn-Mayer. With his usual largesse, Cecil bought two clipper ships, the *Bohemia* and the *Indiana,* to use as permanent sets, and then put in a radio station at the studio so that he could keep in touch when he was sailing in coastal waters in either of them or his own boat, the *Seaward.* After taking out a staggering loan from the Chase Manhattan Bank, he completed plans for a total of forty-one productions to be made in 1926–27, three of which he would direct; the rest he would supervise.

Jeremiah Milbank, although a practical businessman, was a dedicated Christian and had once considered becoming a member of the clergy. Therefore, when Cecil came to him announcing his desire to make a film on the life of Christ, he did not hesitate in agreeing not only to finance the venture, but to donate any or all profits that might come to him through the film to charity. Cecil agreed to do the same. Thus, *The King of Kings* began production with a kind of reverent commitment not common in films. Though Cecil took no author's credit, the original shooting script shows page after page written in his hand. He had taken Jeanie and three other writers* on the *Seaward* to put together the first draft. Gladys Rosson had gone with them, typing the script as they worked on deck. Cecil recalled that "When the *Seaward* changed course, the sea breeze was just right to lift the pages of the script and scatter them over the broad bosom of the Pacific Ocean. All hands were called to

action stations, and we managed to retrieve the soaked pages with harpoons and boat hooks and to dry them out."

Cecilia was a now young woman of eighteen, and she and her father were extremely companionable. Cecilia took an interest in the business side of her father's career, and he discussed things with her openly and candidly. He was loving, but never equally close to his adopted children. Katherine was at a boarding school in Santa Barbara acting in and directing the school's dramatic club. "Katherine is a 'dark lady of the sonnets' type" was how one classmate described her.

Richard had proved to be a bit of a discipline problem. "I was expelled from the nursery school at UCLA for indecent behavior," he recalled. "Two years later I was also expelled from the Hollywood School for Girls.* (It was actually coeducational in the first and second grades when I went.) I won't describe to you why I was expelled—but a seven-year-old can do plenty. Father wasn't much of a disciplinarian although he had to discipline John because John was an uncontrolled, impulsive, and unruly person. All other discipline was sort of invisible, and was imposed by Constance by being shocked. Her idea was that people who were the right kind of people were born knowing the rules. You did not have to tell them. If you broke the rules, her reaction was so painful to the offender that he never did it in public again. Except for John.

"John got into all kinds of trouble. He lost so much money gambling [he was seventeen at the time] that he had to stay on a gambling boat for three weeks washing dishes to pay off his debt. He just disappeared and Constance was frantic. He came back, of course. He was the wild one in the family. He rode his horse home from the private school he attended in Santa Barbara. He was expelled too—for gambling, pitching pennies—by Mr. Cote, the principal, and he did not like being disciplined so he got on his horse and rode home—ninety miles. I remember when he arrived on his horse. Mr. Cote wouldn't take him back so he had to go to military school."

Another family member recalled that "John was fun, he was bright, he laughed a lot and he was giggly, but he couldn't keep up with the family. If you sat down to a family dinner the conversation went very fast, and poor John, there was no way [he could keep up]. Any time he opened his mouth and said something (to his dying day), the poor thing said something stupid. It was sad."

Katherine DeMille added, "Well, even at five or six you could see that Richard was going to be some kind of genius. He was terribly bright, very precocious. He was a lonely child, I think. We were all so much older. He was a bit of a loner. But warm, loving. Father liked to tease him into saying very adult things. I think he had a special feeling for Richard although I'm not sure as a child Richard realized that. . . .

"It was while I was at the Santa Barbara School for Girls—I guess I was fifteen or sixteen—when Father made *The King of Kings*. I didn't have any thoughts about being an actress then—I was just so fascinated by Father's work that during the holiday I used to go down and watch and sit on the set. He always welcomed Cecilia and me—Agnes and Margaret, too. If John had been interested (he never was to my knowledge), I'm sure he would have encouraged him. He let me go into the cutting rooms and work behind the camera. He had a lot of women technicians. He believed in women's abilities. Not many other directors were hiring women for jobs behind the camera at that time.

"I was on *The King of Kings* set a lot and went before the cameras in it as well. So did Cecilia. I think we got fifty dollars which we had to donate to charity," Katherine continued.

Filming the crucifixion scene presented unusual problems. Mitchell Leisen had designed the sets for the film, and this had been the most difficult to engineer. "There were no special effects using dupe film or tricks in those days," he explained. "The only way you could show something was to actually do it and photograph it. There was something called the Williams Process in which they took a positive print, painted out certain parts of it, and made a dupe negative, but that always left a wavy black outline and I said, 'We can't have Christ on the Cross with a wavy black outline.'" He hit on an ingenious solution using casts of H. B. Warner's hands.

Katherine recalled that she "was there [on the set] on Christmas Eve and they had just finished shooting the crucifixion, three crosses on the hill and—I don't know—hundreds, maybe a thousand extras. Everyone had worked about twelve hours and about 8:30 or 9 o'clock Father said, 'Okay, cut. Finished. Done.' And the people began to scurry to get home.

"All of a sudden, his voice boomed across the set. 'Ladies and gentlemen, if you'd stop for just a moment.' And you could hear them saying, 'Son of a gun, what now?' And he said through his megaphone, 'I would like you all to take five minutes—*five minutes*—for you to just think about what you have seen tonight—and to remember that what we've seen tonight is the filming of something that truly happened. I want you to think what it has meant to you. I'd like you to take a few minutes of quiet. I've asked the orchestra to play some music.' He had an organ on the set and first only it could be heard. Then the orchestra joined in. I think it was Bach's Christmas Oratorio [they played]. It was amazing. There were many who wept. Some got on their knees facing the cross—just the sound of the music. In a few minutes, he said, 'Thank you, ladies and gentlemen. Let's go home to our families—

have a wonderful Christmas,' or words to that effect, and they all walked off in total silence....He made *The King of Kings* because he loved the Lord."

Cecil wrote that "All through the production [of *The King of Kings*], every effort was made to maintain the spirit of reverence....No one but the director [himself] spoke to H. B. Warner when he was in costume, unless it was absolutely necessary. He was veiled or transported in a closed car when he went between the set and his dressing room or, when we were on location, his tent, where he took his meals alone."

Leisen added that nobody was allowed "to see Christ get up on the Cross or get off of it. I dropped a curtain in front of it, and when he was in place, we'd raise the curtain. Harry Warner was never allowed to smoke on stage, nor was anybody else in the cast. They also had to sign agreements that they would behave themselves for the next year and not get divorced or cut up in a nightclub."

Cecil "had a fervid attachment to mysticism," his niece Agnes remarked. "He consider[ed] himself a theologian. He believe[d] with sincerity that he [was] spreading the word of God and fostering the brotherhood of man. He believe[d] himself a dedicated person and his pictures, partially at least, instruments of religious faith."

After *The King of Kings*, Cecil was never to look at things quite in the same way again. He thought a great deal about his father and began to identify more with him. Both Julia Faye and Jeanie Macpherson remained close to him, but the relationships were becoming more patriarchal. He saw himself as their protector, and indeed, he took very good care of them for the rest of their lives. But the sexual part of their relationships with him were on the wane. He was to claim that during the making of *The King of Kings* and for a time thereafter, he lived a chaste life.

Agnes deMille in one of her earliest choreographic appearances, Hollywood, about 1915

Although she had not possessed Margaret's fragile beauty, Agnes had been a pretty child. But during her teenage years at the Hollywood School for Girls, she later recalled feeling "imprisoned in someone else's body—[I was] heavy, deep bosomed, large hipped, and on my face there developed seemingly overnight, a large hooked nose—my father's nose. From that unmarked day I looked in the mirror and realized I was not going to be a beautiful woman. I gave up caring how I looked, except in costume, because at the same time I became interested in dancing."

Agnes's desire to be a ballerina had begun as early as 1915 when at age nine she had seen Anna Pavlova dance in concert in Hollywood. Not until she was thirteen (considered late for a dancer) was she permitted dance instruction. Her father had been obdurate. He considered dancing "at best exhibitionist acrobatics, and certainly a field that offered neither intellectual nor spiritual challenge. Worse, the woman dancer entered a field long and closely associated with prostitution. Men did not want their women dancing publicly." Agnes struggled to learn what she could on her own.

Finally, Cecil, sensing how much it meant to Agnes, intervened and secured an audition for her with Theodore Kosloff, formerly a member of the Imperial Russian Ballet. Kosloff had made quite a reputation for himself by directing two hundred and twenty-five Russian dancers in a series of choreographic dramas a few years earlier at the Winter Garden Theatre in New York. The most startling of these dramas was the ballet *Cleopatra*, which starred Gertrude Hoffmann and had a score by Anton Arensky. Miss Hoffman was clad in little more than a string of blue and white beads. Despite (or perhaps because of) periodic rude interruptions by the police, this ballet was extremely successful on Broadway, unique, because never before had the two worlds crossed.

Cecil had seen the potential in Kosloff's work of presenting sex in the guise of art and had hired him to create an erotic dance for *The Woman God Forgot* (1917). Kosloff appeared as an Aztec warrior. Agnes was invited to watch him film his dance, "naked in feathers, leaning on a feathered spear.... His gestures were real classic pantomime, involving clenched fists and the whites of the eyeballs, a positive style which gave the camera something substantial to focus on.... Every expression was performed with a force that could have carried him across the room and over the wall. I was awe struck," Agnes remembered. "I went home and doubled the number of knee-bends I performed every night before bed."

In order for Anna to get Bill to agree to dancing lessons, Margaret's fallen arches were given as an excuse. And after all, if Margaret had dance instruction, so must Agnes. Kosloff seemed to have been in on the conspiracy and put Agnes through her audition himself. "He said my knees were weak, my spine curved, that I was heavy for my age and had 'no juice' [meaning she was not limber]." Nonetheless, he took her on as a pupil. The ideal ballet body is long limbed with a small compact torso that creates a beauty of line. Agnes's torso was long, her hips broad, her legs and arms "abnormally short," her hands and feet "broad and short," and as she also observed, "What I did not know was that I was constructed for endurance and that I developed through effort alone a capacity for outperforming far, far better technicians. Because I was built like a mustang, stocky, mettlesome and sturdy, I became a good jumper, growing special compensation muscles up the front of my shins for the lack of a helpful heel [a wide stretch of the Achilles tendon to take the shock of running or jumping]."

The young woman got no encouragement at home. Anna refused to allow her to practice more than forty-five minutes a day (on a barre fitted in her small bathroom).

"Why did I not simply disobey Mother?" she later questioned. "Because I cannot remember disobeying her in any single instance after the age of ten, never at any time. And because behind my mother stood my father, whom I loved with all my heart and whom I did not wish to flout....

"Pop was too smart to forbid me outright to continue with my chosen work. He knew that direct frontal attack would only serve to crystallize my determination; he bored from within. He sought to make me doubt the validity of the art itself. And I listened to him in anguish because he was an artist, in my eyes—a genius. He counted on this deference. He refused to go to my classes, to go to any performance of dancers, to read about them or look at pictures. At mention of any incident in the ballet school...ice would form on his mouth and he would sit silently sipping his cocktail until the subject had been dropped."

Agnes seemed oblivious to the growing problems between her parents. Home life at the William deMilles' was more cultural and intellectual than "up on the hill." Anna had her single-tax followers to tea. Sunday evenings, she would entice ("using

This photograph of Margaret deMille, Agnes's younger sister, was taken by Clarence Bull, a leading photographer of the day

a trip through the studio as bait") visiting concert artists, like the great violinist Efrem Zimbalist and his wife, opera singer Alma Gluck, and Metropolitan opera stars Lawrence Tibbett and Rosa Ponselle. "They were never asked to perform, of course, but they usually did....

"The evenings manifested a kind of chemical frenzy if only because of the elements thrown together. There was always a famous English author or two out West on a temporary contract, Somerset Maugham, Elinor Glyn...Rebecca West."*

In the summer of 1925, Agnes traveled with her mother and Margaret to England. It opened her eyes to a new world, another culture. Shortly after her graduation from high school in 1922, to please her father, she had given up dancing and had taken a general course at the University of California at Los Angeles, but in London she attended the Royal Ballet and spent two full days in the Reading Room of the British Museum studying the history of ballet.

Bill wanted her to write. She was not sure she had any talent. Anna's only involvement in her daughter's education was to refuse to allow her to take the compulsory course in sex hygiene—a battle she did not in the end win. All this parental disapproval of the dance as a career notwithstanding, occasionally Agnes staged dances for the student rallies "mostly to Chopin, mostly about yearning for beauty and always accompanied by sorority sisters who were not trained." But her studies came first, and in June 1927, just as Cecil began work on *The King of Kings*, she was graduated *cum laude* from college. To her shock, the day after "they had stood side by side" watching her take her degree, Anna and Bill told her that they were going to be divorced. Her world had fallen apart. Her home was broken, her father gone. She had given up the dance to please him—now she had regrets, although little time to think about them, for Anna immediately departed on "a desperate pilgrimage through Europe" with Margaret and Agnes "dragged at the tail" of their mother's grief. "The trip was so bleached by her anguish," Agnes wrote, "that I cannot recall any part of it without melancholy. No theaters. No restaurants. No dancing. Just evenings by the pension window, staring at the suicide wallpaper while Mother sat in her bedroom writing, writing endlessly home to Hollywood."

Under the California community property act, half of Bill's savings (he had been buying bonds since the war) went to Anna. In the beginning, this made him bitter and antagonistic. Before Agnes left with Anna and Margaret, he told her—to her hurt and astonishment—"You know, Agnes, [your mother] has done nothing that a good housekeeper could not have done." Her father had discovered a meaningful sexual relationship, but Agnes later said, "My mother had been a good mother to Margaret and me, such a sprightly, charming, inventive, and faithful wife and so eager always to help him in any of his creative endeavors, that for him to say that— she was nothing but a good housekeeper— so shocked me I could not reply or even look him in the eye."

Anna returned with the girls from Europe to live in New York in late August. Margaret went off to Barnard, but Agnes remained at home. One of the first things she did was to join the ballet company in Max Reinhardt's production of *A Midsummer Night's Dream* at the Century Theatre, but she was only a member of the *corps de ballet*. She knew now, however, what she wanted. She had a vision of a new form of ballet: dramatic, comedic, American in content, ballet that could entertain and hold its own in a Broadway show. Not until that very year had ballet in its classic form reached the Broadway theatre. In the show *Rio Rita,* dance director Albertina Rasch had created a few dances in which her female dancers "got right on their toes in the best Imperial Russian Ballet manner." At this time, the distinction between a dance director and a choreographer was easy to make. A choreographer was "a gentleman, preferably Russian, who devised ornamental numbers for some well-known ballerina...a dance director was a young man, usually reared in the buck-and-wing school, who operated only on Broadway [or in Hollywood], where his presence guaranteed that a number of young ladies...would kick their legs more or less in unison."

But Agnes had studied with Kosloff, who brought a great sense of theatre to ballet. She was also Cecil B. DeMille's niece and had seen firsthand how art could integrate with the commercial and draw a much larger audience. Her aim was to do character studies, where the dancing was a natural incident to the episode. After disappointing interviews with various Broadway producers who were family friends, she decided she must create her own dances and showcase them, and Anna supported Agnes's ambitions, helping her sew costumes and whatever other "loving drudgery" was required.

Anna still could not reconcile herself to the divorce and especially to Bill's plans to remarry. For a long time the name of his wife-to-be, Clara Beranger, could not be mentioned in the house. Anna was bitter, uncomprehending how *this* could happen to *her.* She threw herself afresh into work for the single tax and for the only person left close to her—Agnes.

In California, Bill appeared to be happier than he had ever been. He and

Director William deMille coaching Richard Dix and Lois Wilson in *Icebound*, 1924, with a screenplay by Clara Beranger

Clara shared their work and that was considerable. She had been writing the screenplays of his films for the past seven years. Clara had been born in Baltimore, had been educated at Goucher College, and had been a newspaper and magazine writer before going to Hollywood (a divorcee with a young daughter), in 1920 to write the scenario of *Dr. Jekyll and Mr. Hyde* for John Barrymore. She had met Bill the same year, had fallen in love with him, and had stood by during his affairs with Lorna Moon and with another one of his scriptwriters, Olga Printzlau.

Cecil attempted, in vain, to change Bill's decision to go through with the divorce (which became final on August 10, 1928). He and Clara were wed on August 13, in a drawing room aboard "The Chief," the Santa Fe Railway's transcontinental special. The newlyweds were anxious to return to Hollywood, where they had just signed to make a film together. Police Judge William Ritt had boarded the train as it pulled into Albuquerque along with Bill, who had been in New York, and with Clara, who had just returned from Europe and was visiting friends nearby. He performed the ceremony as the train roared out of the city on its run to the Pacific Coast, and got off at the next station.

A few months earlier, the deMilles had been invited to the opening of Warner Brothers' *Glorious Betsy*, starring Conrad Nagel and Dolores Costello. They had been told "there was some sort of new-fangled sound effect connected with the production. . . .

"For several reels it was just a regular picture, . . . [then] André de Segurola, playing the part of a military officer, stood in the middle of the picture to address the group around him.

"'Ladies and gentlemen,' he said.

"*He said!*"

Bill immediately had registered his interest in his and Clara's becoming two of "the talkies'" earliest pioneers, and old friend Jesse Lasky had taken him up on his offer to become involved in the company's first sound feature.

They Talk

1928–1932

*To bring in sound meant huge new expenditures, both
in the studios and in the theaters, and the scrapping of
much of the existing studio equipment. All this would
be enormous waste if, after the novelty wore off, the
public preferred their screens to be silent.*

—*The Autobiography of Cecil B. DeMille*

PRODUCTION ON CECIL'S FILM *THE GODLESS GIRL* WAS HALTED
in the middle when he realized he must make the transition from silent to sound. A
few sound sequences were added to the film before its release. Still it was classified
as a silent film, which in 1928—with film audiences dazzled by what they heard as
much as by what they saw—spelled failure at the box office. The picture's born-
again Christian theme did not add to its popularity. It was a story of two young college atheists who are inadvertently involved in the death of a student during a campus
riot, convicted of manslaughter, and sent to reform school, where the two fall in love,
find God, save a brutal guard in a fire, and are finally paroled.

By the time *The Godless Girl* was released, the talkie trend had become a
stampede. In the scramble to revamp production methods, several pioneers were
forced into retirement. Other major producers survived, but not all their studio personnel. Strange new faces—songwriters and musicians hustled out from New York's
Tin Pan Alley—began appearing on the lots. Old acting favorites who lacked a pleas-
ing voice quietly disappeared, and new stars rose in their places.

For several months after Bill and Clara had their first taste of the new sound
film, both of them steeped themselves in the process. Roy Pomeroy, who had created
all the famous special effects for *The Ten Commandments*, had in the last years been
associated with recording methods at RCA on the East Coast. He returned to Hollywood as somewhat of a sacred oracle, and Jesse Lasky hired him to direct the Lasky
Company's first all-talking picture, *Interference*, and as Bill had acquainted himself

109

Writer Jeanie Macpherson and C. B. flank columnist Louella Parsons on the set of *The Godless Girl*, 1929, a movie about a high-school atheist who winds up in a reformatory. Cecil wrote that on his trip to Russia in 1931 he found it was very popular and he was "almost something like a national hero"

with the techniques, he was signed as Pomeroy's assistant. When Pomeroy asked for $3,500 a week for his next film, Bill stepped in to direct it himself. Using his talents for organization, he put together a "racket squad of telephone company-trained sound engineers who were happy to carry on at salaries not exorbitant for technical experts in their field." Bill had been forced to leave Cecil and return to Lasky and Zukor to make the transition to the new medium, as DeMille Productions had run into serious financial troubles between the failure of *The Godless Girl* and Cecil's extravagance in running the studio. Almost simultaneously with Bill's departure, Cecil sold a large block of DeMille Productions stock and signed a contract to make three pictures for Metro-Goldwyn-Mayer. His personal staff (Mitch Leisen, Peverell Marley, Anne Bauchens, and Gladys, Jeanie, and Julia) went with him. The keys to the DeMille studios were handed over to Pathé (headed by Joseph P. Kennedy). Cecil's days as a studio head were over. He now had to make his debut in a new medium—the talkies.

For Cecil's first sound picture Jeanie had written a rather hokey story called *Dynamite*. Charles Bickford had been brought to Hollywood from an illustrious career on the New York stage by M-G-M to play the lead, a condemned murderer who marries an heiress the night before his execution to help her comply with a condition of her grandfather's will that she marry by a certain date. As she *really* loves a married man this had seemed the only possibility (at least in terms of film scenario). Bickford, however, wins a reprieve, is proved innocent, and then insists that his bride honor their wedding vows. After a series of misunderstandings, the pair do eventually end up in each other's arms.

Bickford arrived in Hollywood in time for Christmas 1928, for a three-week interim before the film was to begin shooting. Cecil had learned that Bickford's birthday was January first and rang the actor to invite him to be his guest of honor at a New Year's party at Paradise. Bickford "accepted, with thanks. He instructed me that a car would pick me up at my hotel at three p.m. on the afternoon before New Year's Eve," Bickford recalled. "He asked if there were any specific wines or liquors I was partial to and topped the quiz by asking my preference in women."

"'Which is it to be—blonde, brunette or redhead?'" asked Cecil.

Bickford replied, "Make it one of each. All I ask is that they be dainty, feminine, shapely, beautiful, intelligent and passionate," but he thought C. B. was "having him on."

"I know of only one such pearl of great price and unfortunately she's already wearing a brand," Cecil retorted.

"[Then] just tag the three with my initials—C. B.," Bickford quipped. At that point Bickford recorded, "My impression of him was that of a ruddy stallion, pawing the earth and proclaiming himself monarch of all he surveyed ... my instinct warned me that De Mille and I were destined to clash."

At the appointed time on the designated day, Cecil picked up the star of his film in his gleaming black touring car. To Bickford's surprise, C. B. had been true to his word. Seated inside were three gorgeous ladies—one blonde, one brunette, and one redhead, each wearing "a small blue ribbon on which was emblazoned in gold the letters: C. B."

Bickford was initially entranced with Paradise:

Exclusive of the staff of white-clad, Filipino house boys, there were some sixteen people present. I recognized a former Broadway matinee idol ... two screen *femmes fatales*; two hopeful juveniles, one quite manly; and several screen starlets, one of whom was destined to become a top-ranking star....

...De Mille led me into the library where with great enthusiasm, he showed me his collection of erotica.... Because of my streak of inherent Yankee Puritanism, I suppose, erotica was to me synonymous with pornography and I was square enough to be embarrassed by it....

I managed to display a modicum of phony interest ... [in] a privately printed three-volume edition of shockingly illustrated works of Francois Rabelais. De Mille, in what I was to learn was a typical gesture, insisted that I accept it with his compliments.

When Bickford finally went to his room to dress for dinner, he found his clothes unpacked, a Filipino house boy in attendance, and a red silk Russian blouse laid out on the bed. When told he was to wear it for dinner by the servant, Bickford asked what his host wore.

"Russian blouse. Only always white, yellow or black," he was told.

Bickford asked to see DeMille and, when his host appeared, told him that red clashed with his brick-colored hair, adding, "as guest of honor, I think I should be allowed to co-star at the dinner table. Or, you go ahead and star solo in white, and I'll settle for the feature spot in black." DeMille was not amused, but did send for a black blouse. Together they "marched" back to the main house. "He always seemed to be leading a parade," Bickford commented. "During that short walk, in semi-darkness and with no one watching, I got the impression he was attempting to keep one pace ahead of me."

The evening appeared pleasant and innocuous enough until midnight. Cecil then excused himself. A short time later, his butler approached Bickford and whispered that he was expected in his host's bungalow.

> The big play-room [of his bungalow] was in semi-darkness except for a pool of light in the center, cast from the ceiling by an artfully concealed spot-light. A girl, beautiful, blonde and petite, was dancing. She was nude but for a diaphanous veil which she cleverly manipulated as she writhed, python-like, to the beat [on a record] of Ravel's *Bolero.*
>
> ...she was a bumper and grinder *par excellence.* She finished to enthusiastic applause... [from DeMille, the Broadway leading man, and one of the juvenile actors—the manly one, and the three women who had driven with him to the ranch] but DeMille's fervor caused me to wonder if somewhere on her anatomy she wore a brand....
>
> After the dance...we engaged in a sort of strip-tease dice game. Very naughty but lots of fun, evidenced by howls of laughter from the men and squeals of outraged modesty from the girls as, piece by piece, the losers were forced to discard bits of clothing.

Bickford ended "fully clothed surrounded by semi-nude nymphs and satyrs." His prize turned out to be the beautiful dancer who, he claimed, "was innocent of brands."

The party at Paradise had given Bickford notice that he and C. B. might cross swords. Once *Dynamite* was in production, his instinct proved right. Trouble began brewing at the first story conference when C. B. "ascended a platform on which were his desk and throne chair" and, after a speech on how he came to make films and "a commendably short lecture on togetherness," proceeded to read the entire script aloud. "He had been an actor in his younger days and if one was to judge by his stilted speech and ponderous emphasis upon points," Bickford commented, "his acting must have left plenty to be desired." Before Cecil had finished, Bickford had dozed off. Later he had the temerity to challenge the quality of the script. But by the time the film was completed, the two men had achieved "a genuine respect for each other's abilities and were working smoothly together."

Cecil had made a test of a newcomer, Carole Lombard, to play opposite Bickford, but he settled with Kay Johnson, an experienced stage actress, as he was afraid Lombard's voice, being untrained, might not record well.

"Working with that crude sound equipment was murder," Mitchell Leisen remembered. "There was no way you could dub in any sounds later; all the sound effects had to be recorded during the take. The cave-in in the coal mine [a climactic scene] was tremendously difficult to rig up. Nothing could touch the mikes or they'd go out and we wouldn't have any sound. I set it all up so that the mikes were concealed and papier-mâché rocks would fall, and sound effects men banged things next to the mikes to make more noise. I made vents and put big pieces of cardboard covered with coal dust behind them and on cue, the propman was supposed to turn a fan onto the dust and blow it in so it would look like the dust was rising from the impact of the boulders on the ground. I gave the cue and the rocks crashed, but when I cued the propman, he turned his fan in the wrong direction and the dust blew right into C. B.'s face instead of onto the set." Calmly he called for the scene to be set up again, wiped his face, and waited in the same position. This time it went perfectly. Cecil then fired the man responsible for the first wasted shot.

He remained the benevolent tyrant, lavishing gifts on his stars. After a series of harsh lectures to Kay Johnson, who had flubbed her lines, the greatly distressed actress played a key scene with Bickford with unusual fire. Cecil took from his pocket two twenty-dollar gold pieces and handed one to each of his stars, saying impressively, "Those are DeMille medals. They are only awarded for what I consider magnificent performances."

Cecil, as well as Bill, had now successfully bridged the advent of sound. They also managed to sail safely (if somewhat deflated) through the 1929 stock-market crash. Bill's conservatism saved him. (Once explaining the difference between his pictures and Bill's, Cecil said, "It's arithmetical. Bill always brings his pictures in under budget and on schedule. The only trouble is we can't sell them.")

As soon as Cecil got word of the crash, he immediately instructed Gladys to sell every share of stock he owned. She dutifully called his brokers and gave them an order which was Cecil's standing instruction whenever he was selling: to offer the stocks at a half point above the market. But the sharply falling market never climbed that half point, and Cecil lost close to $1,000,000.

I could not say a word of rebuke to her [Cecil confessed]. She offered no alibis. Gladys never did. Nothing I could have said, not if I had burned her at the stake or flayed her alive, could have tortured her more than the self-reproach I knew she was feeling. I took the blame for not having told her more specifically that, when I said "sell" *that* time, I meant sell that minute at any price.

She was, after all, the same Gladys who, one evening when she was dining with me and I fell asleep exhausted at the dinner table, calmly sat all night with her hand under my chin, so that I might sleep undisturbed by a ducking in the soup plate. She was the same Gladys who, another night when I promised and then forgot to pick her up at a corner near her home on my way to my ranch, was still standing there when I remembered and went back a good hour or more later; and all she said was, "I saw you go by, but I knew you'd be back."

Luckily, Cecil had another $2,000,000 in more stable and fluid investments. And when on February 22, 1930, Cecilia married Francis [Frank] Calvin, a railroad consultant and the only son of Eugene Calvin ("who came out West during Indian times as a telegrapher for Union Pacific Railroad and ended up president"), the DeMilles gave Cecilia a lovely wedding. Their vows were exchanged in Cecil's massive office at home. He gave the newlyweds a house just down the hill a few hundred yards from his own.

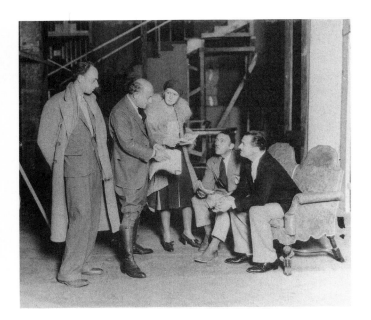

C. B. going over the script of *Madam Satan*, 1930, with Kay Johnson, Roland Young, and Reginald Denny. Mitchell Leisen, now an assistant director, is at left

One of the futuristic sets designed for *Madam Satan* by Leisen and Cedric Gibbons. This was the first movie in which daughter Katherine played a role and it was the first and last musical Cecil ever made

The coming of sound and the Depression created a demand for films that could entertain. Metro pressured Cecil into directing a musical as his second picture on his contract with them. Jeanie turned out a story called *Madam Satan* that managed to mix the seventh commandment with songs (sung by Lillian Roth). According to C. B., *Madam Satan* was "the story of a wife who goes to a masked ball to flirt with her husband because, as he puts it later, he has been wandering 'far from my own fireside in search of—fire!'"

Madam Satan marked Katherine DeMille's screen debut in a recognizable role. Cecil cast her as a society girl—dressed for the ball as one of the wives of Henry VIII ("a horrid fate for anyone's daughter"). She was still a schoolgirl at the time, but Cecil believed she had a future in films. Katherine recalled that "Everybody said, 'Cecil, you must make a musical, everybody's making musicals.' . . . All I remember is this huge replica of a Zeppelin [the masquerade party was held inside it], and I was allowed to play one of King Henry's wives at the costume ball. There were, of course, eight of us and we had these silver costumes—heavy—made of lead—anyway, they weighed a ton—and comes the day that they're shooting. The falling Zeppelin is supposedly struck by lightning, and it's going to go down fast. . . . We were supposed to jump with our parachutes into the great circus net below. When we were told that everybody had to jump, there was a shock of horror. Nobody wanted to do it. Suddenly, Father shouted, 'Katherine!' I said, 'Oh boy, here it comes!'

" 'Katherine, would you step over to the edge and jump?'

"The distance was about twenty feet and there was a strong net, and I was used to swimming and diving, and since Father sounded confident, I said, 'Okay,' and I walked to the edge and jumped into the circus net, and with that, of course, everybody was ashamed, and they followed. No one was hurt and they got the scene in one take."

Leisen called the making of *Madam Satan* "hell. Metro didn't have enough sound stages for all the pictures they were shooting, so each stage had three companies who worked eight-hour shifts. . . . This meant that we had to dismantle the entire set every night before we left and then reassemble it as quickly as possible the next day so we could start working without losing much time. To make matters worse, the party on the Zeppelin was all in two-color Technicolor, which required an enormous amount of light and was so limited in its range, it was harder to design anything than it would be in black and white. The strain was so great I had a nervous breakdown and had to quit entirely for a while. But it was a long picture, and they were still shooting when the doctors let me come back and work an hour a day."

A musical about a Zeppelin disaster proved not to be the kind of entertainment that could satisfy the hunger of a country in a dark, lean time of depression, and was not successful at the box office. For his third and last film for Metro, Cecil reshot his first silent film, *The Squaw Man* (which he had already filmed twice, in 1914 and 1918), with essentially the same plot and characters. The film, starring Warner Baxter, did not fare too much better at the box office than *Madam Satan*. With great relief, Cecil ended his contract with Metro and "humbly hat-in-hand" returned to his old studio (now known as Paramount) after Lasky and Ben Schulberg, the studio's head of production, had prevailed against Zukor's reluctance to rehire Cecil. But Cecil had to accept bruising terms, a tremendous salary cut, lower film budgets than he was accustomed to, and approval by the studio of his subjects.

For his first film under his new contract, Cecil chose to do an adaptation of the Waldemar Young play *The Sign of the Cross*. Zukor agreed and Cecil was back in his stride, feeding the Christians to the lions.

During her last year in California, Agnes had met Douglass Montgomery, a young actor with "a pleasant husky charm."* After watching her dance for the first time, he had told her, with "tears of excitement in his eyes" that she was "a very great performer. You belong to the world." At the moment, she would have settled for belonging somehow to him. But his words had made a strong impact on her. Not long after Agnes, Margaret, and Anna had resettled in New York, "Dug" arrived, cast as the juvenile lead of a Guthrie McClintic production called *God Loves Us*. Agnes and Dug became fast friends, and he encouraged her to go on with her dancing.

Both Margaret and Agnes turned over most of their allowances to Anna to help ease her burden. Bill gave his daughters their financial independence, but at the same time he had also delivered into their arms "a broken woman." Agnes claimed that "to leave [Anna] at any point during the next three years would have been an act of gross cruelty."

The word *choreographer* was virtually unknown in America at this time. Nonetheless, Agnes harbored a dream to become one. Musical shows featured specialties, top chorus-line routines or precision work, but no true ballet. Motion picture houses occasionally presented ballet of a sort, "usually performed in front of jazz bands with cut-glass or *diamanté* music stands." With the single exception of the Denishawn troupe, American dancers were not booked into theatres. John Martin of *The New York Times* was the only critic employed by a daily American newspaper to write on dancing. Despite these discouraging facts, Agnes pressed on in her endeavor.

She chose a small, rather sleazy school at which to study and practice her art.

The studio rooms resounded to the clatter of steel-bottomed tap shoes, "while the dressing rooms were given over to tiny children getting themselves into satin pants and diamond-studded brassieres under the admonishings of their hard-eyed mothers." Dug finally suggested that Agnes hire a rehearsal hall, and a pianist, and give a concert. Agnes, secretly in love with her friend, gave herself over to the idea and to his direction.

"All I know about acting I learned from Dug," she later confessed. "He taught me that every gesture must have some explicit meaning. He taught me to know exactly where the imaginary partners stood, how tall they were and what they were doing at every moment. . . . He taught me to establish with a single gesture the atmosphere and inner rhythm of a personality. He forced me to establish mood with a posture."

Anna entered into the spirit of things and decided that Agnes should give a concert out of town. Santa Fe, New Mexico, was chosen as Anna had some good friends who lived there. Mother and daughter rented a theatre that most recently had been used for prize fights. ("It smelled rather high, and the stage had gone pulpy and rotten. Mother went right out to the local sawmill and got a man with a planing machine to ride over it and remove the fur of splinters. Then she bought putty and crawling over the entire length of the floor on her hands and knees, puttied up the holes crack by crack.")

The concert managed to earn back its expenses ("Three hundred and sixty-four dollars in cold cash"), and the *Santa Fe New Mexican* arts editor hailed Agnes as Isadora Duncan's successor, but the Indians in the audience had been convulsed with laughter, unable to understand why anyone danced on "the very ends" of their feet.

The following December (1928), Agnes gave her first New York concert, sharing the expenses (three hundred dollars) and the bill with another artist, Jacques Cartier, not much better known than she. Anna telephoned all her friends to buy tickets, and to Agnes's amazement, the Republic Theatre was sold out. Cartier occupied the first half of the performance ("blue Indians, Japanese samurai and German elves"). Then Agnes rushed on in her yellow tutu, and from her first gesture, there was laughter. To her bewilderment, she discovered she was perceived as a comedian, she, "who always wanted to die for beauty." The audience even found her heartbreaking *Ballet Class* funny, and at the end cheered and whistled for her to take her solo bows. The next morning, John Martin said in *The New York Times*, "Here is undoubtedly one of the brightest stars now rising above our native horizon," and added that Agnes reminded him of Charlie Chaplin. "She leaves you with the same sort of wistful laughter on your lips and the same sort of lump in your throat." But the words that had meant the most to Agnes had been delivered in a telegram sent to her by her father from Los Angeles: "WELCOME, MY DAUGHTER, INTO THE PROFESSION." William had finally accepted his daughter's chosen art as part of the theatre.

She auditioned for Charles Cochran and Noel Coward, both in New York to cast a new revue. They told her, as kindly as they could, that they were sure she would never find a place in theatre, that she belonged on the concert stage. Her repertoire consisted almost entirely of her own choreographed dances about rape and seduction (*May Day*, about a girl infatuated with a young man who wants only to eat,

New York audiences howled with laughter when Agnes deMille performed in 1929 in her concert piece *Ballet Class (After Degas)*. She had discovered her comic vein

and how she seduces him; *Harvest Reel*, the story of a country girl who is raped; and *Ouled Naïl*, about a prostitute who has problems getting the attention of the man she wants). She had known Dug four years and it was quite evident that the passion she felt for him was entirely one-sided and she "let off steam" in her dances, to Anna's shocked disapproval.

Margaret, meantime, had abandoned college in favor of a career in the theatre and quickly got jobs with George Cukor's stock company and the Theatre Guild.

Despite Martin's good reviews, Agnes's career hit a dead end in New York after she choreographed Christopher Morley's revival of *The Black Crook* in Hoboken, in which she danced a lively cancan. This was her debut choreographing for a group. She also decided the time was right for her to get a partner. John Martin suggested Warren Leonard, a young dancer who he thought had great promise. Leonard was "pugnacious, stubborn and mercilessly idealistic." He was also a thoroughly adaptable and talented dancer and a tough critic both of himself and his new partner. Agnes liked and respected him from the start.

Agnes in *The Black Crook*, a 1929 revival of the first American musical, originally produced in 1866. This was the first play for which Agnes did the choreography

Opposite: Two concert pieces by Agnes in which she also danced: left, *Harvest Reel*, 1930; right, *Ouled Naï* 1935

Martin wrote long columns in the Sunday *Times* about how much he enjoyed deMille and Leonard in *The Black Crook*, but as agents and theatregoers did not read dance critiques, it aided neither Agnes nor the show commercially. (The fact that *The Black Crook* ran for five and a half hours was not a help either.) She took to the road appearing in third-rate moving-picture houses in Baltimore and other Eastern seaboard cities, and performed at private parties and small-time nightclubs. Nothing lasted or seemed to go anywhere, but she had developed a distinctive style of comic balletic dance that evoked laughter. In 1930, Anna finally insisted they return to Hollywood, cashed a couple of bonds, and with Warren Leonard, boarded the train for Agnes's childhood home. Constance and a delegation of cousins met them at the station. Agnes refused to dismount to be kissed. "I wished to be considered a star," she later admitted, "and sneaked out the back of the train, but my presence was discovered by the five-and-a-half-foot Civil War musket I carried on my shoulder [her prop for her ballet *Civil War*]."

Fearful that she might encounter Bill if she stayed at Cecil's, Anna took rooms in a hotel on Vine Street, catercorner from where the old Lasky Studio—now gone—had once stood. They hired the nearby Music Box Theater, a stage manager, and press agent (Agnes O'Malley) and went into rehearsal for eight days prior to the scheduled performance. Agnes spoke to her father only once on the telephone during this time. But Bill came with Clara for opening night and sat on one side of the theatre, while Anna sat with Constance and Cecil on the opposite side. ("On the arm of Cecil [Anna] came down the aisle nodding right and left and bravely trying not to see Pop.")

Backstage, Agnes was more concerned with having her father see her dance professionally for the first time. ("If I were going to let down the family name, I had

chosen the most public possible means of doing so, and the most poignant locality. The emotional circus in the theater was difficult also for him. He sat rigid," Agnes vividly recalled.) After the performance, Agnes O'Malley introduced Oscar Hammerstein II to Agnes. He told her that she had talent—the problem was how to use it.* Cecil gave his niece a party following the program. The house on the hill was blazing with lights. The table shone with Constance's best crystal and silver. All of Agnes's old friends had been invited: the Mayer girls (Irene and Edith, now Mrs. David Selznick and Mrs. William Goetz), her schoolmate (and Cecilia's secret love) Joel McCrea, who was a rising star by this time, Dug, who was now making pictures, her piano teacher, and many of Cecil's staff and colleagues who had known her since childhood. Everyone was there, it seemed, except her father, who had not "of course" been invited. The next day, the entertainment page of the *Los Angeles Times* bannered "DE MILLE GIRL MAKES GOOD." Cecil insisted that not since Gloria Swanson had he seen a young woman of such promise. He proposed to road-show his niece through the United States with her own dance company, with "exploitation on a circus scale." Agnes felt she needed two years to develop. Cecil was startled and withdrew his offer. "Now is the time. There is such a thing as the right moment."

"Father indicated that he also was ready to talk business and I began to shake immediately," Agnes remembered. "Our family has always been very tense about money. I didn't want his money; I wanted him—the father-director—to make a star of me. But he said he would give me six thousand dollars, that he considered I had proved myself worthy of help." Seventy-two hours later, after she told him she wanted to use the money for a European tour, he changed his mind and withdrew his offer, deciding none of his money should go to "unscrupulous European [concert] managers."

"What shall I do then?" Agnes cried, all of her own money having been invested in the Hollywood venture.

"Women's clubs, concert tours—"

"...No manager will touch an American. There are no ballet companies. I cannot get [a job] on Broadway. I have auditioned for every single person in the business," she countered.

"Well, keep trying," he replied.

What she had always wanted was to have her father take over her career. Obviously, this was not to happen. But the Hollywood trip did have two concrete results. Margaret, now twenty and as beautiful as ever, had accompanied her on an interview at M-G-M. Bernard P. Fineman, an attractive middle-aged executive they met with, did not think Agnes's dance talent had a future in film, but as they left his office, Margaret turned to her and "remarked quietly, 'I think I'll marry that man.' " Six weeks later, they were wed in a Tucson courtroom with Agnes and Anna present. The marriage was the second for Fineman, who had been previously wed to silent screen star Evelyn Brent, famous for her "vampy" roles in Josef von Sternberg films.

Upon her return to New York, Agnes moved out of her mother's apartment, first taking an inside room at the Hotel Ansonia, which cost only twenty dollars a week. Within a month, she was able to move to a ground-floor apartment in a townhouse, where she had room to dance. For the first time in her life, she could work half the night without Anna calling to her to "put out the light, dearie."

One of Hollywood's most famous milk baths: Claudette Colbert in *Sign of the Cross*, 1932. C. B. used authentic asses milk, just as the Romans did

"Politically a shade to the right of Louis Quatorze," Cecil voted for Franklin D. Roosevelt in 1932 for one reason: Prohibition, which had brought with it the evils of bootlegging gangsters. He had supported Herbert Hoover in 1928 with the biggest contribution he was ever to make to a political campaign (over $100,000) and still maintained that Hoover's "sheer brain power and his dogged, uncompromising, selfless honesty" placed him in Cecil's esteem above any other public figure he had known. The previous year, Cecil had even been approached by the Republican National Committee to run as their candidate for governor of California, this seeming to be the first recorded overture of the Republicans to place a film personality on their California gubernatorial slate (the second being the choice of actor Ronald Reagan). After due consideration, he had decided that he could reach more people through his pictures than from the state house.

When Roosevelt arrived in Los Angeles on his vote-getting swing across the country, Cecil loaned him his open touring car, the largest of its variety in Los Angeles. (A few years later when the two men met again, Cecil "presented the president with a silver fifty-cent piece of rare type 'for your foreign policy, Mr. President,' and then handed him a Buffalo nickel—'for your domestic policy.' ")

During Roosevelt's visit to Los Angeles, Cecil was shooting *The Sign of the Cross*, a perfect example of the kind of film he felt could carry his message to the public: faith in God, country, and prosperity. *The Sign of the Cross* certainly had equal doses of Christian dogma and vulgarity. It also recreated history in contemporary terms and as lavish spectacle. Cecil himself described *The Sign of the Cross* as "a story of the magnificent faith and heroism of the infant Christian community in Rome."

A synopsis of the story reads:

After setting Rome ablaze, the Emperor Nero finds it politically advisable to blame the catastrophe on the Christians and entrusts his favorite, Marcus Superbus, with their persecution. Marcus's ambition to serve the emperor is tempered, however, by his infatuation for Mercia, a blonde Christian girl, and his predicament complicated by indifference to the attentions lavished upon him by Poppaea, Nero's strong-willed wife. . . . Marcus pleads for Mercia's life before Nero, but the emperor will not relent unless the girl renounces her faith.

The Christians are to be fed to the lions in the Colosseum as part of a series of bloody and grotesque events staged for the pleasure of the emperor and empress. As they await their turn in the dungeon, the Christian prisoners find solace in Mercia's unshakable conviction in God. . . . At the last moment, Marcus enters the dungeon with hopes that he will be able to persuade Mercia to abandon her faith and to live as his wife. Although she admits that she loves him, Mercia speaks glowingly of a greater love and chooses instead to embrace death. Transfixed by the strength of her religious beliefs, Marcus decides to die in the arena with Mercia in expectation of life hereafter.*

Cecil had made a trip to Russia just prior to the filming of *The Sign of the Cross* and had stopped in London en route and seen Charles Laughton in *Payment Deferred* (later refilmed by M-G-M with Laughton repeating his original role). Although Laughton was unknown in America at this time, Cecil would consider no one else for Nero and brought him to Hollywood. As Nero's wife, Poppaea, he cast Claudette Colbert (who until this time had played only a succession of fluffy, lighthearted roles); Fredric March played Marcus, and Elissa Landi was Mercia, the Christian girl.

Laughton, his biographer claims, "daringly for a homosexual, played Nero as one. He supervised his own make-up—plucked eyebrows, rouged cheeks, a touch of lipstick...and he worked out a lisping...voice that proved richly amusing." His performance also gave the film an even more lascivious edge than most of Cecil's films, as Nero is constantly surrounded by attractive young Roman men, and homosexuality was almost never touched upon in American films of this era. Voyeurism was further exploited with scenes of Colbert, apparently nude, bathing in "an Olympic-sized marble pool full of genuine asses' milk" (left standing overnight for retakes the next day, the milk had turned to cheese and Colbert had a difficult time removing the rancid odor from her body); a Roman orgy with a suggestive dance performed by one of Marcus's wanton female guests, dressed only in a rope of flowers draped to cover—narrowly—her nipples and pubic area, and who ends the dance chained to a stone effigy of Bacchus and left to the lust of a gorilla;* and a bloody reenactment of the Christians being devoured by the lions. (For this last scene, lambs' carcasses were stuffed into the Christians' costumes and the lions set loose to feed on them.)

The animals in the film created more problems for Cecil than the actors. During one sequence, an entire herd of elephants stampeded, and one actor (Robert Miles) was nearly killed. The lions never seemed to do what Cecil wanted them to do. They had to be practically starved before they would eat the lambs' carcasses, and at one point they refused to climb a flight of stairs that led to the bright sunlight of the arena. After being told flatly by the lion wrangler, "these cats don't climb stairs," Cecil himself took a chair in one hand and an ax handle in the other and advanced toward them, and when they saw that the stairway was their only route of escape, "up they went."

Jesse L. Lasky and his son, Jesse, Jr. Both Laskys were longtime associates of Cecil's, the father as a producer, the son as a writer

Shortly after Cecil had made his agreement to return to Paramount, Lasky was forced out of his position. Zukor issued an ultimatum that the budget for *The Sign of the Cross* be kept to $650,000. Costumes and sets were fixed at an absolute minimum figure. Mitchell Leisen designed and had built in the open space at the Paramount ranch a detailed miniature Rome with a hidden gas valve that at a given signal ignited the city into flame. The cameraman, Karl Struss, employed a prism lens which doubled the size of the crowds. Nero's palace was largely a miniature set. In midafternoon on October 6, 1932, the last day of shooting, Cecil's assistant Roy Burns rushed up to him in the middle of a take and announced, "We've just used up the budget." Cecil picked up his megaphone and yelled, "Cut." The cast and filming crew were dismissed. Whatever shots were missing Anne Bauchens was instructed to create from the film they had. Amazingly, a final cut was ready within six weeks and the film released in time for Christmas.

Despite the reviewers' disdain of its artistic achievements, they were unanimous in their admiration of the spectacle. Filmgoers endorsed *The Sign of the Cross* unequivocally. The Depression was at its worst, but theatre managers accepted unsecured IOUs "scribbled on little pieces of paper as admission." Cecil claimed nearly every one of them was redeemed when the cash began to flow again. He must have been right, for within a year Paramount had quadrupled in profits its investment in *The Sign of the Cross*, which continued to earn money for many years to come.

The Growth of the Legend

1932–1941

*When you saw him, bald and benign, you could believe
the legends—and the jokes, like the one about
the psychiatrist needed in heaven because "God
thought he was Cecil B. DeMille."*

—JESSE LASKY, JR.

WHILE THE NATION STRUGGLED THROUGH THE HARD TIMES OF
the Depression, Cecil became so rich, rumor had it, that his bathroom contained solid gold fixtures. It did not. The house in Laughlin Park remained virtually unchanged except for its address, which was now 2000 DeMille Drive, the road renamed in Cecil's honor. Cecil's life-style, away from Constance, had always been as extravagant as the spectacles he filmed. That, too, was unchanged. But his power grew in both fact and legend. Most of it during the thirties was used to maintain and strengthen his position at Paramount and to control the men and women he employed.

Jesse Lasky, Jr., who was approximately the same age as Cecilia, applied to his father's old business partner for a job as a scriptwriter not too long after the release of *The Sign of the Cross*. "God, that's what many who worked for him called him," he recalled. "The great man behind the huge cluttered desk. Everything you could imagine was on that desk: photos of presidents he had helped elect [Hoover and Roosevelt], gifts from grateful stars...decorations from foreign governments, endless awards, plaques, and props from one or another of his movies....And under that desk, a terrible weapon: a light which could be kicked on to blaze in the face of some nervous actress, putting her on the spot. But when you walked into that office your attention...was riveted upon the man himself....[he] exuded charm enough to render humans of either sex defenseless, rather as certain insects stun their victims."

True to many legends, he could be a monster, but to most of those he loved, needed, or felt responsible for, he was a benevolent despot. His brother remained his great admirer. In 1931, when Hollywood was hardest hit by the Depression, Bill had been elected president of the Academy of Motion Picture Arts and Sciences and had broadcast an appeal to young people to keep away from the film capital. "Golden opportunities do not await anyone who has the fare to Hollywood," he said, adding, "The motion picture industry is cutting back." His own film career was nearing an end. The type of low-keyed subject matter that he preferred had become passé. By 1933, with the poor reception of *His Double Life*, Bill began to move away from the business of filmmaking.

Cecil still considered him his intellectual superior, and he greatly respected Bill for his refusal to become a C. B. appendage. Bill never had any enthusiasm for Cecil's extravaganzas, and he was not shy in expressing his opinions. The brothers were opposite in many ways. Bill was private about his religion and his politics. (He liked to think of himself as a Jeffersonian Democrat.) Clara was a good wife, a close companion, and a sensitive stepmother—but the second marriage and financial reversals tended to put a distance between Bill and his two daughters. After a short excursion as an actress, Margaret had settled, but not too comfortably, into her role as a Hollywood wife. Her husband, Bernard Fineman, was at this time her father's boss at M-G-M, an awkward situation at best. Agnes remained in New York, still determined to make a successful career as a dancer and choreographer. For a short time, her father sent her fifty dollars a week on which to subsist. But soon that had to stop, and Agnes became reliant upon, and even closer to, Anna, who managed always to find a bond to sell to help Agnes continue with her career. Anna had, in fact, become dedicated to seeing her daughter achieve success in the dance world. ("She married me," Agnes wrote, "and as a wedding gift she gave me my career.")

Agnes had believed her career had taken wings when in 1931 she was hired by producer Max Gordon to choreograph her first Broadway show, a revue, *Flying Colors*, with book and lyrics by Howard Dietz, music by Arthur Schwartz, and a cast that included Tamara Geva, Clifton Webb, Buddy Ebsen (then a tap dancer), Patsy Kelly, and Imogene Coca. But within two weeks she had been fired and replaced by the more experienced and commercial director Albertina Rasch. (Schwartz had been so upset when she broke down and cried after he had fired her that he had kissed her as she wept.) The following year, with Anna acting as her manager, and supplying $1,200 for expenses, mother, daughter, and Agnes's partner, Warren Leonard, launched a brief concert tour, consisting of seven public appearances in Paris, Brussels, and London.

With the help of Romney Brent, a dapper Mexican actor, director, and playwright, and a devoted friend of her sister, Agnes's concert did well in London. Brent was playing with enormous success in a Noel Coward revue, "and had become the darling of the drawing rooms." In the three weeks before her concert at the Arts Theatre Club, Brent introduced Agnes to the *crème de la crème* of London's theatre society at parties given by Lady Sybil Colefax, Raymond Massey and his wife (Adrian Allen), Noel Coward, and Dame May Whitty. "This," he would proclaim to their guests' polite astonishment, "is the greatest pantomimic artist in the world." Agnes's concert was sold out. The critic Arthur Haskell came backstage to implore her to

Marie Rambert, the English ballet pioneer, with two of her dancers at the Ballet Club in the early 1930s, when Agnes was studying with her in London

remain in London to give more concerts and offered his help. Marie Rambert was in the throes of establishing a repertory ballet theatre, and she invited Agnes to remain in London and study with her and give a series of concerts under her auspices. Rambert (who was privately called Mim) was married to playwright Ashley Dukes, who owned a vestry house in Notting Hill Gate that the Dukes had converted into a theatre, called the Mercury, for the use of Marie's company, the Ballet Club (later renamed Ballet Rambert).

In London, Agnes had found "you could be a failure without being miserable. In Hollywood, you had to have success. You had to have fashionable clothes, you had to have a car, or you were just scum. In London, they didn't care. Duchesses went around in old clothes."

Although apprehensive, Anna agreed Agnes must stay. Anna and Warren Leonard returned on the ship on which they had all planned to sail. For the first time, Agnes was "embarked on a project absolutely alone." The Mercury Theatre, which housed Rambert's Ballet Club, was small, seating only 110, but Agnes sensed great things were happening there. She rented a sparsely furnished attic room at the English-Speaking Union on Charles Street off Berkeley Square because it was cheap and was in the center of London.

The Ballet Club was run on a shoestring and mostly supported by Rambert's ballet school, where Marie was chief teacher, and "a young friendly drudge named Antony Tudor," her assistant ("for a fixed salary of £2 a week, room and tuition thrown in"). Everyone else paid Rambert for their classes. Outside income was a necessity as dancers received 5s. 6d. a performance (about $.85 then); choreographers were paid half this amount as a performance royalty and a £10 fee for the ballet (about $35).

Tudor, Hugh Laing, and some of the other dancers lived in a house in Chiswick. The upper floor held Tudor's dance studio, where he taught and rehearsed, and where Agnes, now living a life far removed from the sophisticated world of Romney Brent, spent several hours a day.

"The house reeked of urine," she recalled, "because [the dancers'] dogs were not housebroken and showed no inclination to become so. None of us minded too much. We kept them off the tables and out of the beds...but when they began using the piano for unworthy purposes, the accompanist, Norah...got up in a rage and left. She came back, of course, the next day."

Rehearsals in the practice hall of the Ballet Club ("down precipitous steps at the back...[one] entered a large oak-beamed room with a typical ecclesiastical vaulted ceiling") were only a degree less Bohemian. "The floor was of oak...literally worn into the grain by human flesh," Agnes remembered. "I can still feel the knots, nailheads and joinings under the balls of my feet....Down the length of the walls ran *de rigueur* the barre. At one end of the room hung a large old mirror, at the other, encased in iron railing, stood a potbellied stove which...gave off mustiness but no heat. The pianist with blue fingers sat at her upright...[wearing] two sweaters, a shawl, a coat, [and] an old felt hat....The whole room smelled of damp black woolens. The walls sweated. The gray damp of English winter steamed and thickened on the pale windows. Visitors sat fully coated and hatted....I never put on my pants without looking for mushrooms in the seams."

Ramon Reed, the young Englishman with whom Agnes had an unusual, unforgettable love affair

The DeMilles

A California friend of hers, Elliot Morgan, had sent two introductory letters to people he had known in Oxford: writer Elizabeth Bowen and a Ramon Reed, who now lived in London. Agnes sent each an invitation for tea at the Union. Bowen sent a note of regret, but Reed telephoned. He couldn't leave his house for he was an invalid, he informed her. Hadn't Elliot mentioned that? She said, "No," and agreed to go to his flat for tea. As soon as she disconnected, she reread her friend's letter. "There it was: 'A charming young man, unable to walk, paralyzed in the legs.'" She was to learn soon that for years he had been helplessly crippled by multiple sclerosis. Agnes was about to enter into a consuming relationship that would dominate the next two years of her life.

Two days later, she went to visit Ramon in his small flat in Chelsea, which he shared with a male nurse, Henry Arthur Sharpe* ("a tall, bony, red-faced man with high cheekbones and [an] expression of guarded energy"), and "a huge black tomcat called Solomon."

"He is very young—startlingly young—about twenty-two...," she wrote Anna, "and extraordinarily beautiful. The youth and the beauty grab you by the throat as you see him sitting in his wheelchair. His thinness amounts to emaciation, and in the dead pallor of his face his great dark eyes burn with such intelligence and suffering as to have an almost perfervid quality.... He laughs as though he were in pain. He has masses of dark brown, wavy hair.... I think he is tall; it is hard to tell. His legs are covered with a heavy lap robe and perfectly motionless."

She was to give three recitals in the spring of 1933. On the night of the first, there were two West End openings the same night. The house was only half full, but to her surprise Arthur Schwartz, in London for a show of his own, was present, as were Basil and Ouida Rathbone, actress Constance Cummings—and Ramon in his wheelchair. "I danced *Harvest Reel* as I never danced it before, as I've dreamed I could dance," she wrote Anna. "The dancers in the audience stood up and shouted at the end. Mim [Rambert] said she'd never seen anything like the great tumbling *pas de basques*.... Praise from Mim!... Ramon Reed was all but out of his chair at the footlights.... [When] the auditorium was cleared... I went out and talked to him. He... begged me to come to tea soon.... Then the ambulance attendants [Reed had hired an ambulance for the event] came to help Sharpe, the nurse, get the chair down the steps at the back of the theater. Sharpe... is a rawboned New Zealander with a manner both hearty and sullen.... But there's no question that he's the one in charge."

The next day she went to tea at Ramon's. "He is half-mad with enthusiasm," she confided to Anna. "He criticized in detail with an extraordinary grasp of technique and style and intent. He may prove a real help.... What stumps Mim... are my sixty-four *fouettée pirouettes* on spot.... Oddly enough, Alicia Markova can't do them.... I have so much to learn—so very much. I can run and walk beautifully.... I have a good foot and a hot bounce. I am a jumper, quick off the ground and into the air. (My *entre-chats-sixes* are getting as neat as scissors.) My foot is iron.... That's why I can do sixty-four *fouettées*. My rhythm is... infallible. But, and this is vital, I have no line, and my gestures are never lyrically accomplished.... I'm rump-heavy and too short between knee and ankle and who will teach me a cure for this?"

The English paid little attention to these physical shortcomings. They remained chiefly responsive to Agnes's energy and verve, the jazz style and American folk-dance idiom she so brilliantly evoked, and to her comedic, dramatic style and point of view. At this period in her career, her approach toward folk dancing was more realistic, more ethnological than it would become. Her *'49* was considered "the absolute essence of the Southwest"and her *Blues* and *Striptease* "a good evocation of New York."

All the while she was working on her dance technique and her ability to create new dances, she made several pilgrimages to Haslemere "to study preclassic dance forms" with a disciple of Arnold Dolmetsch.* Rambert noted that her work was touched "for the first time with originality and power."

At home, Anna was becoming alarmed as her daughter's letters reflected a growing and ardent relationship with a paraplegic. Ramon was the heir of a wealthy family whose large country estate in Sussex, called Netherfield Place, had been designed by a pupil of Sir Edwin Lutyens and was opened for public viewing every Tuesday. His mother had died of tuberculosis when he was seven. Five years later his father, Percy Reed, who managed the family's real estate fortune, was remarried to "a young lady who had been a saleslady at a superior men's shop in London," where the Reeds also had a townhouse, which overlooked Kensington Gardens. Ramon did not get on well with his new stepmother but was soon sent to Rugby. At sixteen, he suddenly developed serious visual problems and was hospitalized by a neurologist who was finally consulted. The first night in the hospital, he took a bath and had to inch his way back to bed on his hands and knees. Twenty-four hours later he went blind. Eventually, partial sight returned (he still had problems with peripheral vision), but he never walked again. For a year, he remained in bed, almost immobile, in his room in Sussex, tended by a nurse and infrequently visited in his rooms by his father and stepmother. When he began to grow despondent, Henry Sharpe, who had trained with paraplegics at a London hospital, was hired. "Sharpe took in the situation and ran up the pirate flag, declaring open war on the whole family. The hatred is fierce and mutual and lasting," Agnes explained to Anna. "They say Sharpe is after the boy's money; he says he's trying to save Ramon's life and reason, and it's him I believe."

With Sharpe in attendance, Ramon read for a degree in English literature at Oxford (and also began to learn to play the flute). When this proved too rigorous, he moved to London, where, on his personal inheritance, he set up his own small household at 12 Paulton's Square. He lived a strict regimen: "one-half day up, two days down, and a few outings around the block in his chair," from which Sharpe had to lift him in and out. An ambulance had to be hired for travel.

Agnes met his stepmother one day at tea. Immediately, the family believed she was after his money and became antagonistic. Americans and Hollywood "repel them," she told Anna. "They think I am venal and vulgar." This did not discourage her. When she was not taking lessons or rehearsing, she could most often be found at Ramon's, working on a large gros point chair seat for his dining room set of "Queen Anne beauties" while he read to her from Aldous Huxley or his friend Elizabeth Bowen. They drove in an ambulance to theatre, a film, a day in the country. He sent flowers to her attic room at the Union. Sharpe began to grow jealous and Anna more concerned as her daughter's almost daily letters became voluminous, and detailed accounts of her time with Ramon.

Agnes's second and third recitals were "nicely successful and the London papers each accorded me a paragraph of praise. Jacob Epstein [the sculptor]...said my Degas's studies were 'tragic and tender and beautiful.' The *New English Weekly* printed a sonnet acrostic in my honor and [Arthur] Haskell went out on a limb in large type with 'THANK YOU AMERICA, FOR DE MILLE.' " Her social life outside Ramon's rarefied household began to burgeon. She lunched in a party with George Bernard Shaw, danced at the Derby Ball (a charity bazaar) before the Prince of Wales (who was reported to have told a friend he thought she was a Russian—high compliment at that time for a ballet dancer). She also had lunch with Margot Asquith, Lady Oxford, who "ate three string beans, half a carrot, and two bites of lean chop. 'Is the good lady ill?' I asked the mutual friend who had arranged the séance. 'She will starve.'

" 'Not at all,' I was assured. 'She eats a hearty lunch before dining with someone she thinks will bore her. In this way she doesn't have to stop talking for a minute. I must say, my dear, you got more remarks in than any other young person I've heard try.' "

She met Elizabeth Bowen as well as Rebecca West and began a lasting friendship with both. There was a class with Mim every morning and private lessons with Tudor ("It was Mim, of course, who got paid") and rehearsals. The recitals were hard on her. More than once she had felt "the black weakness engulf" her in center stage, "the breath belt across my ribs like a whip, while I measured in feet the space I would have to cover before I could pause. And afterwards sitting in overcoats, covered with rugs, I would drink an entire quart of milk, sometimes two, before I could stop shivering. It took me a week to recover sufficiently to do a repeat performance."

She was dancing solo thirteen dances in succession, with an equal number amount of costume changes down to her tights, toe shoes, hair arrangements, and makeup to be made in two-minute intervals. But despite her distractions, pressures, and periods of pure exhaustion, she never passed a day that she was not at Ramon's for several hours, nor did he miss her recitals either. An offer in Copenhagen of a paying concert engagement (not to be sponsored with her own money) sent her into a terrible quandary as she both desperately wanted to go and at the same time could not bear leaving Ramon.

"Sow some wild oats," he ordered. "Have some fun. You need it."

...I leaned down to his chair in the London dusk and kissed him....And the world cracked open.

He had not been kissed by a woman since his illness.

There was a long silence....Then he said softly, "You'll come back to me, Aglet? To me alone?...

"You mean you wish me to come back as your lover?...

"Live in your house?"...[He told her he did.]

"I have not the courage to marry you [she warned him]. I cannot face that yet."

He promised that for now this would be enough.

In Copenhagen her engagement was at the National Scala, and there, for the first time, her name was spread across a marquee. She returned to London and Ramon, who "met [her] like a bridegroom." He had filled the house with flowers, presented her with gifts and waited for her to show him her "lovely new negligee." Naïvely, she had believed that he, though crippled, could still make love. She now learned he was totally paralyzed from the waist down. "He had no idea of the situation he'd placed me in," she poignantly recalled. "He didn't beg or whimper. He didn't threaten. He did not even excuse himself. We held hands in terrified silence.... He was going to die and sooner or later depended on me.... I was trapped.... I could have left before morning. I didn't." She made a bed on the floor from sofa cushions and (to Sharpe's irritation) moved in, although she maintained her room at the Union. For the present, she kept her living arrangements with Ramon secret, but she still laced her letters to Anna with anecdotes about him.

Before she had left for Copenhagen, Agnes had a job interview with theatre producer Charles Cochran to choreograph his upcoming London musical *Nymph Errant*, music and lyrics by Cole Porter, book by Romney Brent (based on the novel by James Laver). Cochran had never seen her perform any of her works, but Romney and Arthur Schwartz had both convinced him he would do well to hire her. He offered her a penurious £40 a week and no royalties, but a Porter-Cochran show was the big time, and she did not hesitate to accept the offer.

Rehearsals began on August 17, 1933, four days ahead of schedule and with Agnes "a bit frantic at the lack of preparation." There were to be ten dances including bits and pieces ("Hardly anything for you to do at all," Cochran had said when they had negotiated her fee), one of them a Greek ritual dance that she believed had a real chance. Romney was also directing and he told her "to shoot the works." She asked Porter to write a 5/4 Greek dance for her. To her delight, he returned "the next day with a charming piece with astonishing rhythms and harmony.... He's also done a darling Turkish number [*Solomon*], which our extraordinary little Scotch contortionist will perform on a silk pillow....

"The Keeper of the Harem, the Eunuch, is played by a remarkably fat old 'femascumale' (Ramon's term), Bruce Winston...[whose] chief claim to fame is, however, that he makes hats for Queen Mary. He tells how he sits her in front of a mirror and places the basic toque on the Head, and then tentatively adds, one by one, buckles, lace, feathers, roses and veils.... At length a finger is raised and Royalty speaks, 'Enough!' Winston bows. Another Imperial Hat has been achieved."

She felt the show was rather silly, a "mere excuse" for the star, Gertrude Lawrence, to display her talent with a song and her ability to look divine in the costumes that had been created for her. Cole Porter's "quiet and deferential" presence made a great impression on her. A "finely boned and fastidious little man with a round doll head like a marionette's (Charlie McCarthy) [and] large staring eyes.... He walks mincingly and very gingerly with tiny steps, and he leans on a cane*...but, make no mistake about it, he is the most powerful person in the theater, not excepting Charles Cochran....

"His wife came with him the other day, the legendary Linda Lee [an American heiress], all silver and exquisite, with pale, luminous skin and a veil over her pale hair and face....

"...Gertie and Doug Fairbanks (her steady at present) have taken me twice...to Rule's, the two-hundred-year-old theatrical restaurant...Gertie in her gorgeous streamlined Molyneux, and me in—well what I wear—but I do try to be neat."

Nymph Errant opened in Manchester on September 11 to glowing reviews. Agnes was ecstatic. Her dances had "stopped the show"; "The Greek dance absolutely. For whole minutes—not seconds, whole minutes—Gertie couldn't go on with her lines." But the next morning an inquest was held and Cochran fired the leading man without notice and he turned into a bully where Agnes was concerned. More tap had to be incorporated, especially in the dance numbers performed by Romney Brent's current amour, Doris Carson, who had given Agnes problems all through rehearsals. Agnes panicked, especially after she seemed to be given the cold shoulder by the rest of the company. Lawrence's interest in her had turned cool for reasons Agnes was unable to comprehend. "I'm an outsider...an alien," she wrote Anna. "I have literally been left...standing alone in the lobby while [the company] went to a supper party given by Cole Porter or Gertie." Dance director Carl Randall was called in to rechoreograph Carson's dance (*Georgia Sand*). The show opened at the Adelphi Theatre in London on October 6 to good notices ("the dances got raves, all except the Carl Randall number"*). The Adelphi had been filled with glittering people: Somerset Maugham, Douglas Fairbanks, Cecil Beaton, Noel Coward. There were gala parties afterwards at the Savoy and elsewhere, but Agnes had not been invited to any of them. A member of the company finally confided to her that Cochran, Lawrence, and the others had lost interest because she looked so unkempt and dowdy at rehearsals, and that her residence at the Union gave a "gloomy impression." (Obviously London cared more about success than she had once proclaimed.)

During the Manchester run, Ramon had insisted upon coming with Sharpe while she was in rehearsal and had been taken seriously ill as soon as he had arrived. When she returned to London, so had he, his condition grown worse. When not with him, she was sneaking out to telephone Sharpe every half hour. No one in the company knew about Ramon, and so they concluded that she was "disagreeable, stubborn, self-centered, and definitely unamusing." By opening night, Ramon was well enough to send her orchids and a huge basket of flowers. She wept.

Tears came all too easily over the next few months. She fainted on the street while walking with Tudor, and he thought the action "fake and revolting and said so. Perhaps it was. What I was doing was screaming for help and that was not fake." Still, she returned daily to Ramon. She claimed that by his bedside she was heartened. He neither intimidated her nor was fooled by easy answers. Nor did he try to impose his taste. His brilliance dazzled her; his poetic turn of phrase charmed her. Somehow, Ramon eased her fears. And so she remained emotionally tied to a bedridden invalid.

Nymph Errant had been a success, but as she received no royalties once it had opened, her source of income was cut off. She had a few days of hope for the immediate future when Virgil Thomson considered her for the job of choreographer on his opera (book by Gertrude Stein), *Four Saints in Three Acts*, but in the end she lost out to Frederick Ashton. As Christmas 1933 neared, she was forced to borrow fifty pounds from a London friend of Anna's. Asking help from Ramon was impossible for her. Anna suggested she move to better quarters, and with part of her loan, she rented "a large front room pleasantly furnished on the street [Glebe Place] that goes by Lady Colefax's house. There is no central heat, a shilling gas meter, and baths cost sixpence" (the bathroom was shared). A pay telephone was situated on the landing outside her door. The room with full breakfast cost her thirty-two shillings a week. She bought a tea kettle and a reading lamp and moved in. She no longer slept at Ramon's, but still spent several hours a day there.

Ramon accepted the new arrangement. They shared Christmas alone. She decorated their tree with white candles and he gave her books, bath essence, and crystal earrings that he had selected painstakingly from catalogues. The early months of 1934 contained one disappointment after another. Every plan withered, every avenue was closed. Her father sent her a surprise of one hundred dollars for Christmas, and that supported her through February. Meanwhile, she continued working with Tudor. Ramon was her only "source of strength. . . . He wrote, flat on his chest, stories and poems he never thought to see printed. He read to me by the hour." He listened to her problems (although she did not share her financial woes with him). She served tea in his "delightful" parlor to her friends—Rebecca West and her husband, Henry Andrews, Romney Brent, Mim, Ashley Dukes, Trudy and Arthur Bliss (who brought with them Julian Huxley), and Elizabeth Bowen and her husband, Alan Cameron.

Her room on Glebe Place was cold, and she slept in her coat under floor rugs and a quilt. "Thick, heavy, throat-wrecking" fog rolled in. She began to spend more and more time at Ramon's Paulton's Square flat. Actress Anna May Wong was to make a personal appearance and hired her for fifty pounds to create a dance. "She can't dance and she can't sing. But she has the world's most beautiful figure and a face like a Ming princess, and when she opens her lovely mouth out comes Los Angeles Chinatown sing-sing girl and every syllable is a fresh shock." But the money pulled her through another month.

"There will be an American job one day," she wrote to Anna, "and I will take it. If Uncle Ce would only offer me something! . . . I think I may after all ask him for a loan of a thousand or two. Surely by this time he must believe I'm worth helping."

She never did write Cecil, but Anna discussed the situation with Margaret, who had recently moved back to New York with her husband, and through the family grapevine, it came to Cecil's attention. He did not offer her a loan, but something far better—a contract to do some of the dances for his new film, *Cleopatra*, six weeks at $250 per week and transcontinental (but not transoceanic) fare ("when Uncle Ce's long-hoped-for cable had finally come . . . I flew; I raced; I leaped to accept"). Within ten days she set sail. Ramon was stoic, and though she could see how difficult it was for him, he wished her "Godspeed" after she promised she would be back. As a going-away present, she "gave him a growing garden which covered his bedside table and which he could watch blossom through the lonely spring."

Cecil had been beset with his own problems in Hollywood. The two pictures he had made following *The Sign of the Cross*—*This Day and Age* (starring Charles Bickford) and *Four Frightened People* (Claudette Colbert, Herbert Marshall, William Gargan, and Mary Boland)—had not done well. During the shooting of *The Sign of the Cross*, Cecil had delegated more directorial responsibilities to Mitchell Leisen

than he had ever done before, and as he was always willing to give credit where it was due, the front office became aware of Leisen's contributions (three key scenes, one particularly charming one of Colbert playing with a pet leopard). The studio offered Leisen a contract as a director, and the film *Tonight Is Ours* with Colbert and Fredric March. Cecil's new costume designer, Natalie Visart, claimed, "C. B. never got over the loss of Mitchell. He had to hire about ten people to cover all the things Mitchell did by himself and he was never satisfied. To have to follow in Mitchell's footsteps was an impossible task."

This Day and Age called attention "to the evil of racketeering," and pointed to "the uncontaminated idealism of American youth." Cecil's manner of showing this was to have a group of high school students kidnap a racketeer boss (Bickford) and slowly lower him into a pit full of "very businesslike rats" to force a confession of his crimes from him.

Four Frightened People was the story of four people who flee from cholera and the bubonic plague while on a cruise and find safe harbor in the Malayan jungles. Cecil went to Honolulu for this film so he could shoot a real bamboo forest and ran into tremendous difficulties because the one he chose was covered with lava and the company had to lay tons of sawdust even to walk through. "He shot it all with a two inch lens," Leisen later claimed, "so you saw the people but the whole background was nothing... [I] knew they were in trouble there because I got a telegram from Roy Burns and he signed it, 'One of the four frightened people.'... The audience reaction was terrible...." However, it proved somewhat more of an attraction at the box office than *This Day and Age*.

Zukor issued an ultimatum for Cecil to do a historical picture with plenty of sex. Cecil decided upon *Cleopatra*. Perhaps he would have come to that decision on his own, but at the same time he had to appear with Constance before the Board of Tax Appeals in Washington in answer to a demand from the Internal Revenue Service for $1,600,000 in taxes the federal government claimed was owing them. Eventually, he was to win the appeal, but when he and Constance left Washington, the case had been tabled for a future date and the possibility of having to pay the taxes remained. He was only too happy to start back to work on a project that he liked and one that Paramount approved.

With Claudette Colbert as Cleopatra, Warren William as Julius Caesar, and Henry Wilcoxon as Marc Antony, he began shooting a week before his niece's arrival. Although he did not endorse nepotism, he had kept up with reports on Agnes's career. She could, he acknowledged, create the Egyptian dances for the picture and for the same fee execute one or two of them herself. Agnes had arrived late due to a case of measles contracted on the high seas. She had read the script for the first time while she recuperated at Margaret's in New York, learning with great dismay that she was expected "to dance naked on the back of a live bull."

On her arrival in Hollywood, Constance met her train, and the DeMille chauffeur, Ulysses S. Poe, drove her directly to the studio. Cecil interrupted his shooting to give her a truly welcoming bear hug. Then he stood back from her and with "his quizzical jeweler's eye" surveyed her from top to bottom, and then said, "Lift your skirts, baby. I want to see if your legs have thickened."

She obliged, and he seemed pleased at what he saw. His pleasure faded when they began to discuss the dances he wanted for the film. Agnes was firm about not wanting to "dance dirty." For the moment, she was able to convince him to wait until she had time to create "something mysterious, beautiful, new," in place of the dance on the bull's back.

Cecil's resident dance director was LeRoy Prinz. *Cleopatra* was a historical, not a musical, film. Dance was being inserted in the scenes at court for two purposes—to add spectacle and sex. Under the guise of art, Cecil could display nearly nude women and near pornography. Before Agnes had arrived, Prinz had already incorporated three of Cecil's ideas into his dance sequences: naked girls emerging from clamshells and being fished from the Nile in giant nets; a man with a whip and two women dressed as leopards; a dance in which a goat butts young naked girls around the hall. Agnes was determined to bring a touch of class to the dance sequences for which she was responsible (her official title was Assistant Dance Director and Ballet Artist). Cecil told her she had seven days to present her dances to him but then ignored her presence on the set, forbade her to hire any girls for rehearsals so that she could work out and show him the dances, and sent her "to rehearse in the studio carpenter shops, where the electric saws splitting wood made it impossible to hear a piano."

During this time, she remained a guest in his house, "outwardly friendly and gay." Agnes wrote Margaret a few days after she had arrived, "Uncle Ce keeps a killing schedule. Up at 6:30 A.M., he has breakfast at 7 with Aunt Con in her beautiful east bedroom, the sun pouring through the climbing roses...he drives through the Paramount gate at 8:10...lunches at 12:30 in the commissary...his table is in the center and on a raised platform and all his staff sits with him.

"Back on the set at 1:30....He does everything (sets every camera angle. ...His cameramen, although the best, take instructions from him). He breaks at 7:00. Rushes [reviewing the daily film]...office conferences and business decisions

Left: On the *Cleopatra* set, Cecil directs Warren William as
Julius Caesar. Above: Agnes and Cecil on the set with
Katherine DeMille, who wears her costume for a Mae West
movie being shot at the same time on the M-G-M lot

until 10:30. Home alone at 11 P.M.—dinner (kept hot by Aunt Con in double boilers) . . . conversation with her until 1 A.M. . . . He personally locks up the whole house, speaks to the night watchman [and then reads the Bible in bed]. He never gets more than five hours' sleep. . . . He never smokes, and he takes only a little wine . . . he is on his feet all day . . . a general in full battle. . . . [He has] the unflagging zeal, the undivided strength of the prophet, the fanatic—or alternately, the absolute monarch." Just how absolute a monarch she was soon to discover.

He insisted that if she was to remain on the staff, she must execute the dance on the bull's back. "I've made the acquaintance of the bull," she wrote Anna. "He lives in the back lot, tethered in a pen. As I have always been unreasonably afraid of cows, I could see that this chore was going to present unusual tensions." She finally screwed up her courage and got on his back and was relieved to find that though he was "a great dark tawny brute," he possessed "a strangely subdued manner." She begged Cecil to let her try a seductive dance without the bull. Cecil himself directed a camera test of Agnes's harem dance. Her eyebrows were plucked ("I was . . . rendered as bald as an egg"), her hair greased black. The makeup man painted her entire body with a brown sponge ("You mustn't mind me, honey. Think of me as a doctor. . . ."). The costume was extremely brief, a pleated white gauze skirt "affixed to a jeweled halter around the groin" and an Egyptian jeweled collar held on by surgical tape. In order that nothing crucial would slip during the dance and offend the censors, the collar was readjusted several times, and Agnes bled and suffered second-degree burns as it was ripped from her flesh and new tape applied. Nonetheless, she proceeded with her performance. "Twice the jeweled collar broke and [she] had to stop for repairs." Agnes finally performed her dance, but Cecil stopped it midway and called out, "Oh, no! Oh, no! . . . I am so disappointed . . . it has no excitement, no thrill, no suspense, no sex. . . . What I would like is something like the Lesbian dance in *The Sign of the Cross*."

"Boy!" said the censor, who was standing by. "If we hadn't had the Christians singing hymns like crazy all throughout that dance we never would have got away with it."

"That dance was one of the funniest exhibitions I ever saw," Agnes snapped.

Five minutes later, she was informed that she was off the payroll, and by the next morning, she had "left his house forever"* and had moved in with a "particular friend," Dr. Lily Bess Campbell, a distinguished professor of English literature.

The entire episode was a stunning blow to Agnes. The uncle she had revered "had offered practical help and then thrown me away as trash." Cecil had exercised a great "shaping influence" on her, possibly greater than her father's, and his treatment of her had been wounding. Like Cecil, commercial success was important to Agnes, and now she felt a failure. When she "told [her] father . . . what had happened, he smiled wryly and [revealing much about his own work relationship with his brother] said, "I know! Ce can be tough—particularly with family. I've had some dealings that weren't pretty."

She returned to London, to Ramon, who at least believed in her as an artist.

With *Cleopatra*, Cecil enjoyed a box office bonanza. But the critics were not kind to him, although it was acknowledged that he had demonstrated once again his "rare skill in the handling of mass action." He had contrived a film of great spectacle, filled with modern, easygoing dialogue, with enough of a hint of the salacious to be intriguing and yet not pornographic. And after it was all done with, he had made no overture to win back Agnes's loyalty. "Of course, it was silly of me," she later said, "but at the time I was a lot fonder of that bull than I was of Uncle Cecil."

While *Cleopatra* was being filmed, Katherine DeMille, now under contract to Paramount, had been working on a neighboring set, cast in a supporting role in a Mae West film, *Belle of the Nineties*.

Acting had not been Katherine's first choice of a career. For a time, she had wanted to be an artist and had studied for a year (1930–31) at the Chicago Art Institute. She tried unsuccessfully to write a novel. She took a course in shorthand and typing (using the name Kay Marsh). She returned to California at Christmas 1932, determined to become a film actress. Cecil had refused to help her. "I understood how he felt," she recalled. "He thought that the impression would get around that he was forcing me on the industry because of my connection with him. That's just the way he felt."

This did not stop Katherine. Late in the summer of 1933 while Cecil had been in Hawaii for two months filming *Four Frightened People*, she had made her move. "With Father out of town, I set to work . . . for several weeks I went from studio to studio. . . . I wanted a job but I was not going to let Father's name help me get it. Accordingly, I went under my original name, Katherine Lester." Metro signed her to play the wife of the great Mexican rebel, Pancho Villa (Wallace Beery) in *Viva Villa*. As a result, Paramount offered her a part in *The Trumpet Blows*, with George Raft, and a contract. As she was billed in *Viva Villa* as Katherine DeMille, she must have revealed her relationship to Cecil by the time she was actually signed by Metro. And Paramount had no confusion as to her identity.

A Paramount publicity release (dated January 1935) reported that when Katherine came for a job, a studio executive got C. B. (now returned from Hawaii) on the phone.

"I want to talk to you about Katherine," the executive said.

"I have nothing to do with her business," DeMille answered as gruffly as he could. "You'll have to take it up with her."

"Well, tell me one thing," the nonplussed executive begged. "We want to offer her a contract. Do you have any objections?"

"I have no objections because it's none of my business," DeMille answered as he hastily hung up the phone.

She appeared in supporting roles in four films in the next year, including the Mae West picture and *Call of the Wild*, starring Clark Gable and Loretta Young. Contrary to his original position of total noninvolvement, Cecil had offered her a part as a harem girl in *Cleopatra*. She had refused, feeling that the role was not right for her. Although under contract to Paramount and with a steady income, she remained at home where "a friendly understanding restraint" existed between father and daughter.

Shortly after the completion of *Cleopatra*, Cecil began work on *The Crusades*, an example of what he called "telescoping history." There were several Crusades extending over two centuries. Cecil arbitrarily chose the year 1187 as the focal point and then with writers Harold Lamb, Waldemar Young, and Dudley Nichols, took

Left:
Katherine DeMille
played Alice of France
in C. B.'s next movie,
The Crusades, 1935,
along with Joseph
Schildkraut and
Henry Wilcoxon,
another of C. B.'s
lifelong retainers

Opposite, upper left:
Cecil's personal
approval was required
for every detail of his
films. See his
comment in the lower
right for this costume
for *The Crusades:* "I
like the tabbard [sic]
opening down the
front and lined with
color. C B"

Opposite, upper right:
A viral ailment put
Cecil in the hospital
during the planning of
The Crusades, but he
set up shop and
juggled the myriad
production details
from there

Opposite: C. B. with
the German director
Ernst Lubitsch, who
had just been made
head of West Coast
production at
Paramount as shooting
began on *The
Crusades.* His
appointment was
welcomed by C. B.

characters and incidents from all the Crusades and pieced together a story. This time he had a more interesting role to offer Katherine, that of Princess Alice of France. At Christmas 1934, Katherine had received no present from her father. She was puzzled by the omission; her eyes misted with tears. Cecil put his arm around her. "I purposely bought you nothing this year," he said, "but I want to offer you something which I think will do you more good. My present this year is the role of Alice of France in *The Crusades.*"

In Cecil's version of the Crusades, Alice is spurned by Richard the Lionhearted (Henry Wilcoxon) in favor of Berengaria (Loretta Young), whom he has never seen, in return for financial aid to his cause. Katherine accepted Cecil's offer. ("One simply didn't refuse a present from Father.") Father and daughter now became director and actress. The working relationship was infinitely better than Agnes and Cecil's had been. But it did put a strain on Katherine. She ate out of nerves and gained a considerable amount of weight to her father's nagging irritation, as costumes had to be altered.

During the filming, Katherine received a small shock. She had applied for a passport just previous to the picture's start and had been told that even though she had been adopted by American parents, she was not an American citizen; her Canadian birth made her a British subject. She then applied for citizenship papers, only to discover that there was no record of her entry into the United States and that she had to prove entry to get her papers. An article appeared in the *Los Angeles Times* for the first time giving her original name and including the facts of her entry into the country as she knew them. Her past began to be filled in by letters from people who had known her mother or served in the British Army with her father, some of the orphanage staff and her cousins in England. Her life before she became a DeMille was suddenly becoming real. She was able to prove her legal entry into the United States—but now she had to deal with being "Captain Lester's little girl" as well as Cecil's

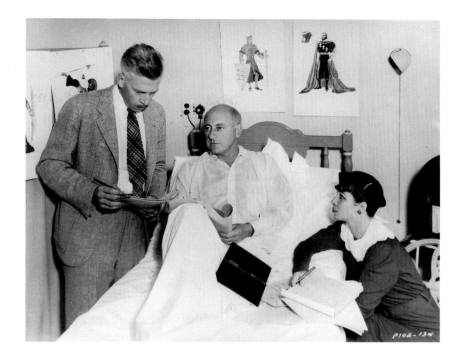

daughter. Her last weeks of shooting were clouded by her confusion and directly after the last shot had been made, she literally disappeared. No one, not even Constance or Cecil, knew where she was. She returned three weeks later, pale, fifteen pounds lighter, and with a request to Paramount for permission to change her name to Katherine Lester. Paramount refused the request. She then asked for time off and when granted it, accepted an engagement with a summer-stock company in Stockbridge, Massachusetts (the same company where Katharine Hepburn had started four years earlier). She claimed she now wanted a career on the stage. She was, however, billed in the play *Topaz* in Stockbridge as Katherine DeMille. The release of *The Crusades* (August 1934) during her stay in Stockbridge would have made a mockery of the use of a name other than DeMille, anyway, as pictures of her appeared in newspapers and magazines across the country.

The Crusades was a resounding commercial success, but the critics were brutal. "As a picture it is historically worthless, didactically treacherous, artistically absurd," *Time* said, adding snidely, "It is a $100,000,000 sideshow which has at least three features which distinguish it from the long line of previous DeMille extravaganzas. It is the noisiest, it is the biggest, it contains no baths."

"The trouble with Cecil is he always bites off more than he can chew—and then he chews it," Bill, who was at the time writing his Hollywood memoirs,* was uncharacteristically quoted as saying.

But Cecil's toughest critics had to admit he had "no peer in the world when it comes to bringing the panoplied splendor of the past into torrential life upon the screen." He had become the master of the screen epic, of the technique of weaving spectacle, sex, and inspiration into a picture "that pulls an audience irresistibly to the edge of its seat."

During the rest of the 1930s, spectacle was to follow spectacle: *The Plainsman*, the story of Wild Bill Hickok and Calamity Jane, starring Gary Cooper and Jean

Arthur, with twice as many horses, Indians, barroom brawls, and teams of vigilantes as had ever before swept across the plains of any Western; *The Buccaneer*, with Fredric March as Jean Lafitte, "dashing pirate of the Louisiana Bayous, who with his army of men helps save New Orleans for America"; and *Union Pacific*, which had Joel McCrea as overseer for the building of the great transcontinental railroad.

Cecil's films with their casts of thousands proved a godsend to Depression-struck Hollywood. "It's like the good old days in Hollywood," one reporter commented. "Extras have money in their pockets, bill collectors wait at the studio casting offices, and the wolf slinks away from many a bungalow door. DeMille is shooting! And when DeMille shoots, the Depression in Hollywood isn't what it used to be...."

Cecil seemed unconcerned that in the opinion of his critics his works were not considered artistically significant. His only fear was that an audience might be bored. "To insure against such a dreadful possibility he would over-pack his vistas, over-costume minor players, and give his actors so much 'business' that the fascinated public hardly bothered to listen to the deathless dialogue," Jesse Lasky, Jr. commented. C. B. signed Lasky as a scriptwriter for *Union Pacific*,* based on a story written by Jeanie Macpherson, now aging and plump.

"[She] always wore only one color at a time," Lasky recalled. "[For this story meeting] it was purple. Purple shoes, purple silk stockings, purple silk dress, purple straw hat transfixed with a purple-jeweled hatpin.... An ancient boa drooped a pair of molting vixens down her heavy purple bosom."

From the clutter of his desk Cecil had picked up a piece of iron and asked,

> "Know what this is, Jesse?"
> "A railroad spike."...
> "A railroad spike," he mocked. "What would you call the quill that signed the Declaration of Independence? A feather?... Sweat, blood, and steel. That's what built the Union Pacific! Yes, and whisky and sin—in portable hells of corruption following the railroad builders, siphoning their wages away in the saloons, brothels, and gambling dens under the tents that followed the ever westward-pushing end of the track!... Once the range belonged to the red man and the buffalo he harvested with arrows. The shaggy herds fed him, clothed him, housed him." His finger stabbed at the purple priestess in his temple of relics. "Get that, Jeanie!"
> "Oh yes, C. B.!"
> Her pencil trembled so violently it could hardly scribble.... Pencils fell from her hands, [her] notebook sprawled down in a splatter of pages. I knelt to help her.
> "Goddamn it, Jeanie, if you can't hold a pencil in your hand, write with it in your teeth," DeMille exploded.
> The hurt in her face was awful to see.

Lasky recalled that as the meeting continued, Cecil's harsh treatment of Jeanie intensified. She attempted to elaborate on the story, bring in new plot ideas,

In 1936, C. B. made his first movie starring Gary Cooper, *The Plainsman*, the story of Wild Bill Hickok. Calamity Jane was played by Jean Arthur, and Charles Bickford was the villain

How will Gary Cooper as The Plainsman get out of this fix? The answer was provided by three scriptwriters, one of whom was Lynn Riggs, who was also the author of the book on which *Oklahoma!* was based

The set design for "The End of the Line," in *Union Pacific*, 1939, which won an Oscar for Best Special Effects, under the supervision of Hans Dreier and Roland Anderson. It told the story of the linking up of the railroads from the East and West with the driving of a golden spike at Promontory Point, Utah

Katherine DeMille' favorite photograph of herself, c. 1935

and each time he would squash her down. Finally, he yelled, "Shut up, Jeanie! If you have to think of the oldest plot in the world, do it on your own time. . . . Now get out!"

As she rose, she dropped everything she was holding. Lasky bent down "to retrieve glasses, pencils, eraser." With a superb dignity, Jeanie "waved away the salvaged pencils and left." Later that day Lasky met with C. B., who to his surprise had incorporated one of Jeanie's ideas in the script, although she had now been removed from the project (her salary, nonetheless, continued). "If that woman doesn't drive you screaming, raving insane—if you can keep from strangling her with your bare hands—she occasionally comes up with something usable," he told Lasky. And then, shuddering, added, "I will take care of my enemies if God will protect me from my friends."

He expected his staff to give him first allegiance over wives, home lives, and personal problems. "Our time was his day or night," Lasky recalled, "we were expected to lunch at the DeMille table [in the commissary] every day. . . . A silence would fall over the vast room of crowded tables as we filed in behind the boss, scripts under our arms, and took our prescribed places. . . . Eating was generally next to impossible! . . . We were always having to defend the morning's work. . . . DeMille kept a Bible beside his plate [and quoted from it frequently without opening the cover]."

Cecil maintained his support of both Jeanie and Julia Faye (whom he cast in a small role in *Union Pacific*). And, although Jeanie was taken off the script of *The Buccaneer*, she did receive an adaptation credit—her last film credit, despite the fact that Cecil called her in for story conferences on other projects, occasionally using her contributions.

On the home front, Cecilia and Frank Calvin had split up and she had moved back home with their two small children, Peter and baby Cecilia Junior (whom everyone called Citsy). The house was brimming with youth again, and Cecil appeared to enjoy every moment of it. John had recently married but still seemed unsettled. Cecil had brought him into the studio at one point, but John had not done well. Richard was attending the Santa Barbara School. A high achiever, he had just won the school's outstanding scholarship trophy and was an editor of the school paper with aspirations of one day becoming a writer. He seldom saw Bill and still had no idea as to his real parentage. He and Katherine had become close friends, confidants of a sort, despite the vast age difference, perhaps because of their special intelligence. Katherine dated, fell in and out of love, but at twenty-six remained without a serious attachment. That was soon to change.

When C. B. had filmed *The Plainsman*, he had put out a casting call for authentic Indians. A young Mexican-American named Anthony Quinn answered the call. "I'm Cheyenne," he told the casting director.

"Say something in Cheyenne," he was requested.

"Ksai Ksakim eledeki Chumbolum."

"Are you sure that's Cheyenne?"

"Of course it is. Would I make it up?" Quinn replied.

Fifteen minutes later, he was in Cecil's private office along with a technical adviser who was supposed to know the Indian language.

"Xtmas ala huahua?" the adviser said to him, in what Quinn was certain was phony Cheyenne, so he replied, "Xtmas nava ellahuahua, cheriota hodsvi."

"Oh yes, he speak good Cheyenne," the man told Cecil.

Quinn was hired. Born in Chihuahua, Mexico, of impoverished Irish-Mexican parents and reared in the slums of Los Angeles, young Quinn had already had several careers: teenage boxer, professional dance contestant, saxophonist in the band of evangelist Aimee Semple McPherson, chorus boy in a Mae West stage production, and several walk-on roles in films. Quinn had wanted to be "Napoleon, Michelangelo, Shakespeare, Picasso, Martin Luther and Jack Dempsey, all rolled into one." What he was saying was that he was determined to be someone. The defiant slum kid had matured into a steely young man, fearful of very little, ambitious almost to ruthlessness, self-educated, hard-edged, and sexually attractive to the majority of women he met.

He encountered Katherine DeMille as he walked out of his dressing room, barefooted, dressed in a torn shirt and loincloth, a feather in his headband, on his way to the set to play his first scene in *The Plainsman*.

"She was dark-haired, with beautiful skin and the most piercing eyes I've ever seen in my life," he recalled. "She looked part Indian, and I thought it was a good omen that I had 'another Indian' there.... She looked over my way and as she did, I realized who she was—the great man's daughter—Katherine DeMille.... I had seen her in several pictures.... I liked the fact that she was there and I was going to show her what a good actor I was...."

The scene she witnessed turned out to be a fiasco and had to be reshot many times. Finally, when Cecil discovered that Quinn was not Cheyenne and Quinn could freely express his feelings about how he should play the scene, the day was won. But by then Katherine had left the set. A few days later, Cecil called him into his office.

"Kid, I just saw the rushes, and I'm going to nominate you for a special Academy Award. I think they should have awards for bit parts for the most outstanding

The Buccaneer, a 1938 swashbuckler, starred Fredric March, center, as Jean Lafitte. Akim Tamiroff glowers at left, and the fledgling actor Anthony Quinn is at right

debut ... [and] you made a great impression on my daughter. She thinks you have a great future, and I do, too."

They shot a test of him dressed in contemporary clothes. A short time later, Cecil began work on *The Buccaneer* and brought the test home for his family to see. "I've tested several actors for the lead," he told them. "I would like your opinion on the one I'm going to show you." The film was run. "Goddammit! I like him!" Cecil exclaimed. "I think he'd be marvelous for Jean Lafitte!"

Katherine disagreed. "After all," she countered, "Jean Lafitte had been a pirate for many years, and this boy looks twenty-one or twenty-two years old." (He was in fact twenty-two.)

Cecil cast Fredric March as Lafitte, but Quinn was put under contract to Paramount and given the supporting role of the pirate Beluche. (Quinn says: "I played a tenth-grade pirate with not the least idea of what I was doing. Merely sitting in front of the altar of success, praying for a place on top of the mountain.") He saw Katherine on the set and suggested she read Thomas Wolfe.

"Why should I read it?" she asked.

"Because if you like Thomas Wolfe, you'll like me, and if you love him, you'll love me, and you'll marry me."

She was not that keen on Thomas Wolfe, but the two began to date, always meeting "away from her own environment." He took her on tours of East Los Angeles, where he had grown up, and to meet his Mexican mother. He took her to Aimee Semple McPherson's Angelus Temple. "I wanted her to share every drop of my experience. I wanted her to accept me wholly and unconditionally," he later wrote.

Quinn went to see Cecil to tell him he wished to marry Katherine. "Remem-

Anthony Quinn had taken a screen test for the role of Jean Lafitte in *The Buccaneer*. He lost out in the casting, but he got the girl; he and Katherine DeMille were married in October of 1937. C. B. and Constance DeMille flank the couple

ber, Tony," Cecil warned, "marry in haste, repent at leisure." Thereafter the wedding plans were left to the young couple.

They were married in Los Angeles on October 5, 1937. "Katie's mother had been Italian," Quinn wrote, "which was close enough to my background. She knew the Latin rules of man and woman—one man and a wall three feet wide for the rest of the world. . . . But the wedding was her wedding. Mrs. DeMille had made up most of the list. . . . Guests sitting in the church, not because two people were promising to love and obey each other forever, but because it was their duty to make an appearance for the old man. [My] mother wasn't included . . . they would have clamped [her] in jail if she had tried to break through and see her only son getting married."

The marriage was off to a rocky start. Their wedding night in Carmel furthered their problems. "The look on [Katie's] face as I slapped her when I found out I wasn't the first man. I felt betrayed, I felt cheated, I felt lied to," Quinn confessed in his memoirs. "Not only could I not make love to her, but I wanted to run away. All the love, all my dreams had turned into a nightmare. The poor, frightened girl packed her things and ran out of the hotel. She said she'd take the train to Reno and get a divorce." After he had let her go, he realized what a fool he had been and

drove over those tortuous winding mountain roads all night racing to get to Reno before her train. Fifty miles outside of Reno, the train came to a stop. . . . I boarded it and looked for Katie's compartment. As I burst through the door, she barely looked up. She was sitting there in silence. She had been crying. . . .

I picked up her bags and told her to follow me. She didn't say a word until we were in the car and the train was pulling away.

"Are you sure that you can live with it?"[she asked.]

"I have to...you are my woman. I have to learn to be your man."

He managed that successfully, but becoming Cecil B. DeMille's son-in-law was quite another matter. Unlike Cecilia's former husband, Frank Calvin, Quinn had problems with this from the very beginning. "To a poor boy," Quinn says, "DeMille was the epitome of success. He was a gracious host at dinner, birthdays, and all social events concerning the family. He was the one everyone tried to please during the family gatherings. In the living room [of the house] he had a special armchair. Beside the chair was a large table with pads of paper, notebooks, a small silver pitcher with a huge amount of pens and pencils. Next to that stood a large collection of pipes, all with a pipe cleaner through the neck and out the bowl....I found him not easy to be around. He was very mannered in his graciousness. The house seemed to belong to royalty rather than a motion picture director."

During the making of *The Buccaneer*, Cecilia had fallen in love with a family friend, businessman Joseph W. Harper. Her second marriage had to be fitted into the schedule of her father's planned publicity tour for *The Buccaneer*. Therefore, her wedding to Harper took place in Kansas City, January 21, 1938, the same night as, and immediately following, the film's premiere there. It was midnight before the vows were exchanged. The *Kansas City Star* unflatteringly noted that "the bride had become a bit weary and even Mr. DeMille's smile had lost some of its luster." Cecil was so tired in fact that he presented his new son-in-law to the press as "Mr. Calvin." Harper smiled, bowed, and replied, "Thank you, Mr. Goldwyn."

After her demeaning experience on Cecil's *Cleopatra*, Agnes was only too happy to return to London and Ramon. He had secured a temporary ground-floor accommodation for her across Paulton's Square, where she only needed to walk a few steps back and forth to his flat. He had lost weight and seemed to be fading, and Agnes had an overwhelming sense of need to help him fight for his life. She worked on the choreography for a comedy ballet based on a scenario written by Ramon* that was being performed in a small London revue, *Why Not Tonight?*, presented at the Shaftesbury Theatre. She had taken up her lessons with Mim and Tudor again. But for the month of August, the Ballet Club was to be closed, and she decided and engineered (against Sharpe's strong objections) a motor trip to the countryside of Wales. Ramon bought a secondhand car, and Agnes had the front seat cut in half, and the back of it hinged, so that it let down to form a bed; that way he could travel lying flat. As he could ride only for short periods of time, they had had the Royal Automobile Club furnish a route where they would have two to three hours between stops.

Sharpe, of course, traveled with them. They ended up in a small village called Brynhyfryd on the River Ceiriog. It reminded her of Merriewold and she was at once at home in the house they had rented (complete with gardener and housekeeper).

She practiced in the sitting room before a great wardrobe mirror that Sharpe had moved for her. They had tea on the terrace in the late afternoon, and then Ramon read while she continued work on the gros point for his antique chairs. On August 19, they celebrated Ramon's twenty-third birthday. They had "champagne and birthday cake with Ramon's name written in pink flourishes over the top." She danced for him, and they became intoxicated, and then Sharpe carried Ramon, "singing at the top of his voice," off to bed.

She brought back to London some heather which quickly faded, but Ramon looked much refreshed. Working with Antony Tudor, Agnes gave a series of recitals at the Mercury which were a great success but earned her only eleven pounds in one week. By November 1934, she had become homesick and asked Anna for two hundred dollars so that she could sail on the *Berengaria* and be home for Christmas. Ramon vowed somehow he would follow her.

Anna helped her put together a concert in New York, and when that brought no offers, they went out to California and stayed with Margaret while they put together two more concerts. After these, Anna went home but Agnes persevered. At last came an offer from the Hollywood Bowl, a single night's performance for a fee of $2,000, out of which Agnes was to pay all her expenses and the salaries of a company of thirty dancers. When she wrote Ramon this news, he replied that he was going to take a freighter and would soon see her himself. When he and Sharpe arrived, Agnes had readied for them a "little new house, bright and jolly, pert with Mexican ollas and painted furniture. He was put to bed laughing with happiness under a handwoven magenta Mexican blanket."

For the next three months, she showed Ramon California, and good friends like Gladys and Edward G. Robinson welcomed him to their homes. He spent long hours on his fringe-shaded patio in the sun. There were picnics and drives through the foothills and to the beach. They dined in Olivera Street by candlelight, and even shopped in Chinatown. ("I ordered Chinese silk pajamas for Ramon, black, lacquer red and mandarin. I could afford three because he needed no trousers.") Friends of hers came to visit with him while she rehearsed. The time was one of enchantment for Ramon.

The Bowl concert had an audience of 18,000 people. Agnes felt she had danced "extraordinarily well." Unfortunately, something electrical went wrong in the midst of the concert, and the stage was thrown into near blackness. "The press was nasty...taking delight in the failure of a de Mille," she noted. "There were no picture offers, which was the object behind all these exercises. It was a bad blow."

Before they were to return to England, Agnes had a team of American specialists put Ramon through a series of tests at Good Samaritan Hospital. "Ag, I've begun to hope again," he confided to her. But the verdict was a dark one.

He returned with Sharpe to England. Agnes was to arrive a few days later, but then the chance she had dreamed of came. George Cukor, Margaret's old friend, was now one of the most powerful directors in Hollywood. He offered her the dances for the million-dollar Metro-Goldwyn-Mayer version of *Romeo and Juliet*, starring Norma Shearer and Leslie Howard, and she stayed.

Romeo and Juliet was the first opulent job Agnes had ever held. She was paid $500 a week, and her contract was for six months. She had her own office–dressing room, a secretary, researchers, assistants, and an enormous rehearsal hall. She reestablished formal relations with Cecil and even went as one of his guests to the Academy Award dinner for the best films and performances of 1935. But the wounded feelings had not yet healed. To Cecil's great disappointment, *The Crusades* had received only one nomination (Victor Milner for photography) and did not win the award. (*Mutiny on the Bounty* won best picture, Bette Davis best actress for *Dangerous*, and Victor McLaglen best actor for *The Informer*.)

She returned to London as soon as her assignment was over, certain she was in love with a German art professor, Edgar Wind, whom she had met just before she had left London and with whom she had been corresponding. Ramon recognized her changed attitude. The romance went quickly askew (when Wind confessed he was in love with someone else), but not before Ramon took seriously ill. Agnes remained by his sickbed for four days.

"Will I be here tomorrow?" he asked her.

"You will. Hold on! Hold on to my hand!"

He recovered this time, but failed again a few weeks later. Leslie Howard had just offered her the dances in his upcoming New York stage version of *Hamlet*. "Ramon, I'll stay," she told him. "I'll give up the job—that's nothing—would you like me to stay here? To be with you?"

"No, Aglet," he said, "this that I have to do, I have to do alone."

"And Ag, don't worry about the work—it will be recognized, I know this."

He died while she was in New York in rehearsal. She "cabled a great sheaf of flowers." He had left her nothing of his estate; most of it had gone to Sharpe. But Ramon Reed had given Agnes a great deal more than money. He had given her confidence, love, companionship, and for an artist, an even greater gift—a sense of tragedy and of triumph. His death, however, had put her in a terribly distressed state and as she was placed under mounting tensions during the rehearsals of *Hamlet*, she appeared about to break. John Houseman, the director, found he had a sensitive problem on his hands. "The play scene in *Hamlet* is a notorious trap," he confessed. "Few theatrical ideas are so cluttered with the bones of bright and pretentious ideas. Agnes...was determined to make a 'mime' of it, while Virgil [Thomson, who had composed the music for the balletic scenes] insisted that it must be performed as '*mélodrame*,' " with the speeches chanted to a formal musical accompaniment. As a result, rehearsals were a misery—with Leslie off in his hotel room trying to arbitrate the insoluble conflict between composer and choreographer. The outcome was a compromise and a mess.

Thomson had decided to use authentic instrumentation and employed a serpent-like medieval instrument. The sound produced was rusty dissonance, and at the final out-of-town preview (Boston) the audience rudely imitated it. "That night the dramatic effect of the play scene was not fully achieved," Houseman recalled. "Next day both 'mime' and '*mélodrame*' were dissolved [in favor of the classic interpretation of the scene] and Agnes and Virgil left, in separate rages for [Agnes] London and [Thomson] Paris."

Howard's *Hamlet* was a miserable failure in New York, partly because John Gielgud had presented a spectacular *Hamlet* the previous season. In England, Agnes searched out Ramon's family, but they were no more gracious to her in his death than in his life. She returned to work with Mim and all her old friends at the Ballet Theatre. But a new and unwelcome chord had been sounded. Now that Tudor, Ashton, and herself, and so many of the others, had become fairly well known as

For the M-G-M production of *Romeo and Juliet*, 1936, Agnes deMille did the choreography, which also involved coaching Norma Shearer

choreographers, they were also competitors and the years during which they had struggled together could no longer be recaptured.

William deMille published his memoir, *Hollywood Saga*, in 1939. "The book is not the best of William," Richard DeMille critiqued. "The humor is slightly strained, a little too cute, just a little too uninvolved. He wrote self-protectively, too restrained, not of facts, but emotions. He was a wounded person when he wrote the book." He tried his hand again in theatre, but none of his projects materialized. After a time in New York, he returned to California. He had given some lectures at the University of Southern California and, to his great delight, was chosen to help develop a new drama department at the university. He accepted enthusiastically. At an age when most men are thinking of retirement, William deMille had found a new career for himself as a college don.

The years since Ramon's death had not been easy for Agnes. She had been living in a sparse two-room studio on East Ninth Street in New York's Greenwich Village. (Her father came to visit once and "was somewhat taken aback. 'How Bohemian!' he remarked. 'No rugs!' " She replied that the lack of furnishings was due to a lack of funds. Later, Clara sent her a rug for the floor and a winter coat.) Once the money from *Romeo and Juliet* had been used up, she was as broke as she had always been, and she turned to Anna for small disbursements, often fifteen or twenty dollars, to carry her through from one week to another. She was hired to do the dances

For most of the thirties, Agnes deMille worked in London. In this Angus McBean photograph she is costumed for her composition *Elizabethan Suite*, 1938

for the show *Hooray for What*, directed by Vincente Minnelli, and was fired, her dances dropped.* She returned to England and an engagement at the Westminster Theatre for which she commissioned Tudor to choreograph the now famous *Judgment of Paris*. It was September 1938. War was looming, after the Munich crisis, and aliens were being sent home by the shipload, Agnes among them.

For nearly the entire year that followed, she was mainly unemployed, although she was hired to stage a ballet for *Swingin' the Dream*, which was a thirteen-performance Rockefeller Center fiasco. She and dancer-choreographers Michael Kidd, Eugene Loring, and Paul Haakon rented a rehearsal room for five dollars a week and coached one another. She saw a great deal of Martha Graham, whom she admired tremendously, danced occasionally at benefits and private parties, joined Mary Hunter's American Actors Company,* and danced at their concerts for a fee of twenty-five dollars. Then in the late summer of 1939, a wealthy young man named Richard Pleasant formed "a gigantic international ballet company," called the Ballet Theatre and sponsored by Lucia Chase. Agnes was not to go on composing vehicles for herself, but was to join nine of the world's most celebrated choreographers—Michael Fokine, Michael Mordkin, Adolph Bolm, Bronislava Nijinska, Anton Dolin, Antony Tudor, Eugene Loring, José Fernandez, and Andrée Howard—to create

150

Antony Tudor
choreographed *Judgment
of Paris* at Agnes's
request; the costumes
were designed by her
frequent dance partner
Hugh Laing

new ballets.* Each choreographer worked separately in private studios with his or
her own group of dancers (included in these ranks were Nora Kaye and Maria Car-
nilova) over a period of four months.

Agnes decided to attempt an uncharacteristic work, not a comedic ballet but
an "exotic work for Negroes using the *Création du Monde* score of Darius Milhaud."
Blacks were not employed by major ballet companies and this was a courageous and
daring project. Most of her dancers were untrained performers, literally, because
blacks had no opportunity for serious dancing in 1939–40. The ballet was called
Black Ritual. "It was danced at its *première* at a pace calculated to kill all excitement,"
Agnes recalled. "We were allotted three performances only.

"And the press was murderous.

"As the Negro troupe performed in no other work, they were . . . considered
an unwarranted luxury. After the three-week season, . . . my girls were dispersed and
the work has never since been performed."

The first season (spring 1940) was successful but when the great impresario
Sol Hurok brought over the Ballet Russe, the Ballet Theatre floundered against such
famous competition. On borrowed money, Agnes took her group out on tour. They
traveled very economically, sleeping in a pullman berth at night, but shifting over to

coaches in the morning. They appeared in nearly every college or university town from San Antonio, Texas, to Chicago, Illinois, survived on sandwiches and pots and pots of tea, and ended up "all nearly dead."

Agnes had netted six hundred dollars. But she was now recognized as one of the world's top choreographers. Her star, if not her income, was rising meteorically. She claimed that "at night in the little personal hours" she added up the negatives in her life. "Youth gone [she was 36 in 1941]. No husband. No child. No achievement in work [not true]." And she would wake "cold and consider the situation. Time was passing.... Prospects...ceased to be bright."

Uncle Ce—"the famous DeMille"—had released *Union Pacific* on April 28, 1939, and demonstrated once again "his special art of the epic." His new film, *North West Mounted Police*, starring Gary Cooper, Madeleine Carroll, Paulette Goddard, Preston Foster, and Robert Preston, was premiered in November 1940. It dealt with the second of two civil wars that split Canada in 1885 and had pitted a small force of mounted police against a horde of rebels seeking to oust the English and rule themselves. Cooper was a Texas Ranger pursuing a gun runner who was now working with the rebels, and so he joined forces with the mounties. As history (despite C. B.'s claims of huge research expenses), the film was totally unreliable. Jesse Lasky, Jr., who with Alan LeMay and C. Gardner Sullivan wrote the screenplay, admitted, "We were giving the customers what they wanted, and the proof of our puddings was that people were crowding the movie houses to, as it were, eat them."

North West Mounted Police was the first DeMille film to be shot completely in Technicolor. Cecil had turned a three-acre lot at Paramount into what looked im-

Dan Sayre Groesbeck, a durable DeMille employee, did the set designs for *North West Mounted Police*, 1940, C. B.'s first all-Technicolor film

In this publicity shot for *North West Mounted Police*, C. B. washes the hair of Paulette Goddard as a half-Indian girl. Costars included Gary Cooper, Madeleine Carroll, and Robert Preston

pressively like the whole of Saskatchewan, the story's locale. Three hundred pine trees a yard in diameter had been planted, the largest trucking job in Hollywood's history. He rechristened Little Bear, the Indian chief who led the rebellion, Big Bear. Sixteen loudspeakers had been hidden among rocks and behind tree trunks to magnify C. B.'s voice so that his least whisper rolled thunderously through the foliage. He advertised the film as "the Mightiest Adventure-Romance *Ever!*" adding beneath it "1000 unforgettable thrills." Miss Goddard's fiery half-Indian siren certainly supplied a few thrills, and there were others—if not 1000, at least enough to make the film one of the biggest moneymakers of the year. Cecil's touch, however irreverent, was golden.

To Agnes, his family, and his staff, he was still considered *God*, and the keeper of the DeMille legend. Agnes could not have dreamed that within a scant five years, she would add her own legend to the name of DeMille.

C. B., famous for his attention to every aspect of
his productions, went underwater to check on
things for *Reap the Wild Wind*, 1942

A Twentieth-Century Success

1941–1946

*"Miss deMille," said the man from the New York Times,
"you don't seem to know what kind of success this is."
I said, "What kind is it? I never had any."
"The biggest success in the 20th Century," he exclaimed.
I said, "Goodness, well, I think I'll ask for a raise."*

—AGNES DEMILLE of the first production of *Oklahoma!*, 1943

THROUGHOUT THE THIRTIES, CECIL NEVER WAVERED FROM HIS course. He remained faithful to the dramatic conventions of David Belasco. Film innovators like Chaplin, Lubitsch, Welles, and Renoir came and went without influencing his style in the slightest. The Depression, war in Europe, and its looming threat to America did not alter his choice of subject matter—action, sex, spectacle, history, and a moral message ending in a rousing climax: Moses parting the Red Sea in *The Ten Commandments*, a train wreck in *Union Pacific*, an Indian raid in *The Plainsman*, a boat capsizing and going over a waterfall in *North West Mounted Police*.

Sea tales held a special fascination for him, and he assumed, therefore, that they would for the public. In summer 1940, he had bought a *Saturday Evening Post* magazine sea saga, "Reap the Wild Wind," by Thelma Strable. He hired three adapters—Jesse Lasky, Jr., Alan LeMay, and an Englishman, Charles Bennett*— and told them, "I want to smell the brine and hear the creak of rigging. I want to feel the bite of hurricanes. I want the birth of America's lifeline on the seas—and to see it threatened by the toughest tribe of murdering pirate-wreckers that ever gutted a ship to steal a cargo!...I want to see the teeth of a reef bite through a ship's bottom— photographed from under water!" Marine photography was a costly and difficult procedure. This did not deter Cecil. And the writers dutifully wrote in scene after scene of divers exploring a submerged hull of a wrecked ship, and an undersea struggle between the two male stars of the film (John Wayne and Ray Milland) "whacking at each other's life lines with hatchets." C. B. was still not satisfied.

A precursor of *Jaws*, *Reap the Wild Wind* featured this giant shark, in another dramatic Groesbeck rendering, one of many such features that earned this film an Academy Award for Best Special Effects

Anne Bauchens came to Hollywood to resume work as Bill deMille's secretary, but wound up as a film editor for every one of C. B.'s films starting with *We Can't Have Everything*, 1918. In 1940 she won an Oscar for her editing of *North West Mounted Police*

The story (based on fact) dealt with America's fight to whip a little island empire of pirate shipwreckers that ruled the strategic Florida Keys in 1840, before the railroad era, when the sea route was the artery of the nation, linking the rich Mississippi Valley with industrial New England. Again and again, ships loaded with teak and ivory smashed up on these reefs. One unscrupulous and avaricious sea salvager (Raymond Massey) hatches and sets in motion an enterprising scheme to contrive wrecks in order to salvage them. Wayne, a captain whose vessels have mysteriously been scuttled, and Milland, a shipping-firm lawyer, join forces to provide the proof to prosecute Massey. They become rivals in love with the same woman, a beautiful, maverick, tempestuous, Southern charmer, Paulette Goddard (who the year before had narrowly missed being cast as Scarlett O'Hara in David O. Selznick's *Gone With the Wind*). The plot was the kind that involved good action, confrontational rows, and ardent love scenes. But unless his writers could come up with a closing sequence that "would galvanize headhunters in an Amazon River jungle," C. B. told them, "we just haven't got a moving picture." After a lot of discredited ideas, Charles Bennett, "scarf tucked Britishly into his blazer," sprang to his feet.

"The first instant that the [two men] start to hack at each other [underwater] you see behind them—rising out of the belly of the dead ship, one great long red tentacle—and then another. . . . Then, faster than a striking cobra, it sweeps around the body of one of the men. It heaves him up, light as a doll in the fist of a giant—for giant it is. A giant squid! The largest monster of the deep. Great eyes like illuminated green balloons, full of malevolent intelligence. Massive slack, big as a circus tent, but with tentacles strong enough to squeeze an elephant to pulp!" The rivals for Goddard's hand and heart were now to be united against "this ink-throwing behemoth, this leviathan! The sea bottom has become an arena where man is pitted against nature."

LeMay and Lasky sat "in stunned silence." To their knowledge no giant squid had ever been recorded seen along the Florida Keys, and this was to be a historical saga—not a horror film. But "DeMille looked ecstatic. 'And in technicolor,'" he breathed, according to Lasky. Bennett had not come up with an entirely new idea; a similar scene had been filmed in the 1916 silent of Jules Verne's great fantasy adventure novel *20,000 Leagues Under the Sea*, the first time that underwater photography had been attempted.

At the start, Cecil actually considered using a real squid but could not locate one large enough in any aquarium. The special-effects department finally constructed a squid with a thirty-eight-foot span, its tentacles made of deep red sponge rubber. A complex electrical keyboard was wired to its ten-foot body where beneath its sponge exterior was a small forest of hydraulic pistons that controlled its movements and the rotation of its eyes.

Four separate camera units were used for the film. The spectacular underwater sequences were photographed partly on the floor of the Pacific off Catalina Island and partly in a huge 1,000,000-gallon tank that was especially built for the picture at the Pacific Marine Museum in Santa Monica.

To direct these scenes, Cecil donned a diving suit and personally attended to the staging of the big fight with the giant squid, maintaining communication with Wayne's and Milland's doubles (the scene was considered too dangerous for his stars) underwater by means of a telephone hookup between his helmet and theirs.

Reap the Wild Wind was Cecil's sixty-sixth film, and during its shooting, he celebrated his sixtieth birthday at a luncheon at the studio. "Now, for the first time," he told the gathering of studio executives and staff, "I am being helped to make a picture instead of being dared to make one."

During the filming of *Reap the Wild Wind*, the DeMille family suffered its first real tragedy. As a wedding present for Katherine and Tony Quinn, Cecil had purchased a neighboring house (Cecilia and Joe Harper also lived nearby in what had become the DeMille family compound). One Sunday, little three-year-old Christopher Quinn "somehow escaped [his family's] watchfulness for a few minutes, trudged across the street...drawn by the magic shimmer of a pond on the property of...W. C. Fields...and was drowned." Cecil and Quinn both ran after him, but were too late.

The terrible incident sent Katherine into a lifelong study of religions that dealt with the afterlife. Cecil drew closer to his other grandchildren, especially Cecilia's daughter, Citsy. C. B. had become especially attached to little Citsy, now a precocious five-year-old child of rare porcelain beauty, somehow red-haired without being freckled, and with enormous, inquisitive gray-green eyes. Cecil had always adored her; now he became almost possessive and overprotective toward her. Her older brother, Peter, remained "down the hill" with Cecilia and his stepfather, who was devoted to and working for Cecil in a business management capacity. Citsy spent much of her time at Cecil's and even slept in a bed in the small anteroom to his bedroom, an area that he had previously used as a private upstairs study and which had to

Citsy (Cecilia Junior), the daughter of C. B.'s own Cecilia, was the apple of his eye: In 1940 she went with him by train to Chicago, and at his home she had her own bedroom just outside his. Until the end of his life, she accompanied him on his trips—to Egypt, Europe, and elsewhere

be crossed in order to get to his bed. This meant he could see the child upon retiring at night and when he awoke in the morning, and that if anything should happen to her during those hours—a fall, a cough, any sign of illness or sleeplessness—he would be alerted and on hand. Constance now slept in a smallish room on the other side of his bedroom connected by a bathroom which all three rooms shared.

Reap the Wild Wind was not released until March 1942. America was at war, and Cecil, with astonishing prescience, had made a picture that exactly suited the needs of the armed services and the public: a historical pageant of American—and for that matter Allied—ideals: freedom of the seas and the right of private enterprise. The press called him "The Old Master." Howard Barnes, the film critic of the *Herald Tribune*, referred to him as a "great showman" (a term that was to stick) and went on to say:

> The film industry cannot fail to give him an obeisance on this his thirtieth anniversary of movie-making.... the fact is this shrewd stage author-actor-director who saw the great potentialities of the photoplay long before it was an important medium, and has stuck to his prophetic insight through thick and thin, always has been a great showman.... he has defined the course of motion-picture progress in no uncertain manner. For he has played the screen long and he has never been wrong....
>
> His latest production defines his thirty years of work in a burgeoning dramatic form almost perfectly. 'Reap the Wild Wind'... is a somewhat startling exhibit at the moment. Hollywood may be retrenching. DeMille isn't. He told me the other day that this new offering of his is more expensive than any he ever made. And he added that he knew perfectly well that we would be at war before the production had a chance to reach the screen. He is that kind of a showman.
>
> For he plays to the gallery, and he rarely fails to get a huge response from the general film-going public. He will never spare any expense to make a show more showy....

What did it matter that John Mesher of *The New Yorker* claimed the plot was "so involved and all these people have so many interests and emotional complexities that we get bewildered... by the story!" Even the intellectuals had to agree that the film was a "celebration of the days of sailing ships" and "every bit a super-spectacle."

The showman evidenced itself in most everything Cecil did. Years earlier, France had awarded him a Légion d'Honneur rosette in recognition of his patriotic World War I screen dramas, and for "his other contributions to the motion picture art." As France fell to the Axis, he announced to the press that as "one man's protest against Pierre Laval and French collaboration with Germany," he had stopped wearing the coveted rosette "until France is once more a free and independent democracy."

About this time, Agnes met Walter Prude, the man she was shortly to marry. She had begun to believe that she would remain a dedicated but unwed dancer. Most of her life she had been told that she was not pretty and "had no sex appeal.... But I could hear people laugh when I danced, I could hear them roar at my comedy, so I must have been attractive in some way." Indeed, though she did not see it in herself, Agnes had matured at thirty-six into a handsome, elegant-looking woman with eyes that flashed intelligence, a quick smile that could light a cellar gloom, and a sense of humor that was witty and engaging. Her posture was regal and her dress—which was once looked upon as careless—was now considered "distinctive."

She still resided in her sparsely furnished "mare's nest on Ninth Street" in Greenwich Village and was trying to subsist on the less than thirty dollars a week she earned from teaching dancing classes. The Ballet Theatre was in limbo. There were no offers for concerts and no money to sponsor one herself. Her company had had to disband as the men received draft notices. Anna was growing old and had very little money left. She had suffered a recent heart attack, and Agnes could not help but feel "a real burden to her" as she was obliged to accept small disbursements to tide herself over. Nonetheless, she practiced every day and created new dances even though she had become despairing that they would ever be performed. And she maintained her close relationship with her dance associates of a decade.

One evening, Martha Graham telephoned to ask her to attend a recital with her. Agnes, who was in the doldrums, was most pleased to accept. "Wear your prettiest dress," the Nefertiti-looking Graham added. "Walter Prude is coming." Agnes did not know who Prude was. It developed he was a member of a concert agency which managed Graham but had refused to represent Agnes.

She did put on her "prettiest dress," a slinky black item ("purchased with tumultuous effort in a mass of quarreling women at Klein's on Union Square for $11.59") that she claimed made her look as though she'd been "pulled from a lake. . . . [But] through half-closed lids I thought I looked pretty good."

Walter Prude was lean, tall, and gray-eyed, "a nice combination of Gary Cooper and George VI of England." He had been born in Baird, Texas, and brought up in Dallas and on the cattle ranches of West Texas. Quite brilliant, he had entered the University of Texas at fifteen, convinced he would study medicine; two years later, he had shifted his interest to music. He had finally left Texas and become secretary to the concert pianist Olga Samaroff (then married to conductor Leopold Stokowski) before joining the staff of Graham's management.

Agnes never stopped "chattering." Still he saw her home and came to tea the next day. Within a very short time, Agnes was in love with this gentle Southwesterner who made her laugh and who possessed "a savage wit laced through his polite manner." Only a few months after their meeting, he was drafted and, following his basic training, was transferred as a corporal to an Army weather station in Tennessee. They corresponded almost daily. He wrote about Army life and she about her first interview with Serge Ivanovich Denham, the head of the Ballet Russe de Monte Carlo.

Through a mutual acquaintance of Denham's, Agnes had learned that the Ballet Russe was considering including in its repertoire an American ballet. In a recent season, Denham had commissioned Richard Rodgers to compose the score for a new work. At the time, the Ballet Russe specialized in the classics or in new works by European choreographers, but was anxious to expand its repertoire. A young American dancer, Marc Platt, had developed an idea for a ballet called *Ghost Town* about the gold rush. He and Rodgers had collaborated on the scenario. Presented on November 12, 1939, it had been poorly received, mainly because of a complicated story and cluttered choreography. Not daunted, the Ballet Russe wanted to give an American ballet one more try.

The last ballet Agnes had done for the group and had taken out on tour had been her *American Street,* and it had contained one dance she called "Rodeo," uncomplicated by story. The dance had been composed of the basic movements of cowboys and horses in the rodeo—galloping, bucking, and jumping. Agnes locked herself in her studio for three days working on a series of studies based on but expanding on "Rodeo." "Draining great pots of tea," she wrote it all out. The story she had written for the ballet centered around a Texas cowgirl "who dresses and acts like a man in an effort to stay close to the head wrangler with whom she is infatuated. She succeeds only in annoying all the cow hands and laying herself open to the mockery of the women. In the end she puts on a skirt and gets her—or rather a—man."

Denham liked the scenario and was impressed with her choreography.

"Whom do you want for a composer?" he asked.

She replied, "The best, Aaron Copland."

Copland came to interview her, brought by Franz Allers, the conductor. There being only one chair in her studio, Allers, the oldest of the three, sat on that. Agnes perched on the piano bench, while Copland lay on her bed, "propped up with chintz pillows." When she told him the story of the ballet, he hedged, "Couldn't we do a ballet about Ellis Island? That I would love to compose." He gave in twenty-four hours later as he saw she would not change her concept. ("You be arrogant," the feminine and yet indomitable Graham had told her. "You're every bit the artist any one of them is!")

That afternoon, "over buttered scones," Agnes and Copland had blocked it out minute by minute. "It scarcely deviated by a gesture in the final version," Agnes later wrote. Copland had a completed first section within a few weeks. Denham wanted the well-known artist Pavel Tchelitchew to design the scenery. Tchelitchew did not like the idea of painting something as "banal" as an American landscape. He finally suggested an almost unknown American designer, Oliver Smith (figuring no doubt that he had no reputation to put at stake). The tall, youthful, red-haired Smith (to become one of the theatre's finest set designers) hastily agreed to do the scenic art.

Agnes then told an appalled Denham that she must have complete artistic control and wanted to dance the leading role. Denham at first was adamant in his refusal of both requests. "I really think at that moment I came into my own as an artist," Agnes has said. After much argument, she won final veto on all artistic questions and the right to dance the premiere performance. She asked only fifteen dollars for her performance for the one night. "If you don't like me," she told Denham, "you can then replace me. The cowgirl is a portrait of me...."

Rodeo was premiered by the Ballet Russe de Monte Carlo at the Metropolitan Opera House in New York on October 16, 1942, with Agnes in the lead as the cowgirl, Frederic Franklin as the champion roper, and Casimir Koketch dancing the head wrangler. At exactly 9:40 P.M., "chewing gum, squinting under a Texas hat," Agnes turned to face what she had been preparing for her entire life. *Rodeo* made

Elizabeth
Montgomery's
sketches for costumes
for Agnes deMille's
ballet *Three Virgins and
a Devil*, 1941, hang in
the choreographer's
apartment today

The Ballet Theatre
production of *Three
Virgins and a Devil*,
1941, with Annabelle
Lyon at left, Agnes
deMille in the middle,
and Lucia Chase

dance history and made Agnes famous even beyond the confines of the dance world. The lusty American theme seemed just right for a wartime audience (it has proved itself a marvelous ballet for any era). Agnes's choreographic style was now "inimitably deMille"—action from start to finish (reminiscent of Uncle Ce), not classical, but all dance and danced drama. The opening scene, a wild rodeo dance—imitative of prancing, bucking, galloping horses—sets the mood. Dance critic Walter Terry was to write: "The movements of the ensemble support, enhance, and color the activities of the principals and lesser characters are all part of the choreographic fabric which captures with brilliance, humor and touches with pathos an episode from life in the hearty, healthy, happy west."

The ballet received twenty-two "roaring" curtain calls on opening night. Anna raced home, "and turned on the coffee and turned on the hot chocolate and got the pies out, and kept open house. Everyone kept saying, 'Aren't you proud, Anna? Aren't you proud? Isn't it wonderful?' And she said, 'Not particularly. I've *always* been proud. I was proud of her when nobody wanted her and nobody would hire her, and she was absolutely alone and she kept working every day. Then I was proud.'"

"I don't really say *Rodeo* influenced dance at the time," Agnes has said, "but that night certainly changed my life." Within twenty-four hours, the verdict by the critics was that *Rodeo* was the first great American ballet, and it opened the way for other important American works. But ballet in Broadway musicals, despite Albertina Rasch's occasional dance arrangements, which presented a line of girls on *pointe*, was still almost nonexistent. George Balanchine had choreographed Richard Rodgers's jazz ballet *Slaughter on Tenth Avenue*, for the 1936 Rodgers and Lorenz Hart musical *On Your Toes*. Knowing balletomanes considered this a historic turning point. But six years had passed with only one other musical, also by Rodgers and Hart, *I Married an Angel*, combining ballet of any skill or importance into its production.

On *Rodeo*'s opening night, Theresa Helburn and Laurence Langner, of the Theatre Guild, and Oscar Hammerstein II and Richard Rodgers had occupied a box looking, according to one report, "like four young birds waiting in their nest for their mother to drop a particularly choice morsel down their throats." At this time the Theatre Guild was close to bankruptcy. Theresa Helburn had an idea that a musical of consequence could save them, specifically Lynn Riggs's joyous folk drama, *Green Grow the Lilacs*, which the Theatre Guild had produced as a straight play in 1931, not too successfully.

She approached Richard Rodgers and Lorenz Hart, who had been a successful team for twenty years. Hart was an alcoholic and—what Helburn did not know—the team was at the point of breaking up. Rodgers had given Hart an ultimatum: either he was to hospitalize himself for a cure, or Rodgers would form a new alliance with Oscar Hammerstein II.

"Well, you couldn't pick a better man," Hart told him. And then as he left added, "There's one more thing. I really don't think *Green Grow the Lilacs* can be turned into a good musical. I think you're making a mistake." And so Rodgers and Hart had become Rodgers and Hammerstein.*

Oscar Hammerstein had written the book and lyrics for Jerome Kern's *Show*

Agnes deMille in her gh-spirited *Rodeo*, 1942, he most popular ballet based on American hemes, with music by Aaron Copland

Against Oliver Smith's striking Western set, the cowhands of *Rodeo* do their leaps, in one of the many revivals of the ballet

Boat and *Music in the Air*. But he had suffered a decade of ill-matched partnerships and theatre failures. Four days before he signed to do *Green Grow the Lilacs*, he had completed the libretto and lyrics to a modern, black version of Bizet's opera *Carmen*, which he had retitled *Carmen Jones*. At the time, *Carmen Jones* seemed an uncommercial project at most, although he was convinced it contained some of his best work. Three weeks later, it was optioned by Max Gordon, but Hammerstein was given the time to write the Guild musical first.

Agnes had heard about the Theatre Guild project while she was rehearsing *Rodeo*. The subject lent itself ideally to her style of choreography and she immediately wrote Laurence Langner suggesting herself as choreographer. That was how Rodgers and Hammerstein and Langner and Helburn happened to be in the audience at the opening of *Rodeo*. After the performance, they wired her: WE THINK YOUR WORK IS ENCHANTING. COME TALK TO US ON MONDAY. Agnes was hired. But the project was no overnight success story.

Rodgers and Hammerstein wrote a literate, imaginative show, and the Theatre Guild hired the inventive Rouben Mamoulian as director. Mamoulian had directed the Guild's highly successful 1927 production of *Porgy*, the play that provided the basis for George Gershwin's folk opera, *Porgy and Bess*, which was also under his direction. Equally at home in films and theatre, Mamoulian had made film history in 1935 with *Becky Sharp*, the first feature film shot completely in Technicolor, and his pictorially exquisite 1941 version of *Blood and Sand*, in which many of his images were styled after the great trio of Spanish painters Goya, Velázquez, and El Greco. Agnes's inclusion in the project added the highly uncommercial idea of the use of

164

Agnes deMille in her *Rodeo* costume for an early publicity photograph

ballet. Backers were instantly leery. Retitled unwisely at this point *Away We Go!*, it was envisioned as a folk opera. The response of potential investors was "No gags, no girls, no chance." This translated into "No money."

The show did have girls, but their legs were covered in period costumes. And the story of the courting habits of an Oklahoma farm community at the turn of the century did not seem compelling; nor could investors foresee how a musical with integrated music and book would be commercial. Such integration, though not unique, had lent itself more successfully to the operetta or the earlier comic opera. Until this time, the book of a musical was mostly a tool to present the songs or a star performer. For two decades, musicals had been topical and contemporary—at least those that had succeeded. *Away We Go!* was "a sentimental look at bygone Americana." And more in keeping with folk opera, it contained a choreographed ballet and a fight in which the hero (Curly) kills the salacious heavy (Jud) with his own knife (DuBose Heyward had used this same device in *Porgy and Bess*, where Porgy kills Crown).

For six months after Agnes had agreed to do the show, Theresa Helburn, Rodgers, Hammerstein, and singers Alfred Drake and Joan Roberts "took to the penthouse circuit in their effort to interest investors." The results were discouraging.

Nonetheless, Agnes packed her dream of doing a Broadway musical along with a blank notebook labeled *Lilacs* and made choreographic notes in it on trains and in hotel rooms as she toured *Rodeo* with the Ballet Russe across the country. What she visualized was perhaps far more innovative than what Rodgers and Hammerstein had expected. Dance movement would define character and the ballets would integrate and help to tell the story. And she would add sex to the benign script by bringing to life in dance the dirty postcards that Jud was said to collect.

By letting Lubov Roudenko replace her for a few days of the *Rodeo* tour, Agnes was able to meet Walter Prude in Tennessee and to spend sixteen hours with him on Thanksgiving. The visit was not totally satisfying as they had very little time alone. But Agnes was truly in love. She rejoined the company in Los Angeles in time for opening night.

As a child, she had once dreamed of doing solos on the stage of the Philharmonic Auditorium. Now here she was, "with the most famous ballet company extant, in my own work, a score by our leading composer, brilliant *décor* and for my partner a great virtuoso." Despite this, nothing meant as much to her as her father's presence, nor was any critic's approval as meaningful as his. Agnes for years—for her entire life—had danced for her father, and this was the moment she had always prayed would come.

"The orchestra played splendidly. We danced and acted as never before, and my father sat throughout hearing the laughs turn into hands, hearing the hands turn into calls. I faced about at the end, dripping and breathing and spent, my arms filled with carnations and roses, toward the wings and there, in the exact spot I had stood as a girl waiting to see Anna Pavlova, there under the great column spots stood Pop, smiling and radiant. He was waiting for me.... I dropped the flowers and was gathered home. His suit still smelled of cigar smoke ... he patted my hair awkwardly.... 'I am so proud,' he said. He could not go on.... We stood quietly together. My grease paint came off all over his suit lapel."

She parted with *Rodeo* in California and returned to New York to begin rehearsals on *Away We Go!* (although all the money needed for the show had not yet been raised). She worked in the foyer and men's and women's lounges at the Guild's old theatre on Fifty-second Street, which they did not clean for lack of a cleaner's salary. Her contract with the Guild called for a meager cash payment of $1,500 (for eight weeks' work); no royalties, no further rights of any kind (meaning touring companies, foreign productions, or a film sale, although her dances could—and would—be used in all of these), and an additional $500 if the show was able to pay off all its costs. She hired dancers, not chorus girls, and Marc Platt (who was also her leading dancer) and Roy Harrison as her assistants, and kept three rehearsals going at once.

"I was like a pitcher that had been overfilled," she later wrote, "the dances simply spilled out of me. I had girls and boys in every spare corner of the theatre sliding, riding, tapping, ruffling skirts, kicking." And to Walter, who had just been transferred to Omaha, she confided, "We live in the basement. I see sunlight only twenty minutes each day. The dust from the unvacuumed Guild rugs has made us all sick, and I put away three Thermos bottles of coffee an afternoon. I look awful."

Richard Rodgers recalled that Mamoulian objected that the dancers she hired were not very pretty. Agnes had won, "but Rouben retaliated," Rodgers recalled, "by preempting the stage of our rehearsal theatre for the book rehearsals and forcing Agnes to use whatever other space she could find. One day ... our chief stage manager came over to me and said, 'Sneak down into the lounge and take a look at what Agnes is doing.' There was Agnes, leading her dancers through some of the most dazzling routines I'd ever seen anywhere. If something could look that great in the men's room, I had no doubt it would be breath-taking on stage."

Agnes remained unsure, terrified, *certain* that what she was doing was not enough, that the dances were being created too hastily to be good.

Evenings were spent writing letters to Walter and listening to the war news, which in the winter of 1943 was encouraging. The Germans surrendered at Stalingrad and in North Africa, and the Allies triumphantly invaded Italy. Benito Mussolini was to fall from power in a matter of weeks, but all Agnes could think about was the short time (five weeks) she had to get her dances ready for the March 11 New Haven opening.

With no advance sale and little publicity, the phenomenal audience reception at the opening of *Away We Go!* at the Shubert Theatre in New Haven would have been reassuring, except for the Broadway crowd's lack of enthusiasm. "The wrecking crew," as Ruth Gordon called them—the agents, lawyers, producers and "first-night hounds"—had made the trip up from New York to see how Rodgers had done without Hart. They apparently were unable to convince themselves that an out-of-town audience knew anything about theatre, and they "spread the word that the show wouldn't make it."

The name was changed to *Oklahoma!* and the company moved to Boston. To Agnes's delight, the Guild now agreed to pay her $50 a week for the run of the show. At the same time, she was doubtful she would ever collect it. "There's hell ahead," Agnes wrote Walter on March 10, "and unless we pull the show up very quick we're sunk."

Walter had asked her to marry him and she had agreed. She had hoped to shop for her trousseau in Boston, but there never was any time. The play was reorganized in the two weeks there, with two numbers removed and the entire "Oklahoma!" number restaged, and then Agnes took sick as an epidemic of German measles spread through the company. Four days later, she was back at rehearsals, but Marc Platt had injured his foot and was ordered not to dance for a week; Joan McCracken, the second lead dancer, had collapsed from exhaustion; and two other dancers were also down with measles. But "the matinee went on today in good order," Agnes wrote Walter. "This is a remarkable troupe. The actors are dumfounded. They've never seen such stamina before; they've never worked with real dancers."

They returned to New York with only two days to rehearse before the opening. Platt's foot was still bad. The first night had not been sold out. The Guild subscriptions had fallen very low, and the Broadway crowd were saving themselves the embarrassment of seeing Rodgers and Hammerstein fail. Agnes had ten front-row balcony seats (the only time she ever had seats to the show) and could not give them all away. Anna was there with Margaret, now divorced from Fineman and working as a buyer at Macy's. Agnes had borrowed a black evening dress from her and stood at the back of the St. James Theatre with Rodgers. Platt insisted he would dance the opening, even "if he lost his leg." A doctor anesthetized it. He danced (to marvelous reviews) on a frozen leg and foot and had to be cut out of his boot afterwards.

> The curtain went up on a woman churning butter; [Agnes remembered,] a very fine baritone [Alfred Drake] came on stage singing the closest thing to lieder our theater has produced. He sang exquisitely with his whole heart about what a morning in our Southwest is like. At the end, people gave

Overleaf, right: Agnes deMille's choreography for *Oklahoma!*, 1943, revolutionized dance for theatre: gone were lines of chorus girls and boys interrupting the story; now cowpokes and their rural sweethearts and tavern cancan girls danced their roles. Left: For a 1969 revival of *Oklahoma!* Miles White designed new costumes

an audible sigh and looked at one another—this . . . was music. They sat right back and opened their hearts. The show rolled. . . .

The barn dance opened Act II. Marc Platt in an ecstasy of excitement rode the pain to triumph. Virile, young, red-headed and able, he looked like Apollo and moved like a stallion. The audience roared. . . .

. . . They were howling. People hadn't seen girls and boys dance like this in so long. Of course, they had been dancing like this, but not just where this audience could see them.

Within days the theatre was a mob scene with everyone wanting to buy a ticket to the new hit, pushing and shoving to get to the box office. A policeman had even been called in to keep order. Agnes knew that *Oklahoma!* was a success. No one involved quite understood at the time how great a success. *Oklahoma!* had changed the fashion abruptly and irrevocably in American musicals, which would now integrate book, music, and dance. And it brought back the period piece. And Agnes's abilities "to express moods and feelings, rather than to devise formally traditional exercises," made her the foremost and most sought-after choreographer for the new wave of storied dancing that her ballets for *Oklahoma!* had made the rage. Suddenly Agnes deMille was famous. When she entered Sardi's (then *the* New York after-theatre restaurant), she was recognized and given a front table. *The New Yorker* did a profile. She was photographed with her dancers for *Vogue* (the full-skirted dance costumes in bright ginghams, ballet shoes for street wear, and straw hats with flowers, all designed by Miles White, had become the fashion news of the season). Theatrical managers, agents, and dancers telephoned so frequently that Agnes changed her number. People besieged her for tickets to *Oklahoma!* (she could not even get one for herself). John Martin reported that "the current year was becoming known on the street as the 'de Millennium.'"

So she went to Laurence Langner and said, " 'Laurence, I'm not greedy, but $50 a week is not much to live on. Will you please, in view of the show's success, make it $75 a week.' And Laurence looked around the room as if I'd caught him on a fish line and said, 'Oh, I don't like these conversations at all. Just remember, you haven't got a legal leg to stand on.' I said, 'I'm not standing, I'm not sitting, Laurence, I'm on my knees. I want to get married to a lieutenant [Walter had recently been promoted] who is about to be sent overseas. Please help me.' So then he mopped his brow. He had literally burst into a sweat, and said, 'I couldn't justify such a raise to the backers. I couldn't possibly.' And that was that."*

She began to listen more intently to the offers she was getting from Hollywood and which she had earlier refused to consider. Sam Goldwyn dangled a $750-a-week contract before her. It was more money than she had ever dreamed of earning, and though she loathed the thought of Hollywood, she felt forced to consider it and telephoned Anna for her advice.

"I can pay you back everything. I can help now. I can be a real help."

"What are the terms?" Anna asked.

"A seven year contract. . . ."

"Never," she shouted through the phone. "Never, not for any money. Your freedom is . . . beyond price. You must be able to choose. . . . Think only of the kind of

work you want to do. Don't ever speak to me about paying [me] back!"

Agnes turned Goldwyn down. Then in May she was asked to do a new comedy, *One Touch of Venus*, with a book by S. J. Perelman, music by Kurt Weill, and lyrics by Ogden Nash. The book was disappointing, but she was assured that Perelman was working on it and that it would be in good order for the start of rehearsals in August, with Elia Kazan as director. They offered her a $10,000 advance and a handsome royalty. Walter had a furlough due in June. This meant she would have money for her trousseau, wedding dress, and the time beforehand for a wedding and a honeymoon, so she accepted.

She preceded Walter to Los Angeles, where they were to meet, by two days so that she would have time to make all the preparations. The small, charming All Souls Episcopal Chapel in Beverly Hills was chosen for the ceremony to be held June 14. The reception was to be at her father and Clara's home, after which the newlyweds would train back to Hobbs, New Mexico, where Walter was stationed, for a week together. Agnes wore a tan gabardine suit, to match Walter's summer khaki officer's uniform, and a new straw hat. Her dance assistant, Mary Meyer Green, was matron of honor; Mary's husband, Dennis, a six-foot-four-inch Englishman, was Walter's best man. Agnes walked proudly down the aisle on her father's arm to the music of a Norwegian country wedding march played *fortissimo* by the organist. Her matron of honor claimed that as Agnes started down the aisle she snapped her fingers smartly, " 'And!' [Agnes] said as an upbeat and stepped out. One does not loiter on an entrance or the audience leaves," she had learned. Her father pulled her back, his arm "like a vise," and they "proceeded with propriety" to the altar.

Only nine guests were present, not including the wedding party and Clara. Anna had not been well enough to make the trip, and Margaret could not afford the time. Her Aunt Constance, Cecilia, and Cecilia's husband, Joe Harper, attended for her side of the family.

Though Cecil was no longer an ardent admirer of President Roosevelt, he seldom failed to listen to one of his fireside chats. One evening in April 1942, Roosevelt told the heroic story of Navy doctor Corydon M. Wassell, who had been stationed in Java when the Japanese invaded that country. Ordered to leave behind twelve badly wounded American sailors in the face of the Japanese advance, Dr. Wassell had defied his superior officer and remained with the injured, knowing that he would be captured by the enemy. "But when he was faced with the enemy's imminent arrival, he decided to make a desperate attempt to get the men out of Java," Roosevelt revealed. "He asked each of them if he wished to take the chance, and every one agreed. He first had to get the twelve men to the sea coast—fifty miles away.... The men were suffering severely, but Dr. Wassell kept them alive by his skill, and inspired them by his own courage.... On the sea coast, he embarked the men on a little Dutch ship. They were bombed and machine-gunned by waves of Japanese planes. A few days later Dr. Wassell and his entire flock of wounded men, all thought to have been too gravely injured to move, reached Australia safely." (The president had been wrong in his count. Dr. Wassell had saved *fifteen* wounded sailors.)

The story was a natural for film, and Cecil wasted no time in purchasing the rights to Dr. Wassell's story, which novelist James Hilton had already written for a magazine syndicate. Jeanie did a treatment (although once again she received no on-screen credit), and Alan LeMay and Charles Bennett wrote the screenplay, which they proceeded to embellish with flashbacks that added the love stories of several of the men, including Dr. Wassell (played by Gary Cooper). The film was premiered in Washington, D.C., and in two theatres in Little Rock, Arkansas, Wassell's hometown, on April 26, 1944. The critics found it moving and rousing film entertainment, but were reluctant to endorse it as a factual war movie.

"Actually it is a hopped up melodrama," Bosley Crowther wrote in *The New York Times* on June 11, 1944, shortly after its general release. "True, such a thing did happen. But not this way, we'll bet a hat! And not with the increments of incidents that DeMille and his scenarists have devised.... The truth has been shown grimly in actual [newsreel] films.... So it is not in the least surprising that folks should start in resentful shock [as Crowther had] when DeMille (or anyone) shows them hoopla warfare in a technicolor blaze."

But *The Story of Dr. Wassell* proved to be just the kind of surging drama to meet the wartime demands of inspiration and entertainment, and was one of Cecil's most successful endeavors.

The war personally affected only one member of the DeMille family, Richard, who was first trained in the Army Air Corps photography school, at Lowry Air Force Base, Denver. He was then attached as a corporal and assistant film editor to the Motion Picture Unit of the Army Air Force 18th Base Unit at "Fort Roach," Culver City. Richard had worked as a telephone boy on the set of *Reap the Wild Wind*, attended Columbia College in 1940–42, and then the University of California at Los Angeles the following year, before his induction into the service. In 1944, he married

Richard DeMille
in 1988

For *The Story of Dr. Wassell*, 1944, C. B. again turned to Gary Cooper to play the heroic Navy doctor who braved a Japanese air bombardment to bring his wounded men to safety. Laraine Day costarred in the enormously popular movie

a lovely ballerina named Rosalind Shaefer. He had matured into a restless, insecure intellectual. Citsy recalled that her "Grandfather once said, 'It's a tragedy when a great mind goes wrong,' and he was talking about Richard. No one had told him the truth about his parentage yet. Maybe they didn't tell him because he never fit in with the family's concept of how you thought. Richard was a rebel, more liberal in his thinking than pleased Grandfather." Small of stature, a maverick by nature, he was perceived by one of his peers as "troubled, rebellious, stigmatized at carrying the name DeMille, but truly brilliant."

Richard disagrees that being a DeMille ever presented a personal problem to him. "I thought everybody's father [referring to Cecil] was famous. I didn't know this had anything to do with being special. This is what fathers do—they're famous.... He hoped I'd stay out [of the industry]. He really did not want any more DeMilles being in the movies because there had been enough. He never said this, but I think that's what he felt.... There was very little direction by either parent.... He never said to me, 'What are you going to do in life?' I didn't have the foggiest notion what I was going to do in life, so I just bumbled along going through school. There was very little control of any of the children—a total lack of manipulation. We were allowed to be ourselves. I was basically an idea person, and Father and everybody else in the family were action people.... I was a stranger—it caused some hassles."

But such independence does not seem to be what the DeMilles' three adopted children really wanted. John was now a bank teller, had been married since 1934 to Louise Denker, and was the father of two,* so he was exempt from military service. Katherine was trying desperately hard to be the wife Quinn demanded she be, but after the freedom of choice her background had assured her, this new subordinate role was not easy. She made an occasional low-budget movie, seldom appearing in the lead. Her career was more or less over, mainly because she chose not to pursue roles seriously. Quinn was "insanely jealous" of her when she did work, so her idleness pleased him. Little else did. He continued to play parts he considered demeaning—"third-rate gangsters," Mexican bandits, and poor Indians, "who were always getting the shit kicked out of them by the big strong white man." When Quinn had met Katherine, he had believed he was headed for stardom. By the mid-forties, a decade had passed and he was still playing the same roles but in lesser films. Once he and Katherine had married, his relationship with Cecil had become rocky, and since *Union Pacific*, his father-in-law had not cast him in a picture.

With three children* and the daughter of a DeMille to support in her accustomed style, Quinn felt a heavy responsibility to succeed on the grand scale. "[DeMille] considered his grandchildren by Cecilia his only grandchildren," Quinn says. "The others—Richard's, John's, Katherine's and mine—were just interesting objects....I never understood it. He treated Katherine like a beautiful doll he'd acquired someplace, somewhat daughter—but not really a daughter. When I married Katherine, she owed her father $5,000, which I paid off." Believing also that his marriage would benefit if he could move his family out of the DeMille complex, he went to Cecil for a loan to buy a house in Santa Monica. Cecil asked him for collateral, which shocked and offended Quinn. ("Grandfather wanted it to be a business deal," Citsy recalled. "He felt Tony would keep his pride that way. Tony had an opposite point of view. He did not think family asked for guarantees.")

Cecil was uneasy about Quinn because he could see that Katherine was unhappy. (A few years later Quinn would confess, "Katie would read Krishnamurti. That was her way of escaping to a never-never land. I was even jealous of him. He could bring her the peace I could never supply.")

Julia Faye and Jeanie Macpherson, both now in their sixties, remained part of the family circle. Cecil supported them and still used Julia in small roles in his films. They came to the house, but not as often as before. Though Gladys had replaced them as a sex partner, there seemed to be no animosity among the three women, or Constance. Citsy believes "Grandfather turned to Gladys for sex because she worked with him. It was convenient. There she was, taking notes. There she was, in love with him." More often now when he traveled, Constance remained home, and Gladys and Citsy accompanied him. Cecilia worked for him along with Harper in a business capacity. Father and daughter were still close, and it was Cecilia to whom he confided all his business and family concerns. "One of Grandfather and Mother's favorite things to do," Citsy says, "was plan estates. They loved to do that—like a bucket of gold coins. I'm sure Grandfather's whole will was written at Mother's instigation. She did not want...[the other three children] to have anything to do with power. She wanted it all, and he respected that, and so...[the other three—Katherine, John, and Richard] were taken care of generously and separately with sizable trusts."

Citsy also recalled that her grandfather "drank only moderately—an ounce of bourbon in an old fashioned....He made the drink himself every night, with bitters and sugar. He had a big seltzer bottle that he used. He loved wine but he only had it at special dinners. He was a very, very modest drinker and eater, very disciplined. He took care of his body, his weight, and he could not accept less of those close to him.

"He suffered with tremendous work pressure. I don't think he ever made a movie that Paramount wanted him to make, always a movie they *didn't* want him to make. He was always spending great sums of money—on his life-style and his pictures—so the pressures were enormous. If any one picture had gone under, it could have broken the studio, his budgets were so high [over $4,000,000 for *Dr. Wassell*]. He was always onto another project, always thinking of the new styles, new art, what stories to film, how they related to modern man. Not only what was current. He *made* things current. He changed the way women dressed, their bathrooms, their homes—he changed the world fashionwise."

Every Monday night from June 1, 1936, until January 22, 1945, Cecil was the director and host of *Lux Radio Theatre*, a popular weekly show that under his aegis dramatized successful films, cast with the original stars whenever possible. The show attracted an audience of over 40,000,000 listeners and made Cecil's voice immediately recognizable and DeMille a household name. In terms of personal publicity and money (he received a $100,000 yearly salary), *Lux Radio Theatre* was a great boon to Cecil. However, California's November 1944 general election ballot carried a proposition (number twelve) to abolish the closed shop in the state and give every Californian, union and nonunion, the right to obtain and hold any job. The American Federation of Radio Artists assessed each of its members one dollar to fight Proposition Twelve. A payment was required and refusal meant automatic suspension. Cecil was for (and ultimately voted for) this proposition, and not only refused to pay the token assessed amount, but would not permit his sponsor, Lever Brothers, to pay the dollar for him. Lever Brothers had no alternative but to cancel his contract. Cecil never regretted his stand, but the last radio adaptation under his direction, *Tender Conrad* (a few years later, ironically, to become a picture labeled "Red" by Joseph McCarthy's probe into Communism in Hollywood), starring Olivia de Havilland, June Duprez, and Dennis O'Keefe, was a sad parting. *Lux Radio Theatre* managed to survive another decade under a series of directors, its audience diminishing yearly. But it was generally associated with Cecil's name, the aura of his personality hovering over it until its demise.* Even more ironically, Mitchell Leisen was hired to replace Cecil. "DeMille never actually directed any of those things," he said. "They always had somebody else to do that.... I earned $3,000 a week for a couple of hours' work, but I tried to copy him and they didn't like it.... I only did seven of them."

For two years following the release of *The Story of Dr. Wassell*, Cecil gave his energies to the founding of the DeMille Foundation for Political Freedom (with his lawyer, Neil McCarthy, and William M. Jeffers and Sidney Biddell, who helped Cecil in production), whose purpose, Cecil wrote, "was to work for political freedom and the right to work." The precepts were generally conservative, and the foundation attracted some of the richest and most powerful corporate executives in America who were antiunion, as well as many agitators who were anti-Semitic. The stigma was to adhere to Cecil throughout his life, although he spoke out clearly against these factions, as he made his way across the country speaking at large gatherings, battling to get his union-curbing policy incorporated into the legislature of every state's constitution, succeeding in some.

And as he traveled, his thoughts were turned "to the birth of freedom, and the beginning of the death of slavery in Colonial America." He recalled that one Sunday afternoon when he was reading a book on Colonial history, he came across a

For more than eight years Cecil hosted the weekly *Lux Radio Theatre*, which broadcast adaptations of successful movies. Virtually every star in Hollywood appeared on the program; here Marlene Dietrich, Clark Gable, and Jesse L. Lasky are guests

description of how white men and women had been bought and sold as slaves in the eighteenth century. "I was familiar with the indentured servants, of course; but these were slaves, convicts from England, shipped to the American colonies to be sold by private transaction or at public auction, in conditions often as degrading as those which aroused the nation's conscience against Negro slavery a century later." In typical DeMille fashion, he hired six researchers who spent two years "consulting 2,500 historical sources for authentic data about the period." Then he signed Jesse Lasky, Jr., Charles Bennett, and Fredric M. Frank to write a script titled *Unconquered*; with the "special DeMille brand of theatricality, [it would] ultimately submerge all but the pageantry."

Unconquered had the same $4,000,000 budget as *Dr. Wassell* and was set in Pittsburgh in 1763, when the city was just a log fort in the heart of unfriendly Indian country. "We [the writers] churned out a massive (190-page) screenplay under the master's eye," wrote Jesse Lasky, Jr. "The film opened with dear old C. Aubrey Smith, that paragon of British virtues, as a judge at the Old Bailey (recreated on stage nine) offering murderess Paulette Goddard [later proved innocent] the choice between the gallows and indentured servitude in America. Her decision [to go to America] was not exactly surprising."

Cecil's first consideration for the role of Abby Hale, the beautiful English indentured servant, had been Deborah Kerr, who was then new to Hollywood. As a bargainer, Cecil's rule of thumb was: "Cut the price in half, then argue like hell." One of his associates recalled, "He suggested with more than an inference that the actress's career in America would be greatly accelerated by her appearance in a DeMille film." The agent refused to budge from the $72,000 plus expenses that Miss Kerr had received on her last film. Goddard's agent asked for $100,000 and settled with Cecil (who considered he had won a victory) for the same $72,000.

Bosley Crowther called *Unconquered* "Just about as subtle as a juvenile comic strip and cut on a comparable pattern," which he could forgive except that he found the picture "as viciously anti-redskin as *The Birth of a Nation* was anti-Negro long years back." The *Los Angeles Times* sneered, "sensationalized history." But the film set a record in box-office highs. The *Hollywood Reporter* wrote, "DeMille pictures have a way of infuriating non-DeMille fans into cold rage, a glow matched inversely by the people who like his odd product. Those latter people are the ones to whom Mr. DeMille caters and so far they have never failed to roll up a fat profit for the provider of their vicarious adventures." The pressure was tremendous on Cecil, but *Unconquered* more than tripled Paramount's huge investment, if it added only another title of dubious critical esteem to Cecil's list of sixty-seven films.

By the summer of 1943, the war in North Africa was over. Hope rose that once a landing was made in Europe, German resistance would collapse. Agnes prayed the end would come before Walter was sent overseas. Once again he was being transferred—this time to California. She promised to join him there just as soon as *One Touch of Venus* had opened.

Oklahoma! continued to play to packed houses. Four of its songs were in the top ten of the "Hit Parade."* Agnes's weekly stipend, modest as it might be, looked encouragingly long-lived, and the advance from *One Touch of Venus* had made her financially comfortable for the first time in her career. At last, she had made contractual provisions for a royalty if the show succeeded. Now independent of Anna, she hoped to have a nest egg to set up housekeeping for herself and Walter when the war was over.

Superficially *One Touch of Venus* "was just another of the recent musical comedies with an innocuous plot and contemporary setting." The story was simple. A museum curator (John Boles) unearths a long-lost statue of Venus which he places

Unconquered, 1947, reunited Gary Cooper and Paulette Goddard, who had also played in C. B.'s *North West Mounted Police.* This time Goddard got her man

on display. A young man, Rodney (Kenny Baker), has just bought an engagement ring for his fiancée. In a moment of fancy, as he views the Venus, he places the ring on the statue's finger. Thereupon, as in the Sleeping Beauty legend, he brings Venus (Mary Martin) to life, and she falls instantly in love with him—the man who has been responsible. Venus then sets to work to woo him away from his intended bride, the boring mother-dominated Gloria (Ruth Bond), but, Venus soon realizes, "once a goddess always a goddess" and "in a blinding flash," she is transferred back into stone. Rodney is desolate for he has fallen in love with her. But then, miracle of miracles, a young woman enters looking remarkably like Venus and coming coincidentally from his hometown.

Rehearsals for the dance numbers began in the great studio rooms of the American Ballet School as soon as Agnes returned from New Mexico. The heat that August was overpowering. "Kurt Weill, the composer, sat at the piano, bright eyes gleaming behind thick glasses. Maurice Abravanel, the conductor, sat beside him. Weill had composed a stunning six-minute bacchanal which they now played for the cast four-handed.... This piece was, in Weill's opinion, the finest orchestral composition he had turned out since he had come to America from Germany, on a par with his great early work, *The Three Penny Opera*, [and] *Mahagonny*."

Agnes blocked through two ballets the first week with "the gentle-voiced," short of stature, and marvelously intelligent composer almost always present. Agnes recalled that Weill "used to score [his own orchestrations] in the rehearsal room...through the chaos of shouting, counting, orchestral reading and rows.... His concentration was absolute.... He composed and orchestrated in ink because he made no mistakes." Mary Martin, she claimed, looked like "the Sugarplum Fairy, a pretty, rather unimposing Southwestern girl with a straight body and a flat Texan voice as carrying as someone calling cows, almost unsexed like a choir boy's, of trumpet clarity....

"...She was irresistibly charming...and she was a very real problem. She couldn't walk. She walked like Miss Atlantic City 1927. She couldn't stand. She couldn't raise an arm simply....

"'I'm not very good at this, [she confessed]. I'm going to need lots of help.'" Within one week Agnes had her moving with Olympian elegance.

Five weeks later the company trained to Boston for their out-of-town tryout. None of the previous personal misfortunes such as Agnes had suffered in this city with *Oklahoma!* recurred, but it was obvious that the show needed much work, and the activity was tremendous as scenes shifted, songs came and went, and tempers were strained. Finally, on October 7, 1943, it opened in New York (in "Version V," according to Agnes) during a rainstorm with real thunder and lightning effects outside the Imperial Theatre. Her reviews were excellent, surpassing even those of *Oklahoma!* and—the show was a hit. ("Two triumphs...were Agnes deMille's ballets.... [And] coming just a season after *Oklahoma!* [they] confirm that Agnes de-Mille has replaced George Balanchine as Broadway's leading choreographer.")

Agnes wasted no time in joining Walter in California, but after a few weeks he was transferred again, this time to Jefferson Barracks, St. Louis, and no family or dependents were permitted to accompany him. Agnes returned to New York. A month later, Walter followed, but was allowed only a forty-eight-hour pass on his

Planning *One Touch of Venus*, 1943. From left: Kenny Baker, [E]lia Kazan (director), [S]. J. Perelman (book), John Boles, Kurt [W]eill (glasses), Cheryl [C]rawford (producer), [M]ary Martin, Paula Laurence, [u]nidentified woman. [B]aker, Boles, Martin, [an]d Laurence were in the cast

Mary Martin's costumes for *One Touch of Venus* were designed by the famous couturier Mainbocher

way overseas. Agnes took him to see both *Oklahoma!* and *One Touch of Venus*, wanting desperately his approval, to show him what she had accomplished. But Walter's response was cool. "Our little shows seemed [to him] cute as store windows and just about as important," she wrote, "...related in no way to the vast, the momentous and quickening impulses in which he now lived." When they parted after his time was up, it was to be for two years. Work was the only cure for the emptiness she felt and she went right back to it.

Ballet Theatre requested a new work. Agnes decided upon "a gay and bawdy romp in the style of Watteau, a composite selection from Gluck." A young composer, Paul Nordoff, wrote a thirty-five-minute score complete with overture which "although only one third original Gluck, was so perfect in style and vivacity that the musicologists detected no forgery." Named *Tally-Ho!* or *The Frail Quarry*, the story revolved around the charmingly decadent young men of a French court, and the frail quarry are the women they pursue. The ballet's main characters are a studious husband, who neglects his pretty wife; the wife, who seeks to make him jealous; and a prince eager to help her oblige. Walter Terry was to call it "an engaging comedy, which derives much of its humor from a juxtaposition of aristocratic elegance with primitive instincts."

Directing the ballet turned out to be anything but comedic for Agnes, who also danced the role of the Wife with Hugh Laing as the Husband, and Anton Dolin as the Prince. "Anton (Pat) Dolin* is basically kind," Agnes explained, "...but he could never resist wicked Irish mockery. He could never resist taunting Hugh....

"...[T]heir styles were irreconcilable. I began to devise the scenes so that they never appeared jointly. Inasmuch as the story depended chiefly on their interrelation, this proved a drawback of consequence." Tension began to mount, and it did not help that Walter's letters were infrequent and when they arrived the censor had done a hatchet job on them.

The Los Angeles performance went better than she expected (seventeen cur-

179

tain calls; Agnes took three bows by herself); the critics called it "pure Gainsborough." But she knew New York audiences were tougher.

"I should say something cosmic, I suppose," she wrote Walter on the eve of the New York opening, "but like you on the eve of our marriage, 'I've said I love you and that covers everything and I'm dead beat.'...

"...If you were here I think I'd be having a drink, and then I'd have a hot tub and you'd rub my back and feet and then maybe you'd read me some poetry and put me to bed and hold my hand. This is not an important work, but it had a point, or I believed it had. I wonder how much shines through?"

When she arrived at the theatre, she was stunned to find a box of violets on her dressing table with a card from Walter [arranged through Anna], and when she finally staggered up the stairs to her studio long hours after the New York premiere, somewhat reassured by the audience response and a good review by John Martin, there "beside the bed stood a young apple tree in full bloom, its arms spread out over the quilt, the blossoms pallid and clear and unmoving in the breathless room." And on her pillow lay another card from Walter. She had not been so moved since her father had come that one time in Los Angeles to see her dance. After all, Walter understood how very much her work meant to her and how badly she wanted him to share some part of her feeling for her art with him.

"Every worker recognizes his own devices," Agnes wrote in a self-revelatory review of her own work:

> I can name mine easily....I have an affinity for diagonal movements on the stage, with figures entering at one corner and leaving at the opposite....Why in one corner and out the other?...Could it be because the first fine choreographic design I ever saw was the *Sylphides* mazurka danced by Lydia Sokolova with the Diaghileff ballet?...But behind this reason, there must be more.
>
> I use a still figure, usually female, waiting on the stage, side or center, with modifying groups revolving about, always somehow suggesting the passing of time and life experience. Why does the woman waiting seem to me so emotionally pregnant? One woman standing alone on the stage while people pass until a man enters upstage behind her. Why upstage and why always behind and why the long wait? I cannot be sure, but I remember waiting for years, seemingly, shut away in my mother's garden. My father was absent most of that time and I longed for him to come home to release me from the spell. Possibly the answer is somewhere here.
>
> Why is my use of circles, open or closed, a constant? The avoidance of symmetrical design, with the exception of the circle, my acute difficulty with all symmetrical design, even including square-dance pattern, which one might think was my native language? My repeated use of three female figures, a trilogy which because of plurality takes on symbolic force? And the falling patterns—the falling to earth, the swooning back, the resurrection, the running away always to return to a focal point—seem also to be insistent; and more important, more gross and unbearable, the breaking of all lyric line with

a joke, as though I could not trust emotional development but must escape with a wisecrack....

...I seem to be obsessed by an almost Henry Jamesian inability for hero and heroine to come together happily, and by that other bedeviling theme, the woman as hunter....

...[B]ecause I am a choreographer, I respond through my instinctive gestures....

"There is a further personal identification in choreography because most choreographers compose on their own bodies," she added, observing that they have a tendency to favor their most spectacular abilities and to eliminate their weaknesses.

At dawn on Tuesday, June 6, 1944, the Allied Expeditionary Force crossed the English Channel and invaded the northern coast of France. Walter was not in the invasion forces, but in the course of the months that followed, he flew active bombing missions over Germany. Finally, letters from him came through. He was unharmed. Agnes "lived from moment to moment."

Work was the immediate answer to her sense of loneliness, and happily she was asked to choreograph a new Civil War musical titled *Bloomer Girl*, with a score by Harold Arlen and lyrics by E. Y. ("Yip") Harburg. She took the job "in order to do a ballet about women in war," thankful that she would at last have a chance to put on stage what was in her heart. Arlen had played her one of the score's outstanding songs, "The Eagle and Me," an "impassioned, tuneful plea for racial understanding," and she had been moved and impressed. But the book of *Bloomer Girl* was "superficial, somewhat silly, if entertaining...and had very little seriousness of purpose or artistic cohesiveness."

The story centered on the rebellious daughter, Evelyn (Celeste Holm), of a prosperous hoopskirt manufacturer who supports her maverick Aunt Dolly Bloomer (Margaret Douglass) in a campaign to replace hoopskirts with the item of clothing that would eventually carry her aunt's name. The ballet Agnes conceived did not have much relevance to the plot, but it did set the scene and give the show a subtext of some consequence. The producers gave Agnes a free hand, but they were under the impression that the ballet would have the lighthearted comedic touches for which Agnes was now famous. What she presented to them once the show was in rehearsal was a passionate antiwar ballet of great tragic strength. It opened with some girls saying good-bye to their men, who were going off to war. Then the body of a dead soldier was brought on stage, and after a ballet sequence, the widow was left standing alone beside his body. Agnes was pleased with her effort ("a rushing, running thing with a steady beat that sounded like the wind," she later called it). In near repetition of her failure to please her Uncle Ce in *Cleopatra*, Arlen had told her, "No. No. No. This is all wrong. Where is the wit? Where is the humor?... This is tragic. This isn't real de Mille. This isn't what we bought."

Furiously, Agnes shouted back at Arlen, "How the hell do you know what real de Mille is? I think this is the realest thing I ever did. It is not *Oklahoma!* if that is what you mean. If you wished to buy *Oklahoma!* you're a little late."

Finally, after everyone had cooled down, Agnes "whipped up a happy ending in which everyone returned from war unscathed and there was great rejoicing." A

week later she showed this version to John Wilson (the producer), the director, and Arlen and Harburg. But the new ending did not lighten the tone of the preceding ten minutes of the twelve-minute ballet. Harburg wailed, "Oh, my God. Can't we get rid of this somber, dreadful ballet? . . . Women will faint. They'll weep. They'll leave the theater."

"You don't know women," Agnes countered. "They'd rather have their grief talked about and shared than made light of."

The final decision was to eliminate the ballet unless Agnes rechoreographed it. Harburg's proposal called for the ringing of victory bells and was, in Agnes's words, "all very Fourth of July—war was over, nobody died, and peace was declared in ten minutes." She composed four ballets in four weeks. By this time, the show had had three directors and six writers, all demanding authority. "Vilification was rampant," Agnes bitterly remembered. " 'I'm going to have your paranoids removed,' yelled one author to another at the close of a gala rehearsal. 'Homo, Sweet Homo,' sang someone under his alcoholic breath." Agnes and Harburg finally came to a compromise on the ballet. The Fourth of July touches would be toned down and the soldier's body removed. In Philadelphia after the first out-of-town rehearsal, Wilson told Agnes, "[The ballet] is beautiful, but it's going to ruin our show. The whole War Ballet in its entirety has to be deleted." He offered to give her the ballet material for her own property to perform elsewhere later and to replace it with a singing chorus for which she would not be responsible.

After considerable pleading on her part, he finally agreed to let the ballet be presented in the first performance in Philadelphia and then to cut it. Since there was to be only one performance, Agnes had the dancers do her version without the happy ending. There was silence at the end of the ballet, "no one breathed. . . . Women bowed their heads." Afterwards, one woman handed Agnes her son's Navy wings and Yip Harburg conceded, "Goddamit! I've begun to like the dreary thing." The ballet was to remain, and after the New York opening (October 5, 1944), Agnes had the satisfaction of having Wilson confess to her, "Darling, it gives me great pleasure to state we were quite, quite wrong." The Civil War ballet had received the highest single praise of anything in the show and given it a stature the flimsy material could

Agnes deMille's famous Civil War ballet for *Bloomer Girl*, 1944, lifted the musical above the frivolous feminism of the plot to express the anguish of women left at home during the bloody four-year conflict

not have attained on its own. With the war painfully prolonged and a predominantly female audience, *Bloomer Girl* played over 600 performances and Agnes deMille became the first woman to equal the accomplishment of Irving Berlin, George Gershwin, and Cole Porter: she had three hit musicals running simultaneously.

In November 1944, Theresa Helburn and Laurence Langner asked Rodgers and Hammerstein if they would do a musical play based on Ferenc Molnár's *Liliom*, which had been successfully produced in 1921 by the Guild in a straight dramatization by Benjamin F. Glasser, with Joseph Schildkraut and Eva Le Gallienne, and again in the 1940 revival featuring Ingrid Bergman and Burgess Meredith. *Liliom* was the story of a shiftless but charming carnival barker (Liliom) in Budapest and a young factory worker (Julie), who loves him and is left pregnant with his child when he commits suicide rather than be arrested for an attempted robbery. Sentenced by God to sixteen years in Purgatory, he is finally allowed to return to Earth for one day to atone for his sins. He searches out his daughter, but when she refuses a gift of a star from him, he is whisked away from Earth presumably to Hell.

Rodgers and Hammerstein quickly replied in the negative to Helburn and Langner, and stated their reasons: the Hungarian setting lent itself more to operetta than to musical theatre and the difficult dialect was unsuited for lyric writing. The settings were gloomy, the mixture of realism and fantasy hard to adapt for a stage musical, and the ending bitter and downbeat.

Langner and Helburn pleaded with them to think about it for a few days. During that time, Rodgers came up with a musical concept for a song in which Liliom discovers he is to be a father and "sings first with pride of the growth of a boy and then suddenly realizes it might be a girl and changes completely with that thought."* Having conceived a song for a character, the collaborators were more inclined to accept the idea that *Liliom* could be musicalized. After several discussions, they decided the story might be set in New England rather comfortably, which would avoid the Hungarian dialect "zit, zat, and zose." They agreed tentatively to do the show. Now Molnár's permission to adapt *Liliom* for a musical had to be obtained. Molnár had previously refused to allow Giacomo Puccini to adapt it for an opera ("I want it to be remembered as Molnár's *Liliom*, not Puccini's *Liliom*," he had said). Molnár, in the United States since the war, was invited to see *Oklahoma!*, and he consented.

The Guild gathered virtually the same staff that had worked on *Oklahoma!*: Rouben Mamoulian as director, Miles White as costume designer, and Agnes as choreographer. "Remembering the nervous tension during the preparation of *Oklahoma!*, Dick and Oscar warned Mamoulian at the outset that he had to maintain a good relationship with Agnes. The two worked much more closely in this production, and the prologue was in fact a joint effort," one observer commented.

From the start of Agnes's involvement, it was agreed that the work—now called *Carousel*—was to open with a ballet pantomime that would introduce the main characters and set the scene. Liliom—now Billy Bigelow—spots the lovely Julie at the amusement-park carousel where he is the good-looking but troublesome carnival barker. Julie is attracted, but uncertain. Finally she acquiesces. This was the first chance Agnes had to do a show ballet that moved the plot forward, and she dug right in with great enthusiasm and success. Agnes admitted that "*Carousel* was a tough

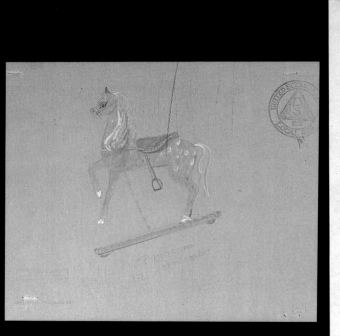

Spanish Dancer in Carnival opening

COLOR SKETCH for CENTER of S.R. TRAVELER
ORNAMENT (FRAME SAME AS S.W. ORNAMENT)
for CAROUSEL   DES. by Jo Mielziner

show for the choreographer because it was based on a strong and well-written play and there seemed small need for dances." The second-act ballet was her hardest challenge, for it brought on a lot of characters the audience had not previously seen. She "struggled and strained, but at last the bosses avowed themselves pleased." They departed for their out-of-town tryouts feeling confident.

The opening in New Haven stunned everyone. None of the second act came off as they expected. A conference was called immediately following the performance. In two hours, Mamoulian, Rodgers, and Hammerstein had drastically cut half of Agnes's ballet, five completed scenes, and two songs.

Just before the Boston opening, the tragic news came that President Roosevelt had died, putting a terrible pall on the dress rehearsal. That night the revised ballet and the new ending were tried out. "Well," Rodgers said with relief to Agnes when the curtain came down to thunderous applause, "I wouldn't have given you a nickel for it this afternoon.... It's all right now, kid," he added, hugging her. "You've got a hit." New York confirmed this was the case when *Carousel* opened at the Majestic on April 19, 1945.*

Agnes had reached her apogee. She had choreographed four consecutive Broadway hits; *Rodeo* was now considered a ballet classic. She could not possibly read all the scripts that were being offered her, and Hollywood was constantly on the telephone. At last she was financially secure. She bought a mink coat and furnished her apartment for Walter's return.

But the war dragged on, and that winter Walter was sloshing through the mud and snow with the First French Army in Bavaria as a liaison officer. The German Army had capitulated. Agnes's greatest fear was that he might now be transferred to the Pacific front. As summer approached, he wrote her that there was a possibility of his being transferred to London. It seemed to Agnes at the time a miracle of sorts that she had just been offered a musical movie titled *London Town* to be filmed in London. Private permits to travel to England were next to impossible. Despite her apprehensions about the script, she accepted the assignment.

The film industry in Great Britain had never had any success in the making of musicals. *London Town* was an attempt by the Rank Organization to disprove the maxim that this genre was impossible outside Hollywood. The project had been the idea of American director Wesley Ruggles (brother of actor Charles Ruggles), who had written the screenplay and was also set to produce and direct. Ruggles had started his career in silents as a Keystone Cop and then in 1917 became a director. His most famous film had been the 1931 adaptation of Edna Ferber's *Cimarron*, the only Western ever to have won the Academy Award for Best Picture.

The story of *London Town** had to do with backstage theatre life during the war. Agnes arrived in England on June 2, 1945, the date of her second anniversary. She read the script that night and found it "far, far worse than anything" she had expected or ever attempted. The next day Ruggles had her look at the costume sketches and had the score played. "The songs were terrible and so were the dance ideas." One scene called for a grand piano forty feet by eighty, made of white satin and "while twenty girls in evening dress played it, a group of witches were to dance around a caldron on top."

For five weeks Agnes struggled with an impossible situation, but with a de-

In this Cecil Beaton photograph, the board of the Ballet Theatre is meeting, c. 1946. Standing: Agnes deMille and Oliver Smith; seated: Jerome Robbins, Lucia Chase, and Aaron Copland

Opposite: Rehearsal for *Tally-Ho!*, April 1946, four days before the birth of Agnes deMille's son, Jonathan Prude. John Kriza and Janet Reed rehearse in foreground, left. Diana Adams is doing the arabesque at right

lightful star, Kay Kendall (in her first starring role). Walter had not yet been transferred, and it appeared now that he very well might remain stationed on the Continent. Then on a hot July night the doorbell suddenly rang in Agnes's flat. She expected no one and walked dully to the door. Outside stood a soldier who handed her a newspaper.

"Your evening paper, madam," he said.

Finally they had been reunited, but only for twelve days. After that, they would be parted for another three months while he did a tour of duty. Then in August, a month later, an atomic bomb was dropped on Hiroshima. Walter was rerouted to New York. But Agnes was contracted to remain four more months in London. They spent a weekend together and then parted again. A few weeks after he departed, he called from New York to wish her a belated happy birthday. Agnes was the one to give him the true surprise. "We're having a baby!" she shouted over the bad transoceanic connection.

The week before she left for home, Walter had been formally demobilized and had accepted a job as assistant to Sol Hurok, and she had been offered a new Rodgers and Hammerstein show, *Allegro*. The ocean voyage aboard the *Empire Ettrie*, a captured German freighter, took seventeen days. The small ship crossed in a wild November sea. Agnes was neither sick nor cold.

One day in the spring of 1946, Jeanie Macpherson called Cecil to tell him she was too ill to come into the studio for a story conference on *Unconquered*. That night he learned that she had been taken to the hospital and rushed to her side. The doctor confided that she had inoperable cancer and had only a few weeks to live. From the

moment he learned this, Cecil spent part of each day with her at the hospital. "There were misunderstandings between us sometimes," he confessed later, "but when for the last time I left the hospital room where Jeanie was dying, I could be glad and grateful that they had all been healed."

Jeanie's death marked the end of a very special era in Cecil's life. For two decades, with Jeanie's presence to remind him, he had been able to keep alive the vivid memory of those first years in Hollywood. "He once told me Jeanie could have had anything," Citsy recalled. "All she had to do was ask. Of course, she never asked.

"Jeanie was the great love in his life—outside of Constance. He talked about her a lot. She shared with him that most important time when you are in your thirties and you're going up. From what Grandfather said, I knew the thrill he and Jeanie had had in what they were doing together—the films, the pioneering in a new industry, watching time after time the major successes of their collaboration."

Difficult as she might have been in the last years of her life, Jeanie had been a focal point of Cecil's career, often dictating by her creative ideas the path his films would take. The early social dramas, the sex comedies, the religious epics and spectacles were in good part Jeanie's inspiration.

He had always invited a harem. Anne Bauchens was still his editor, Gladys his right hand and his mistress, Florence Cole and Berenice Mosk his studio secretaries for more than twenty years, Constance his wife and guardian of his home, Julia his charge, Cecilia his confidant, and Citsy his adored granddaughter. But Jeanie had brought fire to his life, and with her death, despite the years that had passed since they had been lovers, that flame lost a large part of its incandescence.

Costume design by David Ffolkes for *Brigadoon*, 1947.
Agnes deMille's choreography was set to music by Frederick Loewe;
lyrics and book were by Alan Jay Lerner. The Scottish setting and never-never-land
plot were a combination that Broadway loved

A Display of Endurance

1946–1959

The power to dominate the mob came out of his guts,
the very core of his nervous life. When I began to direct
I recognized what went into these spectacular displays
of endurance.

—AGNES deMILLE

AGNES DID NOT SPEND THE REMAINING MONTHS OF HER PREG-
nancy reclining on a sofa. Almost immediately upon her return to Walter and to New
York, she took on the choreography of an unworldly tale of two hunters who lose
their way one night on a murky brae amid Scottish woods and fall upon a quaint village they had not noticed moments before. This is the magical *Brigadoon*—a town
created when a village minister asked God to "make Brigadoon and all the people in
it vanish with the Highland mist. Vanish, but not for always. It would all return jus' as
it was for one day ev'ry hundred years. The people would go on leadin' their custom-
ary lives; but each day when they awakened it would be a hundred years later." The
musical team of Alan Jay Lerner and Frederick Loewe, who had written two previous
unsuccessful musicals—*What's Up?* in 1943 and *The Day Before Spring* in 1945—was
responsible for the book and score. This, their third show, was to make them two of
the brightest stars on Broadway.

Before *Brigadoon* was a perfect vehicle for Agnes's talents. The show was perhaps too
highly romantic. But the fresh setting, the charm of the story, and the strength of
such Lerner and Loewe songs as "The Heather on the Hill," "Almost Like Being in
Love," and "Come to Me, Bend to Me" counterbalanced any shortcomings. The
start of her association with *Brigadoon* was touched by the magic of her private life. At
home she now had a ten-month-old son, Jonathan Prude, born April 24, 1946. She
went through all the trials of rehearsals and out-of-town tryouts fairly light of heart.

189

She created one extremely rich ballet that encompassed the chase where the hero (David Brooks) inadvertently trips and kills the villain (James Mitchell), who has threatened to destroy the miracle of Brigadoon.

The show opened to rave reviews at the Ziegfeld Theatre in New York, on March 13, 1947, and played 581 performances, and 685 at His Majesty's Theatre in London. Sadly, two weeks after the opening, Anna died of a heart attack. But if Agnes thought that after *Brigadoon* she might now rest on her laurels and her royalties, she was mistaken. For it was not long before Rodgers and Hammerstein interrupted her short respite from the theatre to ask her to work with them on a new show, *Allegro*.

Allegro was the first original musical Rodgers and Hammerstein wrote. Hammerstein had been responsible for the concept. In the beginning, he planned to write a broad-scale work about a man from cradle to grave, which would deal with what ambition does to a man's integrity. Because of a close friendship with his own doctor, he chose medicine as the man's profession. Rodgers, whose father and brother were doctors, liked the idea. They decided that in order not to have a rambling story, the action would be limited from the hero's birth to his mid-thirties. Even so, they realized that they needed "something like a Greek chorus to bridge the scenes, comment on the action, and talk and sing directly to the actors and the audience." This meant they had to achieve "a smooth interflow of narrative, songs and dances," and this led them to a daring decision to place the show in the hands of a single guiding person who would be director, choreographer, and musical director. They both agreed on Agnes as that person.

> When I first heard [the score of *Allegro*, Agnes recalled], I was so shocked and disappointed I went home and told my husband I was absolutely taken aback, and he said, "Don't do this show."
>
> And I said, "But it's the first time a dancer has been permitted to do a

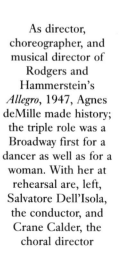

As director, choreographer, and musical director of Rodgers and Hammerstein's *Allegro*, 1947, Agnes deMille made history; the triple role was a Broadway first for a dancer as well as for a woman. With her at rehearsal are, left, Salvatore Dell'Isola, the conductor, and Crane Calder, the choral director

David Ffolkes and
Agnes deMille helping
with costumes at a
Brigadoon rehearsal.
Her recasting of
traditional native
dances profited
immensely from her
vast knowledge of
dance history and
feeling for folk forms

The dancer and actor
James Mitchell played
the villain in
Brigadoon, a role rich
in dramatic expression
that produced some of
Agnes deMille's finest
choreography

directorial job, and it's the first time that a woman has been allowed to do such a job, and I don't know that I will ever again get another."

And he said it was no opportunity if it was a bad show. And I said, "Well, I love the men. I trust the men. And they're marvelous professional workers and I'm sure they'll pull it through. I'm going to take the chance."

Hammerstein had been working a full year on the first act, and when he gave the opening pages to Agnes to read, "she found them so beautiful that she cried." When she received the first scenes of the second act, she called Hammerstein, much alarmed.

"Oscar, you're writing several plays at once. You're all over the map," she warned.

"Well, I'm deep into act two. When I'm finished we'll get together." By now production had been set and Hammerstein was working against a deadline. He finished one week before rehearsals began.

"Oscar, what is this play about?" she asked.

"It's about a man not being allowed to do his work because of worldly pressures."

"That's not the play you've written," she countered. "You haven't written your second act."

Hammerstein's comment was, "But we're already committed to the theatre in New York."

Agnes began rehearsals with a script that had no valid second act, an unwieldy cast of forty-one principals and about a hundred more in the chorus, dancers, and staff, a complex set by Jo Mielziner consisting of "an intricate series of platforms, treadmills, pendulum stages, curtains and loudspeakers in front of a huge screen on which images were flashed" and with financial pressures by the Theatre Guild to bring the show in on time. Hammerstein, Agnes recalled, "was giving me sections of a new story line and script every morning, and with the dancing chores I simply could not keep up, so I told him he would have to step in and stage his rewrites, and he did."

"Agnes is supreme as a choreographer," Rodgers later commented, "but to our dismay we found that she was unprepared to take on the additional chores of directing the dialogue and staging the musical numbers." This was unjust, for it is doubtful one person could have successfully handled all three jobs on such a massive enterprise. In the end, Hammerstein functioned as director on all book scenes while Agnes staged the songs. "It was not a satisfactory solution by any means," Rodgers commented.

"Now you'll learn something . . . about the *geschrei* we go through," Hammerstein told his young protégé, Stephen Sondheim, just seventeen that summer, who worked on the show as a "go-fer," fetching coffee and typing scripts. Sondheim was not disappointed. Rehearsals were a nightmare with his mentor writing new scenes at five in the morning to be incorporated each day, songs being moved in and out, and Agnes often on the edge of a collapse.

The show's premiere at the New Haven Shubert Theatre in September 1947 was a disaster. In the first act, a set collapsed, causing a five-minute break while it was repaired, smoke from a trash fire at the back exit of the theatre panicked some of the audience and sent them rushing to the exits, and Lisa Kirk, one of the stars of the show, fell into the orchestra pit as she was singing "The Gentleman Is a Dope." (Two cellists caught her and hoisted her back onto the stage, and she continued with the number to a great ovation.)

By the time the show reached New York, the technical difficulties had been smoothed out, but Hammerstein had never been able to solve the problem of the loose second act. It opened at the Majestic on October 10, 1947, one night after the well-received Jule Styne musical *High Button Shoes*. *Allegro*, as it came from the team who had given life to both *Oklahoma!* and *Carousel*, promised to be an even bigger hit. One critic called it, "An out-and-out failure." However, Brooks Atkinson at *The Times* wrote that "[Rodgers and Hammerstein] have created a first act of great beauty and purity, as if *Our Town* could be written to music." Most of the critics found that the rambling story had failed to inspire any live ballet. This could well have been the case. More likely, Agnes's talents were too fragmented by her responsibilities to concentrate on her strongest suit—dance. But *Allegro*, despite its failings, was interesting theatre. Audiences attended it for 315 performances, and Agnes retained the credit "Direction and Choreography by Agnes deMille." Noting this, Brooks Atkinson added to his comments, "Rodgers and Hammerstein seemed to be trying to create a musical play from the inside out, as if music and ballet were a single form of expression...all contributing equally to the whole impression."

The experience on *Allegro* for Agnes was both painful and instructive. Twenty-five years later she was to recall the experience with blurred memory:

> When I was beginning my career, I had no endowment and was very poor. I felt sorry for myself, naturally, and as it turns out, quite foolishly, for in many ways the hardships were beneficial. I played the piano for rehearsal, I arranged and copied music, I designed costumes, shopped for material, cut and stitched, packed, pressed, and hung. I learned lighting, lit and ran performances, I rehearsed groups and myself, I took charge of printing, wrote copy and advertisements, organized photographic sessions, signed leases, devised and signed contracts, made up the payroll and kept the books. I also devised all my dances and performed them. The first time I walked into a theatre as a director-choreographer, I was the master of the situation, although I had never directed before in my life, and the job was an enormous Rodgers and Hammerstein musical. There was nothing technical that could daunt or bewilder me, however; I'd done it all before on some scale or other. The theatre was my tool.

All of her claims to experience were certainly true, yet *Allegro*'s demands had been too much for her and she really had not been "the master of the situation." The show could not be called a commercial success. And even had she been able to bring some binding and innovative ballet into the show, dance could not have covered for the lack of story coherence in the second act. Hammerstein always took the blame for this, but Rodgers somehow felt Agnes had let them down, and sadly they were never to work together again.

For *Fall River Legend*, 1948, Agnes deMille drew on the story of Lizzie Borden, who was accused of the ax murders of her father and stepmother. Nora Kaye plays Lizzie here, Peter Gladke is the father, and Lucia Chase is the stepmother

For the next year, perhaps because of the pain and humiliation and difficulties connected with *Allegro*, Agnes moved away from the musical comedy. However, the association had taught her a great deal about story and the need to sustain it. She applied this knowledge to her first love—the ballet—and worked out a scenario for one of her most fully realized works, *Fall River Legend*, based upon the true story of Lizzie Borden, an unmarried woman of Fall River, Massachusetts, who was accused of killing her father and stepmother with an ax in the year 1892.* Lizzie was acquitted of the crime and lived out her life in her hometown. But in Agnes's version, written for the Ballet Theatre, she is condemned to death on the gallows.

Ironically, Agnes achieved in her ballet (consisting of a prologue and eight scenes) exactly what Hammerstein had failed to do in *Allegro*—she had followed the story of a person from cradle to death. Morton Gould composed the music, a moving, tortured score with some lovely melodic passages. Agnes had created the leading role especially for Nora Kaye, but illness kept the famous ballerina from dancing the New York premiere (April 22, 1948). Alicia Alonso stepped in to dance the role for her. Kaye assumed the role shortly after and the part was to become associated almost exclusively with her. *Fall River Legend* was a brilliant success and reestablished Agnes as one of the strongest creative forces in American theatre.

Next she took a brave step in agreeing to direct a Broadway production of Benjamin Britten's opera, *The Rape of Lucretia*. In the late nineteenth and the early years of the twentieth century, opera had been performed at regular Broadway houses as well as at the opera house of the period. With the advent of operetta and musical comedy, however, Broadway audiences became attuned to lighter entertainment. But the previous season Gian-Carlo Menotti's *The Telephone* and *The Medium* had met with astonishing success. Since Britten's opera was more intimate than one thought of in grand opera and contained only six characters and a so-called chorus of two (a man and a woman), it was not unreasonable to assume it at least had a chance in commercial theatre. But Menotti's work told two good contemporary stories and the writing was popular. *The Rape of Lucretia* was a grim, starkly tragic telling of André Obey's *Le Viol de Lucrèce* (adapted for Broadway by Ronald Duncan) and concerned the seduction of Lucretia, wife of the Roman general Collatinius, by the Etruscan prince Tarquinius.

In February 1947 Agnes deMille directed Benjamin Britten's *The Rape of Lucretia*, with (at left) Giorgio Tozzi as Tarquin and Kitty Carlisle as Lucretia

A Display of Endurance

Despite Agnes's talent for choreographing rape and seduction, and the opera's often lyrical prose and atmospheric music, New York audiences did not welcome the work. It opened at the Ziegfeld on December 29, 1948, and closed a few weeks later. Still, for Agnes, staging the opera was a minor triumph and certainly no mean accomplishment for a choreographer. Opera had a certain cachet attached to it and there was great respect for those connected with it. The theatre world henceforth looked at her with unabashed awe.

Agnes now took time off to be a wife and mother. But when she was asked to choreograph a musical version of Anita Loos's best-selling novel *Gentlemen Prefer Blondes*, she found she could not refuse. Though on the surface the book about Lorelei Lee, the little girl from Little Rock who rose from humble beginnings to become Harry Winston's best customer, was not unusual, it had great flair and a marvelously brash score by Jule Styne and Leo Robin that helped conceal its mediocrity. Lorelei Lee was played by Carol Channing, "a towering amazon of a girl with big wide-open eyes." From the wildly festive mayhem of the opening number as the *Ile de France* is about to sail from the French Line pier with the blonde, brassy Lorelei Lee and her brunette friend Dorothy (Yvonne Adair), through scenes depicting the tourist attractions of Paris, to a glittering finale at the Central Park Casino, with Lorelei sheathed in dazzling red sequins, *Gentlemen Prefer Blondes* was "splashily mounted." Agnes had to trade her more serious inventions for a kind of glitz usually saved for the genre of Hollywood musicals choreographed by Busby Berkeley. The challenge was great and the result spectacular. *Gentlemen Prefer Blondes*, which opened on December 8, 1949 (just six months after *Oklahoma!*'s 2,248th—and last—performance), was a runaway hit and would, along with the irrepressible Miss Channing, regale audiences at the Ziegfeld for 740 performances.

Gentlemen Prefer Blondes was exactly the kind of commercial success that Agnes's Uncle Ce could applaud (and did, for he was in New York at the time of the opening); naughty but yet naïve, expensive, expansive, and thoroughly entertaining. His niece's grand success appeared to ameliorate all the differences they once had. Agnes might have been hurt by Cecil, but she had always admired him and could not have helped being genuinely pleased at his approbation.

Because he had not had the benefit of a college education, Cecil was fond of saying, "I have been accused of not being able to read, but no one has ever said I can't add." Then he would proceed to tell a story that emphasized his shrewd way with the dollar. His favorite tale went back to his early days in movies when they poured chemicals from the film-developing room down an empty gutter that ran to a nearby sewer.

"The chemicals discolored the gutters and we were warned by the City of Los Angeles to dispose of the solutions in some other way. A kindly soul came along and offered to haul away the hypo for twenty-five cents a tank," Cecil would begin. "I did a little figuring and found he couldn't make expenses that way. While I am a great believer in human kindness, I never heard of anyone doing anything for nothing so I refused his offer.... A few days later he came back and ... said he would pay me twenty-five cents a tank ... I told him I would not sell the stuff at all but would go fifty-fifty with him if he let me in on his secret."

Agnes deMille did the choreography for *Gentlemen Prefer Blondes*, 1949, the hit musical based on Anita Loos's hilarious novel. Miles White designed the costumes

195

Cecil would pause dramatically and open his top desk drawer and take out a shiny block of silver.

"I've kept this all these years," he'd say, "as a reminder to be careful when someone wants to buy something from me. It's solid silver. You see this man had discovered that the silver in the hypo could be reclaimed. I learned his secret and it paid most of our chemical bills for quite a while."

Cecil was very much the mule trader despite his lavish personal life-style and the size of his film budgets. And though Paramount was always asking him not to discuss the costs on his films, as the amounts seemed vulgar, he paid little attention. He was in New York when *Gentlemen Prefer Blondes* opened because his latest film, *Samson and Delilah*, starring Victor Mature and Hedy Lamarr, was to be premiered a week later, and he had come to sound the drums. As a mask for the sexual overtones of the film that had created extreme censorship problems, Richard Condon,* the head of Cecil's publicity department, deluged women's clubs and fashion and retail outlets with Edith Head's pseudo-Minoan designs. Tie-ins with over seven hundred manufacturers had been arranged "to flood the market with everything from Delilah sandals to perfumes and costume jewels.... In the name of the Bible and History." Condon sent out hundreds of packets filled with educational materials on Minoan civilization to schools, churches, and movie exhibitors (though the research was impressive, little of it was reflected in the film) to counteract groups like the Legion of Decency, which chastised Cecil "for producing a film portraying Samson and Delilah as a morally corrupt couple yet billing it as a religious film."

The most talked-about item in the film was a cape made entirely of peacock feathers worn by Hedy Lamarr. Stories had circulated that this was the same cape worn by Gloria Swanson in the scene in the lions' den in *Male and Female*. Cecil was furious that the public might believe he had used a "left-over" from some other De-Mille epic and told *The New York Times* that he had personally followed molting peacocks around his ten-thousand-acre Paradise ranch, "catching feathers as they dropped and saving only the best for Delilah's cape."

"Of course, he didn't go out and gather dirty bird feathers," *Samson and Delilah*'s top designer, Edith Head, declared. "My own staff helped collect them [from Paradise] and bring them in. We sorted them by size, color and brilliance. It took days. A 'left-over' indeed. DeMille never used anything that was left over from something else; he was too egotistical for that."

Edith Head was now in charge of Paramount's costume department as well as having become one of the top designers in Hollywood, and perhaps the most famous. Not since the early days of her association with Cecil had she got on well with him. Their temperaments clashed. Unlike the women in his personal harem, Head refused to either do his bidding or accept his word as final. Cecil fought back by insisting on Head being a part of a team of designers, and threatening instant dismissal if she did not follow his instructions.

"I always had to do whatever that conceited old goat wanted, whether it was correct or not," Head related later with great bitterness. "He never did an authentic costume picture in his entire career, and in my opinion that made him a damn liar as well as an egotist.... I thought of him as a freak, trying to play God. He never treated [his staff] as if we were talented—we were supposed to feel honored, and *know* we were good simply because we were working for him.

"I will never forget the day I mustered up the strength to complain that he never complimented my sketches. He snapped back at me, 'If I didn't like them, I wouldn't let you work for me.' " To make sure that finished costumes were the same as the sketches he had approved, he kept a photostat of each on file in his office and sent back any costume that contained any new or deleted element even if she, as head of design, felt the final version was an improvement. Head insisted a call to his office "with its stained-glass windows, vaulted ceilings, bear rugs, enormous oak desk ...and his elaborate lighting setup" was meant to intimidate any recalcitrant employee and did. "He would flick a switch and shine a bright beam directly into my eyes....when I realized that taking off my glasses would reduce the effect, [I removed] them before entering his inner sanctum."

Cecil had been considering doing another Bible story for years. Finally, the idea of *Samson and Delilah*—in his words, "the greatest love story ever told"—came to him. However, the story from Judges 14–16 refers to *three* women in the super-strong Samson's life; one is his Philistine bride who betrays him, the second her sister, whom he not only rejects but then, presumably along with her entire family, home, and guests, destroys; and the third—years later—is "a woman in the valley of Sorek, whose name was Delilah." Most schoolchildren know that Delilah tempted from him the secret that his strength came from the length of his hair, then had it cut to make him vulnerable to capture and blinding, and how, when his hair grew again, he vented his vengeance by pulling down the temple on himself and his enemies.

As a film drama, the Bible scenario would not work, but before Cecil called in Jesse Lasky, Jr., and Fredric M. Frank for their first story conference, he had the answers. Make Delilah a composite of the first two Philistine women whom Samson scorned, have her miraculously escape death when he "unleashes a holocaust," and then a few years later have them meet again (Samson of course not realizing it is the same woman). "The woman scorned becomes the instrument of high tragedy. We understand why Delilah seduces the secret from Samson. We have the magic formula—love becomes hate becomes love!" Lasky wrote of that first conference. "We can now prepare the treatment and screenplay for an ideal DeMille film."

Cecil had recently hired Phil Koury, a former reporter and movie critic for the *Kansas City Star*, as his executive assistant. Koury attended most of the story conferences held "in the small box like, single-story building [called the 'bungalow'] that sat with quiet dignity in a corner of the vast Paramount studio grounds." Cecil used his home office for company affairs, private meetings, and film showings. When not actually filming, he would work there until noon and then depart for the studio, a distance of roughly two miles, taking a swift driver as little as five minutes, an element, according to Koury, "important [to the staff] because of the ceremony attendant upon his arrival....At the moment DeMille headed his car down the winding private roadway [from his home] a call was made by Gladys to the studio—'Mr. DeMille is on the way.' " The staff was then alerted. If he had sent word in advance that he wished to see one of them, he or she was expected to be seated in the bungalow outside Cecil's office awaiting his arrival. Koury added that Cecil's "progress from garage to his office was unimpeded...the street door to the bungalow was propped

Left: In *Samson and Delilah*, 1949, Cecil B. DeMille returned to the Bible for his story for the first time in more than twenty years. Hedy Lamarr and Victor Mature starred, with George Sanders, Angela Lansbury, and old retainers Henry Wilcoxon and Julia Faye among the cast. Above: Norman Rockwell painted Mature as the blinded Samson in his chains. The temptress, Lamarr, wore this peacock-feather cape

open, an assistant taking a stand at the garage entrance across the street to seize Mr. DeMille's inevitable valise as he stepped from the car."

The bungalow contained a succession of small staff offices that opened into a narrow hallway running the length of the building. "At the far end," Koury recalled, "like a jeweled crown on a stick, were Mr. DeMille's quarters." Writers were not allowed to go off independently to write, but were expected to work in the bungalow so that they would be on hand at all times and so that Cecil could control their daily output. "He felt he could drive them to greater literary heights if he kept at them," Koury commented. "He once told me, 'I fracture my writers. I keep at them until they are half crazy and in the end the blood and tears will get me what I want. I rarely accept their first efforts.' "

Koury made notes on some of the story sessions on *Samson and Delilah*. "You have got to get it down where I believe it. Joe and Mabel down behind the cotton mill by the Los Angeles River. When you get [Samson and Delilah] on that basis, it will be true," C. B. told his writers one time. And another: "When Samson comes into this wonderful place to take refuge—when [Delilah] pulls him in, he sees this little girl that he kicked out. The little girl who has run away from home to go to hell. We must play with that situation like a cat plays with a mouse. It's beautiful stuff. She may keep her back to him for a while . . . and then she turns around. He sees who she is. And he cries out, 'Jesus H. Christ! *Delilah*!' "

Edith Head's verdict on Delilah, played by Hedy Lamarr, the actress reputed to have the most spectacular face and figure in films, was somewhat more restrained.

"Beautiful, yes," she agreed. "A great actress? I had my doubts. . . . Dressing her wasn't easy. . . . She [had] specific demands about how things should fit. DeMille wanted her to look voluptuous, but she was small-busted and she wouldn't wear padding. She told me she couldn't act if she felt she had unnatural proportions. So I draped her and shaped her until I finally achieved DeMille's required sensuousness. . . . Often when she would come into my salon for fittings, she'd float past my secretary, one hand dramatically placed on her forehead, and immediately plop down on the floor, complaining that her back gave her constant pain, that she had never been the same since she had had children. She'd get up to fit a dress but in between pinnings she'd plop down on the floor again, which gave me the impression that her back wasn't really aching; she was just lazy. We fitted a multitude of rather bare bras and skirts for her role as Delilah, but the real work came from helping her get up off the carpet!

"We ran into constant sexual discrimination with the censors. . . . It was okay for instance to wrap Victor Mature [Samson] in a loin cloth with his navel showing, but if Hedy's navel was exposed it was censored. If I stuffed it with a pearl, we got by." Head was to regret giving in to Cecil on the peacock cape. "I have always had the feeling that it was entirely wrong. I doubt very much that there were any peacocks around or nearby in the days of Samson and Delilah. Nor would anyone, even Delilah, have worn the kind of cape that I designed—or any of the other costumes for that matter. I suppose only scholars would know that the costumes were not historically correct, but it bothered me terribly."

While *Samson and Delilah* was in production, Cecil was asked to play himself in a scene for *Sunset Boulevard* being filmed on the Paramount lot with his onetime

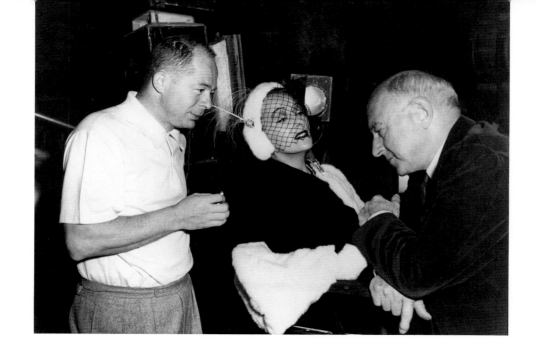

C. B. portrayed himself in seven movies. Probably his most notable appearance was in *Sunset Boulevard*, 1950, directed by Billy Wilder (left) and starring Gloria Swanson

leading lady Gloria Swanson. Edith Head was the designer for that film as well, and she created a bizarre hat for Swanson to wear in her scene with DeMille that had a large, single peacock feather as the focal point. As *Sunset Boulevard* was not a De-Mille film (Billy Wilder was the director), she did not hesitate to use this leftover feather from Delilah's cape.

"Mr. De Mille took direction like a pro," Swanson recalled. "Erich von Stroheim [playing her devoted butler in the film], on the other hand, kept adding things and suggesting things and asking if scenes might not be reshot—very much in his grand old manner of perfectionism regardless of schedule or cost."

Cecil was having lunch in the commissary just before the last scene of *Samson and Delilah* was being shot. Jesse Lasky, Jr. and Fredric Frank—who had both been on the payroll as writers for a number of years (Lasky longer than Frank)—were discussing some final details when Cecil, beaming across the table, said, "Well, that's it, fellahs. Good job. You're finished.... Collect your final check and go home after lunch."

"You mean we'll be—off salary?" Lasky asked in shock.

Cecil admitted that was the case. "Just like that," Lasky later commented. "After years of diligence.... Working till nine or later most nights. Saturdays on the ranch. Or the yacht. Nightly projections at his house. All ended—to be cast adrift on the seas of unemployment as casually as a dismissal of strangers. It was too much.... It was also illegal. Our Writers' Guild required ... two weeks' severance pay." Lasky went to the unit's business manager, Roy Burns, and insisted he be paid what was due him or he would report the infraction to the Guild.

"For *two lousy weeks'* pay you'd stick a knife into *him*!" Burns said.

"Moments later the famous booted stride thundered toward us down the hall.... [C. B.] closed his eyes a moment, wounded to the core.... 'Caesar had his Brutus—' he said. 'I have you.'... His hand moved slowly toward his pocket.... 'I was going to say thank you for giving me your devotion, and a script to be proud of—a film that will outlive us.... I hope you will accept—for your devotion and effort—above and beyond the call of mere duty—these tokens of my appreciation and esteem!'"

Cecil bestowed upon Lasky, who had worked for him for ten years, "one of his mint fifty-cent pieces—in lieu of two weeks' salary." Lasky pocketed the token, and Cecil walked away smiling.

Samson and Delilah was voted the most popular picture of 1950 and became the biggest box-office money-maker to that date, outgrossing *Gone With the Wind* (which as it kept on reaping in receipts from replays won back its title as number one the following year). Cecil received his usual "mixed bag" of reviews. When the Academy Awards were handed out, *All About Eve* won the Best Picture award. *Sunset Boulevard* was voted the Best Story and Screenplay. Both the stars of those films— Bette Davis and Swanson—were overlooked in favor of Judy Holliday's performance in *Born Yesterday*. *Samson and Delilah* was not totally ignored. It won Best Costume Design Color and Best Set Direction Color.

Gone With the Wind was the one film that Cecil wanted desperately to overtake in revenue, popularity, and esteem, and David O. Selznick, its producer, was the single Hollywood producer he considered a true competitor. Besides Margaret Mitchell's great Civil War epic, Selznick had been responsible for such giant movie entertainment as *King Kong, A Tale of Two Cities, A Star Is Born, The Prisoner of Zenda, Rebecca, Spellbound,* and most recently, *Duel in the Sun* and *The Third Man*. Both men approached their films in much the same way. ("Great films are made in their every detail according to the vision of one man, and through supporting that one man," Selznick claimed.) Both men agreed on giving their audiences a big show with plenty of lust and sentiment. But whereas Cecil believed in sex, religion, and spectacle, Selznick affirmed he must add to his films an "idealism worthy of a Thomas Mann."

He once wrote to his father-in-law, Louis B. Mayer, who was considering having DeMille film *Joseph and His Brethren*:

> Cecil B. DeMille is, of course, one of the most extraordinarily able showmen of modern times. However much I may dislike some of his pictures …it would be very silly of me, as a producer of commercial motion pictures, to demean for an instant his unparalleled skill as a maker of mass entertainment…. As both professionally and personally he has in many ways demonstrated himself to be a man of sensitivity and taste, it is impossible to believe that the blatancy of his style is due to anything but a most artful and deliberate and knowing technique of appeal to the common denominator of public taste….
>
> But there has appeared only one Cecil B. DeMille. Nothing is more appalling than second-rate DeMille; the result is the vulgarity without the showmanship which makes his work acceptable and even applauded by those of taste, albeit tongue-in-cheek; there is the size and spectacle without discrimination; there is the "big theatre" without the rough but clever balance of characterization and character relationships; there is the indiscriminate use of resources to the ultimate extent, without any realization of why they are being used, but instead only the hope that the sheer weight and volume will produce a result, and there is the final resultant expense without the final resultant gross….

A Display of Endurance

[But what must not be forgotten is that] what can be superb in a De-Mille film can be disastrous in a film of more integrity; and what can be superb in a film of more integrity can be disastrous in a DeMille film....You must go "whole hog" in one direction or another.

After receiving this letter,* Mayer abandoned the project.

In April 1948, Selznick had announced to the press that he planned the following year to film a circus drama entitled *The Greatest Show on Earth*, admitting to *The New York Times* that "the idea of doing a picture with that title and the cooperation of the Ringling Brothers and Barnum and Bailey Circus must have occurred to a lot of people over the years, but we [Selznick International] plan to give a conception of what actually happened during an entire season at the circus. It won't go back to Barnum—that is, it won't be a historical film—it will be contemporary, with personal stories included against the background of the circus." At the same time Selznick revealed that he had made a deal with John Ringling North, president of the circus, for a "profit-participation" arrangement, and that background shooting in the projected Technicolor production would start in the circus's quarters in Sarasota, Florida, that winter. A crew was then to follow the Big Top to Madison Square Garden and on the road, and wind up at the Selznick lot in Culver City. It was to be the highest-priced picture he had ever produced: $6,000,000 (*Gone With the Wind* had cost $4,000,000).

The Greatest Show on Earth, 1952, an appropriate title for any DeMille extravaganza, was filmed in part at actual circus performances. James Stewart took cues for his role from famous clown Emmett Kelly (second from left) and Betty Hutton learned trapeze techniques to do her own stunts

Selznick had no writer assigned yet to develop this story. The title belonged to North who used it as his circus's slogan. Aware of how important his cooperation would be in the making of the film, North drove a hard bargain, requesting a 50% interest with no investment other than his permission for Selznick to use "The Greatest Show on Earth" as a title, the circus grounds as sets, and his contracted performers as technical advisers as well as acts in the film. Lawyers fought out these terms for several months and just when a deal appeared to be struck, Selznick changed his mind, withdrew, and devoted his energies to a projected version of *War and Peace* (never to be made by Selznick).

Cecil has claimed he had fostered the same idea a decade earlier. Whether that is the case or not, at this stage he stepped in and closed a deal with North granting him 50% of gross *after* the film recouped twice its negative cost, an upward sliding scale from that point, and a substantial fee for acting as the film's technical adviser ($250,000).* On July 24, 1949, Cecil and North called a press conference. Like Selznick, Cecil announced that "This is not to be a history of the circus.... We will tell the story of the circus and its people in relation to all other people." North commented that he hoped Ann Sheridan (a personal favorite of his) would have a starring role. Cecil smiled tolerantly but did not commit himself to any casting.

Unlike most DeMille films, *The Greatest Show on Earth* was to be based on an original screenplay, and for nearly a year, writers came and went as Cecil tried to piece together a suitable story. Phil Koury wrote that "DeMille's antics during this period were not of a kind to endear him to his writers. He flayed them in conference, then openly at staff luncheons. There were moments when he seemed close to panic. Costs were piling up. More than $50,000 had gone into writers' salaries. There were thick stacks of material, conference notes, bits of plots and miscellaneous ideas—but nothing drawn together into dramatic sequence."

Then Cecil had an idea. Cecilia's son, Jody Harper (Citsy's half-brother), was eight years old at the time and loved to watch films with his grandfather. "When Jody says, 'That's the bad man, grandfather,' or 'That's the good man,' I know all is well with the story," he told the staff at lunch one day. By this time five writers had been on the script and he turned to one and asked him to bring him an outline of a circus story that Jody could understand. The writer came back a few days later with seventeen typewritten pages that began:

> Once upon a time there was a circus and the boss of this circus is a strong, tough young fellow called Brad Gable. Brad lives and breathes circus ... he eats and drinks circus. Brad is in love with Holly, the flyer, but Brad could never tell Holly that he loves her. In fact, he hardly admits it to himself. He knows it isn't good for the boss of a circus to be in love with a performer. When this happens he gets to worrying about her because she might fall and be hurt. She becomes more important to him than the circus, which shouldn't be....

Cecil was delighted, and on this simple approach to character, he overlaid a story he lifted from the old silent circus film *Variety*, which had starred Emil Jannings and in which the two members of an aerialist team, a husband and wife (one the catcher, one the flyer), were insanely jealous of each other. As the anger between them mounted, so did the suspense, with the audience fearing the worst—that one would cause the other to fall. Now there was Brad, the circus manager, and Holly and Sebastian, the two flyers, and as the sixth writer set to work, Angel, the elephant girl who also loved Sebastian, and Phyllis, the wise-talking, softhearted iron-jawed woman. Cecil had most of the elements of a good story but he needed a plot twist to intensify the drama. A seventh writer was brought in and the last plot device set in place; a new character was added: Buttons the clown, in reality a doctor on the run from the FBI for a "mercy" killing, who never removes his clown makeup and who in the end reveals his identity to save the circus manager's life after a train wreck.

The script now ready, Cecil figured the only way for him to learn about the circus was to tour for six weeks with Ringling Brothers. With Gladys by his side, his granddaughter Citsy, one of the writers, a publicist, and Phil Koury, he joined the circus in Milwaukee (where he was photographed carrying Gladys over a mud pond) and took the northern swing with them. Koury describes him as "a stalking figure in breeches, boots and open shirt, peering through a camera 'finder' at Bengal tigers within a foot of striking range . . . scaling rope ladders to aerialist platforms. . . . " During one performance he was placed in a bucket seat and raised a dizzying forty feet above the highest aerialist platform to see how the circus would photograph from that high angle. He came down, mopping his brow, and advised the circus manager, "It's 101 degrees up there and you need air in this tent. You can get it by opening a slit in the top." Perforations to admit air were later added to the Big Top.

"His pace did not slacken even as the trip wore on," Koury continued. "Only a few of us knew the extent of his fatigue when the day was over. . . . On more than one night, at dinner, he slipped into a sort of semi-consciousness. . . . Gladys Rosson held up his head to keep it from striking the dishes. When he awoke he went right on with his meal as if nothing had happened."

He filmed the majority of the picture on location with the circus. His star performers (Betty Hutton and Cornel Wilde as the aerialists, Charlton Heston as the circus manager, James Stewart as Buttons, the clown, Gloria Grahame as the elephant girl, and Dorothy Lamour as the iron-jawed woman) did many of their own stunts, which meant a four-month stint with the circus experts before filming was begun. Hutton and Wilde learned all the high-flying acrobatics they were to do, and no tricks were used when the jumbo elephant's hoof was raised only inches above Gloria Grahame's beautiful face. Sixty of the circus's best acts were also filmed, as well as a dangerous climax where the circus train crashes and the animals break loose.

For the first time the Legion of Decency gave a DeMille picture a "B" rating which meant it was considered morally objectionable in part for *all* persons. Cecil was dumfounded. "It's a lot of Goddamn hogwash," he told Koury. "Morally objectionable to boys and girls! This is a picture with clowns, elephants, flyers in the air, horseback riders. . . . " But it had not been these aspects of the film to which the Legion had objected. The character of Buttons was the culprit. "With those Catholics, a little euthanasia goes a long way," Cecil commented.

The "B" rating did not hinder the success of the picture, and except for *The New Yorker*'s apathy ("all the wonders of the Ringling Brothers and Barnum and Bailey can't save this picture from becoming rather boring"), the other "class" critics found the film to be authentic, moving, and marvelously entertaining.

The Greatest Show on Earth was Cecil's sixty-ninth film. During all those movies and all those years, he had never won an award or been honored by the Academy, although a few of his technical staff had received Oscars for *Cleopatra* and *Samson and Delilah.**

But *The Greatest Show on Earth* was chosen Best Picture of 1952, and then, as a crowning glory, Cecil was presented the coveted Irving G. Thalberg Memorial Award honoring his long, distinguished career. Cecil's speech to the Academy reflected his bitterness for their years of neglect: "I wish to thank you all for the great patience you have shown me over the years. It was exceeded only by my patience with you!" And after the ceremony, he told a reporter, "They've given me one [Oscar], but I've won eleven!" And to make the evening complete, son-in-law Anthony Quinn was singled out as Best Supporting Actor for his role in *Viva Zapata* as the brother of Mexico's great revolutionary hero (played by Marlon Brando).*

Katherine and Quinn had their fifth child, Valentina Andrea Quinn, on December 26, 1952, but by this time there were serious problems in the Quinn marriage. Within a year's time, Quinn went off to make five movies in Italy. In the last, *La Strada*, he played the brutish Zampano and became an international star. (Cecil hated the film. "Why make a movie about a man's faults?" he said to Citsy. "The picture made me want to take a bath.")

Quinn describes his scene with Katherine before he left for Europe:

> Katie and I sat in a corner booth of a fashionable restaurant that jutted out over the sea. In a few days I'd be leaving for Europe, alone, and in spite of my gut-searching with the psychiatrists we were no nearer the answer [to the problems in their marriage]....
>
> She, too, was looking. Her bedroom was decorated completely different from the rest of the house. It was almost monastic. She had very few paintings on the walls. Those she had selected were pictures of saints and philosophers. On her night table beside her narrow single bed she had photographs of the children and me when we'd all been young. The books beside her bed also were evidence of the world she'd retreated to: Gandhi, Krishnamurti and endless books on Moral Rearmament....

After a long discussion of their past problems and Quinn's hang-ups about his sufferings as an underprivileged child, Katherine countered:

> "Really, Tony, doesn't it seem ridiculous to put yourself and all the people you love through hell because of a twelve year old boy?...My God, you have kids of your own now; would you let them tell you how to live?...I can no longer fight for [your] approval. I frankly don't give a damn....I only pray for my children's approval and God's. If after those [psychiatric] sessions you can't make peace with our lives, I'd rather you found it somewhere else. It's been a long fight and I've found I can't win...."

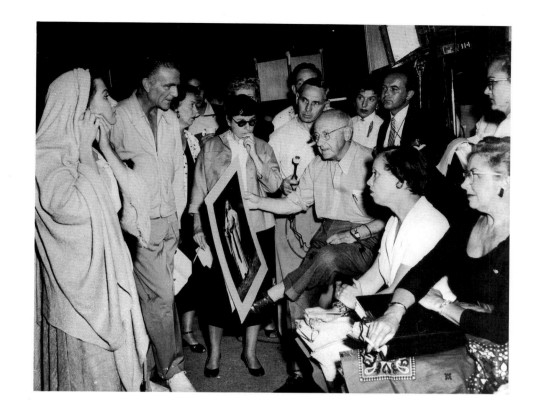

In 1956 C. B. shot a second version of his 1923 blockbuster, *The Ten Commandments*. At left, stars Yvonne De Carlo and the durable Henry Wilcoxon listen as DeMille discusses a costume with designer Edith Head (in dark glasses)

That night, Quinn had a nightmare and ended up screaming and on the floor. Katherine rushed in to see what had happened and shook him. Still not fully free of the dream, he grabbed her by the throat and "almost choked the life out of her. I picked her up and tried to put her to bed. She jumped out of my arms.

"'Leave me alone,' she screamed. 'Don't touch me. I can't live like this. I won't live like this. You're crazy...you're crazy.'

"She was right," Quinn admitted. "We couldn't go on like that." He left for Italy. The marriage was over in all but name.

Within a short time after Quinn's return, his friendship with Cecil began to grow. But now their relationship was on an entirely new plane. Though still married to Katherine, Tony was living a fully liberated life. However, when invited on his own to Paradise ranch, he did not go. "I hated the atmosphere," Quinn says. "My wife borrowed it once. I couldn't wait to get away. It made me uncomfortable. It seemed a place made for pleasure, not enjoyment."

Cecil was in the early-preparation stage of a remake of *The Ten Commandments*. Why retell this story? "The world needs a reminder," Cecil wrote, "of the law of God," especially since the horrors of World War II and "the world's awful experience of totalitarianism, fascist and communist, had made many thoughtful people realize anew that the law of God is the essential bedrock of human freedom."

Actual work on the script was begun in the spring of 1953. "COME WADE WITH ME IN THE RED SEA," he wired Jesse Lasky, Jr., who by now had forgotten his anger at C. B. (or perhaps felt properly chastised for not having been called back to work on *The Greatest Show on Earth*). Lasky readily agreed to be one of the four writers on the project.* From the very beginning, Cecil had decided upon Charlton Heston as Moses. ("My choice was strikingly confirmed," he wrote, "when I had a sketch made of Charlton Heston in a white beard and happened to set it beside a photograph of Michelangelo's famous statue of Moses. The resemblance was amazing.") The casting of the Pharaoh Rameses was also done very early on.

Cecil was in New York in the summer of 1952 with Citsy, Gladys, and an executive assistant, Donald Hayne (who was also helping to edit Cecil's autobiography, then being written), and the group attended an evening performance of *The King and I*, which starred Gertrude Lawrence and Yul Brynner. At the end of the second act, Cecil went backstage, told "Brynner the story of *The Ten Commandments* from the viewpoint of the Pharaoh, I offered him the part, he accepted, we shook hands, I went back to my seat in the theater, Yul became King of Siam once more; and I did not see him again until we were ready for him to become King of Egypt." That took place about six months later.

Lasky's area of the screenplay was based on what he called "a rather bogus assumption . . . that, for [C. B.'s] purposes I was the company Hebrew. The fact that I'd never been bar mitzvah, or even inside a synagogue, and had in boarding-school days been a leader of the Christian Endeavor Society, was completely ignored. He needed a Jew, so Jesse was elected." He was given, as his initial scenes to dramatize, the first Passover feast. Lasky approached it with "a deep sense of reverence and emotion" and then, believing he had written a scene that came "as much from the heart as from cerebral research," returned confidently to C. B.'s office. After Cecil read it, Lasky claimed, "suddenly he was seized by one of those senseless rages that seemed to sweep away reason. . . . I had failed in every respect! . . . I had reduced a great moment in the saga of mankind to Hollywood theatrics! . . . Then, with spluttering finality, [he] spat on my scene!"

Lasky walked out of the office and returned to his own and began to pack up to leave. A knock sounded at his door. He opened it and faced C. B. "Packing, Jesse?" he asked. Lasky nodded.

"Not removing any DeMille property?"

Lasky attempted to control his fury. C. B. continued: "You're—walking out on me—just because of . . . a petty difference of opinion on a scene? I can't believe it. . . ." A curving smile came over Cecil's face, and he said, " 'And the Lord God took dust and mixed it with spittle—and from this he made a *man*.' . . . Not a spoiled child but an adult, who can stand up against criticism. . . ."

"Where in the Bible did you find that quotation, Mr. DeMille?" Lasky asked.

Cecil told him to find it himself and to "keep looking." The quotation was not to be found, but Lasky unpacked his books and went back to work.

Not long before they were to go into production in Egypt, Gladys was told she had cancer. Cecil was beside himself. While Gladys lay dying in Good Samaritan Hospital, Cecil called in the top specialists, and when no one could offer hope, he turned to Dr. Max Jacobson, a charlatan whom a friend of his, Albert Dekker, suggested. Jacobson dispensed numerous addictive drugs to clients (which he then continued to supply for high fees), among them the hallucinatory LSD. Gladys died on June 14, 1953, before Jacobson could administer anything to her, but Cecil, who had been told he had a minor heart condition, now turned to this man for medical advice.

In a scathing indictment, Citsy declared, "Max Jacobson was a cuckoo doctor, who treated Dekker and Alan Jay Lerner and the Kennedys, and he was, of course, finally disbarred. But I know for a fact that he gave Grandfather experimental drugs when he shouldn't have. The man was nuts. I think if it hadn't been for him, Grandfather would have lived much longer. I think he killed him...he was absolutely crazy. I don't know where this Svengali thing was because, if you looked at him, he was disgusting, everything Grandfather always hated. He was sloppy, his posture was awful...and he shot Grandfather full of all these experimental drugs."*

The void that came in Cecil's life after Gladys's death was filled by work on *The Ten Commandments* and suffused by Jacobson's drugs. He spent more of his free time at Paradise, often joined there now by Yul Brynner. "Good old pals just didn't exist any more," Citsy explained. "Yul was extremely bright, spoke many languages, and had no fear of Grandfather (there were very few men who didn't [fear him])."

The Ten Commandments was to be the first film that Cecil made in Europe. Egypt was chosen as the location where the scenes of the Exodus were to be shot. But the country was in great turmoil. King Farouk had been exiled in the summer of 1952, and in 1953, General Mohammed Naguib became president of the new Republic of Egypt. Cecil started immediate negotiations with Naguib and by early 1954 felt that the country was stable enough for his crew to go to Egypt to begin construction on the huge set of the gates of the City of Rameses (using the old drawings of the 1923 version as their models).

That October, he sailed on the USS *Constitution* with Cecilia, Joe Harper, Citsy, Jody, Donald Hayne, Berenice Mosk, Joan Catterlin (a fairly new secretary), and his butler, Joseph Mullen. In Naples, they transferred to the Italian ship *Enotrea* for the journey to Alexandria. Lieutenant Colonel Gamal Abdal Nasser was now prime minister and the man in charge.

The voyage on the final lap had been difficult for Cecil. Everyone except Cecilia took ill and the stress of the journey showed on Cecil. Cecilia immediately became his right hand. "On the Egyptian location, Cecilia was out at the set every day, no matter how late the night before she had been representing me at social functions which I thought up all manner of excuses to escape....if I was occupied or not, members of the company would come to Cecilia for decisions and would get them quick and right. I do not often use the word 'proud,' but this is one place where it belongs; for is there any word that any father would rather be able to use, to tell his daughter what he thinks of her?"

Two weeks after Cecil had arrived, Yul Brynner flew over to join the company, accompanied by "his old friend and mine, Dr. Max Jacobson" and his wife, Nina. Neither Cecilia nor Citsy was happy to see Jacobson, but there was little they could do to counter Cecil's belief in the man.

In Hollywood, the name of Westmore conjured up a remarkable dynasty almost as well known as DeMille. George Westmore and his six sons were the makeup geniuses of the industry. Frank Westmore, the youngest brother, was following in the footsteps of his older sibling Wally (who was the makeup artist on the silent version) and creating the makeup that would bring to the screen the faces of the biblical figures in this DeMille epic. Thirty at this time, recently divorced, and a young man of great charm and good looks, Frank was an attractive bachelor, and from the beginning of this Egyptian odyssey, Cecil had the idea that he would make an ideal husband for nineteen-year-old Citsy. Also present, and much admired by Citsy, was Major Abbas El-Boughdadly, of the Egyptian Army, along with two hundred cavalry troops lent by the Egyptian government to drive the chariots used in the film. The major was also an attractive man, exotic, and extremely virile. He was not, however, Cecil's choice for a grandson-in-law, and Cecil did what he could to bring Citsy and Westmore together.

"I was spending all my free time...with Citsy," Westmore recalled. "We shared many sunrises together, but not the way I would have liked. She had taken to coming to the make-up department every morning at the crack of dawn, sometimes arriving before I did. She would have the coffee prepared and, more often than not, would be deeply involved in conversation with the handsome Major El-Boughdadly. Citsy was crazy about horses...and our spit-and-polish Egyptian Army man was breaking all the rules by letting Citsy ride his horses. Once he even allowed her to drive a chariot. For that he received one of DeMille's more classic chewing outs...."

"Whenever C. B. saw Citsy and me together he would beam with pleasure....I had the impression that he would not object to me becoming his grandson-in-law." Westmore was not yet ready for a new commitment, but he was more than just a little attracted to the beautiful, red-haired, willful Citsy. But he could see that the major was a formidable rival. "I sensed that C. B. loathed the English-speaking major because Citsy spent so much time trailing after him," Westmore has said.

On the morning of the day they were to shoot the Exodus, Cecil arrived at the location at 6:00 A.M. "Suddenly," Westmore remembered, "I heard him shout my name....to my astonishment he said, 'Frank, I want you to put on a galabia and burnoose and lead this Exodus. I can't trust anyone else.'" It was obvious that Cecil wanted to prove to himself and Citsy that Westmore could be a part of the DeMille team.

He strode off and handed me a walkie-talkie, [Westmore continued.] I didn't dare refuse what was essentially a job for the assistant directors. ...Under the galabia I wore nothing but my underdrawers and paratrooper boots, hardly fit footwear for trudging across a desert. I concealed the walkie-talkie beneath my robe and went to take my place directly to the rear of Charlton Heston. Behind us were the twelve thousand extras and what seemed like millions of animals....

Through the two-way radio DeMille's voice said to me, "I will be at the top of the Gates of Tanis with a tied-down camera, Frank. I will be talking to you and letting you know if I want you to move faster or slow down, or to go to your left or right. You will tell Heston what I relay to you. You will inform my assistants in the rear whether to catch up or go more slowly...."

The sun was high by then and scorching.... Through the walkie-talkie DeMille shouted, "Action!" and fired his forty-five [pistol]. I told Heston to move and we were on our way. Behind me I could hear the huge crowd jabbering in Arabic, kids giggling or crying, animals bawling....After many hours we had moved about two and a half miles in the desert. My lungs felt as if they were clogged with sand....DeMille kept talking to me by radio from

C. B. directs
Anne Baxter and
Sir Cedric Hardwicke
(with glasses) on the
set of *The Ten
Commandments*

The largest crowd
scene ever assembled
in Hollywood history
appears in this second
production of *The Ten
Commandments*. At its
head, in the distance,
is Charlton Heston
as Moses

Yul Brynner, an experienced monarch after playing the King of Siam, took on the role of Pharaoh Rameses

C. B. maintained control of all details in making *The Ten Commandments*. He personally initialed the design for this shofar, "if cost OK," as he wrote in the margin

Opposite: Charlton Heston as Moses in the climactic scene, as he cleaves the waters of the Red Sea to enable the Jews to escape Pharaoh's pursuing army

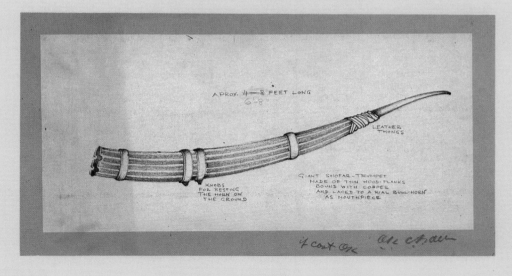

his distant 108-foot-high vantage point atop the gates [of the City of Rameses].

     At about five o'clock, I heard him say, "Frank, will you please tell...." and then his voice stopped.

     Another voice now shouted over the radio, "Something's happened to Mr. DeMille!" This startled the 12,000 extras, who suddenly dropped their spears and torches and raced off across the desert. (Actually, sundown marked the beginning of a Muslim religious holiday.) Westmore hurried back to where Cecil had been stricken (a half-hour hike). Citsy met him. "He's alive, Frank, but he's had some sort of heart attack," she told him. Westmore moved closer to Cecil. Jacobson was with him, pushing everyone aside, yelling at them to stay back. Cecil "was slumped in his director's chair, his face an odd shade of gray and shiny with sweat." Despite Jacobson's admonitions, Cecil insisted on speaking to Westmore. "What happened out there?" he asked in a weak, almost inaudible, voice. Westmore told him about the Arabs running off. "That's all right, Frank," he said, sighing, "I got the shot."

     Against Jacobson's orders, he was carried back on the set the next morning on a stretcher. Three days later, with Jacobson in attendance, he flew back to the United States, and Cecilia assumed command for the rest of the location shooting. Westmore was more or less delighted to look after Citsy, but she was by this time "madly in love" with Major El-Boughdadly.

     The day after Westmore returned, Cecil called him personally to come by the house to see him. Cecil was still bedridden, and Constance led him upstairs to her husband's room. Cecil was hunched up in bed, wearing "a little pointed red cap" (to keep the bald area of his head warm), almost hidden by a mound of books and periodicals. "A beat-up brown card table sagging on wobbling legs" was covered with newspapers and set and costume sketches. Books were piled up on the floor.

     "We talked a bit about the 'flow of true love,' as he put it," Westmore recalled, "and he assured me that he didn't hold me responsible for 'not stemming its tide.' He offered me nonpertinent advice: 'Never give money to a woman. Make her borrow it. Never settle for one woman. Never be humbled by anyone. You can determine almost everything you want to know about a person by examining his feet.' (I had heard about DeMille's so-called 'foot fetish' but had put it down as another ridiculous rumor. Now I realized it was true. A psychiatrist once told me that a foot fetish often indicates a severe genital inadequacy coupled with a rigidly moralistic attitude. Certainly in C. B.'s case, the latter applied, but it was difficult for me to consider DeMille inadequate in any area.)"

     Soon after they returned to Hollywood from their three-month stay in Egypt, Citsy defied her grandfather's wishes for the first and perhaps only time. On July 6, 1955, she was married to Major El-Boughdadly, by the Egyptian Consul in San Francisco, and then returned with him to Cairo to establish their home.

     The remainder of *The Ten Commandments* was shot at the studio with Cecil under constant medical attention and Jacobson near at hand. Vincent Price (in the role of Baka) recalled the shooting of the studio scenes. "In the city building sequence I had to stand in front of a huge, blue velvet screen, stretch out my arm and say, 'Yonder, Pharaoh, is your City of Gold.' Of course, there was nothing there, just acres of blue velvet. So during lunch Cecil took me to the viewing theatre, sat me down and said, 'Now, watch!' And up on the screen came 3,000 extras pulling huge stones, heaving massive logs and enormous carvings. 'That's what the audience will see when you say your line,' said C. B. and by golly when I did the take again after lunch, I really said it with feeling." Reminiscing about the lighter moments, Price recalled the disenchanted woman extra who was overheard saying, "Who do you have to sleep with to get *off* this picture?" During this time, instead of the usual flowers in the center of the luncheon table in the commissary, Cecil had placed a huge, leatherbound Bible. "Not that I ever saw Cecil or anyone else ever open it," Price wryly commented.

The Ten Commandments opened at the Criterion Theatre in New York on November 9, 1956. The reviews were mixed. No one could deny that it was an extraordinary spectacle. But the story had more of the frenzy of soap opera than the religious fervor of a biblical tale. A few weeks later, Cecil flew to England and met with the aging Winston Churchill and was presented to Queen Elizabeth and, moving on to the Continent, had an audience with Pope Pius XII. The film had been nominated as Best Picture (1956), but had lost to *Around the World in Eighty Days*. Pharaoh Brynner had won the Oscar for Best Actor, not for *The Ten Commandments*, but for the arrogant King of Siam in *The King and I*.

Cecil did not allow his physical condition to stop his flow of work. He put Jesse Lasky, Jr., Henry Wilcoxon, and an Englishman, Sidney Box, to work on a script titled *On My Honor*, based on the life of Lord Baden-Powell, the founder of the Boy Scouts. And he acted in an advisory capacity on a barely recognizable remake of *The Buccaneer*, produced by Henry Wilcoxon, starring Quinn and Brynner and directed by Quinn, who recalls only "raw pain" connected with this endeavor:

> I took the picture on a dare from C. B. I hired Abby Mann to write the script along with Jesse Lasky, Jr. . . . [With my help] we wrote what I thought was a wonderful script. . . . We sent the script to Mr. DeMille.
>
> Next day he wanted to see no one but me. I never faced such fury—[he asked:] "Why have you written such a dirty script, a bunch of lies?" . . .
>
> I held my ground. I had all the documentation and references [regarding Lafitte's exploits]. . . .
>
> "What is wrong with the script I shot in 1938?" he yelled.

Quinn told him it was old fashioned. "It was a hit!" Cecil countered, adding: "Are you afraid you can't do as well as I did?" The two men reached an impasse, and in the end Cecil recut the picture to his own specifications. The film was not well received.

William deMille died on March 5, 1955, at seventy-six, after a protracted illness. He had resigned from the University of Southern California in 1953, planning to devote his time to writing, but he had developed cancer shortly thereafter. Constance was ailing and had become somewhat senile. Cecil's thoughts revolved around death, the Bible, and prayer.

"In the Midrash Rabbah there is a beautiful legend about Moses on Mount Nebo," he told one interviewer. "It says that just before God took Moses to Himself

C. B. on *The Ten
Commandments* set in
Egypt, with local
residents who served
as extras

He showed him an immense vision of the victories and defeats of God's people throughout history. One part of the vision was a view of what the Midrashic writer called 'the Temple of Heaven that the earth shall build.' We build that temple by our lives and deeds. I think that . . . the only stones worthy to go into the building of that temple are lives and deeds according to God's Law. And I hope and pray that in that temple my work may be one small stone."

On June 18, 1958, two days after he had testified before a subcommittee of the United States House of Representatives in Washington on behalf of the right to work (and against union control of jobs), he suffered his second, and more serious, heart attack. He made a partial recovery and by August 12, on the occasion of his seventy-seventh birthday, he attended a luncheon in his honor at the studio. There-

On his seventy-seventh birthday, C. B. was feted at his office by old friends. From left: Anthony Quinn, Henry Wilcoxon, Mary Pickford, and Bob Hope. Cornel Wilde looks on from the photograph on the wall

after, he came into Paramount for an hour or so nearly every day. "Against the advice of his family," he flew to New Orleans in early December for the premiere of *The Buccaneer*, and then attended the New York opening at the Capitol Theatre December 22. At Christmas, he came to the studio to distribute his gifts to his staff. With the success of *The Ten Commandments*, he had taken 10% of his share (50% of the gross) and divided it equally among the fifty people he believed had contributed the most to its success.

He visited his office again on January 9, 1959. "We have a lot to do in the next three years," he said in parting.

His condition weakened. A few days later Quinn came to see him. "He was dressed in a flannel robe. We sat in the courtyard near the long hall library. The sun was weak.... I knew it was the last time I would see him. I was sincerely sorry. We both could have learned so much from each other. As I got up to leave, afraid he was growing tired, I said: 'You know in Europe I learned a very nice thing! ... Men hug each other on saying good-bye.'

"I took the frail man in my arms. He made a feeble attempt to hug me. In that minute out of twenty-odd years we became father and son ... [and] I still love him deeply for that minute when he was in my arms."

Cecilia and her husband, Joseph Harper, were at Cecil's bedside when he died twelve days later, the morning of January 21. The funeral was held at St. Stephen's Episcopal Church, Hollywood, on January 23, followed by burial in Hollywood Cemetery in the family tomb, where he was placed to rest between William and Beatrice.

Agnes was in New York, where she had recently added two more Broadway shows to her credit: *Goldilocks* and *Juno*, the latter adapted from Sean O'Casey's *Juno and the Paycock*. Cecil Blount DeMille's death marked the end of an era, but the DeMille dynasty shone brightly and was now in the capable hands of Beatrice's granddaughter.

217

C. B.'s granddaughter Citsy (Cecilia Presley) riding the camera used to shoot *The Ten Commandments* in 1956. Behind her is the primitive camera used to shoot *The Squaw Man* in 1914

Agnes deMille in a photograph by Irving Penn, 1948. She is wearing the flat-heeled shoes and full skirt popularized for women's fashion by *Oklahoma!*'s costumes

Jonathan Prude with his mother, Agnes deMille, bagging lilies at their garden at Merriewold to prevent the deer from eating the blossoms, early 1960s

The Dynasty Continues

*I had no cane. I had no arm. I had no support. I had
no companions. I was alone out there, absolutely alone.
And the curtain went up and I stood exposed. And all
I could think of was, "Let me not drop the bouquet."
I stood alone and Walter's eyes filled with
excitement. . . . I stood without wobbling. I extended my
arms again and the right arm did not waver. I held it
high. And I did not drop the bouquet.*

—Agnes deMille

THE MOST CONTROVERSIAL AND POWERFUL TELEVISION PRO-
grams in the mid-to-late 1950s were Edward R. Murrow's *See It Now* and *Person to
Person*. Murrow was possibly America's greatest broadcast journalist. During World
War II, his voice was almost as familiar to the radio public as was President Roosevelt's. He once claimed to have been "on the side of the heretics against those who
burned them because the heretics so often proved right in the long run. Dead—but
right!" Murrow had always gone against the tide. When Senator Joseph McCarthy
had hit his most virulent demagogic stride, Murrow led a television attack that contributed greatly to the Red-baiting senator's downfall. Hollywood had come close to
destruction with McCarthy as the industry was torn asunder by the probe, accusa-
tions, and innuendoes of the House Un-American Activities Committee.

For all his conservatism, Cecil had not been one of McCarthy's supporters.
"Grandfather refused to be bullied," Citsy contended. "He had his own ideas on
what made a loyal American. And he did not support the blacklist. Eddie Robinson
was one of the blacklisted actors, but Grandfather starred him in *The Ten Commandments*. He saw what McCarthy was and what the witch hunts were and the only way
he could say 'This isn't right' was to hire blacklisted people, which he did."

Agnes, on the other hand, spoke out where she could, and the best soapbox
was Murrow's prime-time television programs. On December 6, 1959, on the program *Small World*, Murrow pitted Agnes in a debate (begun as a "conversation")
with actress-columnist Hedda Hopper, whose extreme right-wing beliefs and position as a member of the press had destroyed many lives during what later became

known as the McCarthy Era. Once the two women got going, Murrow sat back and let the fur fly.

Hedda Hopper [claiming Communist-inspired film writers were attempting to give an erroneous picture of America to the public]: There was a picture made several years ago [1955] called *The Blackboard Jungle* [from the novel by Evan Hunter]. Now, that showed the pupils of a high school—dreadful, dreadful people. That picture did a great deal of harm. I've talked to people in South America, one from Brazil. She argued for one hour. She said you can't tell me the high schools [in America] aren't like that.

Edward R. Murrow: You're mistaken, Miss Hopper. It did not do any harm to America. It proved that America was able to be free enough to tell things on itself.

Agnes deMille: Hear! Hear!

Edward R. Murrow: Which is the best proof you could give to the whole world about freedom.

Hedda Hopper: Yes, but in the other countries you can't persuade them that [the school in the film] was one single high school.

Agnes deMille: Hedda, dear, let me tell you something. . . . We have as English and American people committed every crime in the book. But this is our unique distinction and perhaps honor. At the time of the commitment there was always a man on his feet on the floor of the House denouncing the iniquity. This is our way of living—this way of having the freedom to stand up and say, "This won't do," and if ever we try to suppress our own voices to ourselves just so other people who are less informed will get a glossy picture of us—we're lost. We've given up our big freedom.

Hedda Hopper: And our big freedom is what?

Agnes deMille: The ability to protest freely among ourselves—not to subvert, not to betray—to protest and to criticize freely among ourselves in whatever medium we choose to use. Don't you agree, Hedda, dear? I'm *sure* you agree with that.

Hedda Hopper: Well, that shut me up completely!

Agnes continued to work in the Broadway theatre through the 1950s (choreographing for *Out of This World*, 1950; *Paint Your Wagon*, 1951; *The Girl in Pink Tights*, 1954; *Goldilocks*, 1958; *Juno*, 1959) and into the early 1960s (*Kwamina*, 1961; *110 in the Shade*, 1963). Two of these enterprises were to enjoy moderate success—the Lerner and Loewe show, *Paint Your Wagon*, and *110 in the Shade*, A. Richard Nash's musical adaptation of his own play, *The Rainmaker*. She considered the "rollicking, boom-or-bust" gold-rush musical by Lerner and Loewe her finest, most integrated work. The score, with such songs as "They Call the Wind Maria" and "I Talk to the Trees," was memorable, and Agnes's dances set just the right note to this

A poster for *Come Summer*, 1970, which Agnes deMille directed and choreographed and in which Ray Bolger starred. Stanley Simmons did the costumes

Flanking it are costumes he designed for *The Four Marys*, 1966, a ballet by Agnes deMille

Left and right: Simmons's designs for Agnes deMille's *Golden Age*, 1967

Below: A set design by Santo Loquasto for Agnes deMille's ballet *The Informer*, which premiered in March 1988

Charlotte Greenwood
limbering up for
Agnes deMille's
choreography in
Out of This World,
Cole Porter's 1950
musical. The
direction was also
by Agnes deMille

distinctly American tale about a prosperous mining town that becomes deserted when the gold runs out.*

She had directed the Cole Porter show *Out of This World.** Based on the Jean Giraudoux–S. N. Behrman success *Amphitryon 38*, it did not recapture "the airy grace and sophisticated wit" of the original, and closed in twenty weeks.

"During the forties and fifties," Agnes once observed, "we were all creating the musical as a specific art form. I don't know why especially. Why did operetta burst forth in Vienna in the middle of the last century, except that all the right people were there at the right time." It was not so much a matter of coincidence as of need. With Europe in chaos, Americans were in search of their own roots, their heritage and culture. During the twenties and thirties, the musical theatre had become the province of Broadway, but Americans were insecure and turned toward England and the Continent for culture. Broadway followed suit, and many story backgrounds and characters had a distinctly European flavor. When Agnes burst onto the scene in 1943 with *Oklahoma!*, the United States was at war and in a patriotic state of mind. And there was Agnes, a thoroughly American artist creating a thoroughly American product—dance American style—and in a Broadway theatre, where Americans felt a good deal more comfortable than in a concert hall.

Then in 1961, Rudolf Nureyev defected to the West from the Soviet Union while on tour with the Kirov Ballet in Paris. Believed to be the leading classical ballet dancer of his day, Nureyev almost singlehandedly brought back public interest in the Russian ballet, and on Broadway the tide had begun to turn. By 1962, ballet imports gave the real excitement and backbone to the season, the dance chorus (or "gypsies," as they were known) returned with high kicks, and ballet moved back to the concert hall, and Agnes with it. But she was well prepared.

With music by Virgil Thomson, Agnes had choreographed an elaborate ex-

Gemze de Lappe and
James Mitchell in
Paint Your Wagon,
1951, the Lerner-
Loewe musical, with
choreography by
Agnes deMille

222

James Mitchell in
Agnes deMille's *Gold
Rush*, 1958

pansion of the Civil War ballet from *Bloomer Girl*, and it had been premiered successfully by Ballet Theatre on October 1, 1952. The following year, she had organized the Agnes deMille Dance Theatre and went out on tour with some of her most popular ballets. *The Rib of Eve* was premiered by the Ballet Theatre on April 25, 1956, with Nora Kaye and James Mitchell (from *Brigadoon*) dancing the leads of this "modern morality play...part farce, part satire, part drama" of a restless woman, fearful of encroaching age and needful of adoration. *The Bitter Weird, The Rehearsal, The Wind in the Mountains, The Four Marys, Golden Age*, and *A Rose for Miss Emily* followed in almost annual succession. No one could dispute that Agnes deMille had become the doyenne of American ballet as she had been the force behind ballet in theatre. Now Broadway had been placed neatly behind her, her niche in it secure for all time.

She had found her voice as well, as book after book appeared in the stores: *Dance to the Piper* (1952), *And Promenade Home* (1958), *To a Young Dancer* (1962), *The Book of the Dance* (1963), *Lizzie Borden: Dance of Death* (1968), *Dance in America* (1970), *Russian Journals* (1971), and *Speak to Me, Dance with Me* (1973).

She was a favorite speaker on the lecture circuit and one of those very few venerable personalities who could walk out on a stage and receive a standing ovation before uttering a word. She now organized what she called her "cherished" Heritage Dance Theater.

"At 5:50 P.M. on May 15, 1975 [one hour before curtain]," she recalled precisely, "I stood in the auditorium of the Hunter College Playhouse in New York City giving last-minute instructions to my dance company before a lecture-dance concert. The concert was sold out and the audience numbered quite the most elite and distinguished people in New York.

A scene from *The Four
Marys*, 1966. From
left: Judith Lerner,
Paul Sutherland,
Cleo Quitman,
Judith Jamison,
Glory Van Scott, and
Carmen de Lavallade

223

Agnes deMille at the
White House in 1986
for a state dinner

"Suddenly I discovered that half of my body was dead." She had suffered a massive cerebral hemorrhage.

David Baker, the pianist, remembered that "Nothing had seemed to go well, and she had been raging with all too much energy for something to work—the lights, the tapes, the dancing. And nothing much *was* working. Finally she dismissed the company with just enough time to grab a sandwich and be ready for the performance.... I came down off the stage to sit with her in about the third row on the aisle...After a few moments she turned to me and said, 'I have no feeling in my right leg.' A moment later she turned to a friend seated on the other side and said, 'Mary [Green], I can't feel.' "

A few minutes later, Dr. George Gorham, her private physician, who happened fortunately to be only a few streets away, was at her side and she was taken by ambulance to New York Hospital, where Walter, who had been notified of her stroke, joined her. For many hours, the doctors thought she would die. Her sister, Margaret, was called and joined Walter in his vigil at the hospital. "Shortly before the stroke," Agnes recalled, "there had been [Margaret's] little girl voice on the phone saying, 'Ag, Ag, I'm going to die. It's cancer.' " Now they stared at each other. " 'Mag, this should have been your show, [Agnes said.] Not mine. You were to die first. Oh, Lord, I've done it again [a reference to how, as the elder sister, she had always led Margaret].' We both giggled."

Both her sight and speech went and the doctors gave her only hours to live, but gradually she began to recover, slowly at first—her sight returning. Then the gibberish she had been uttering became articulate speech. But feeling did not return to the right side of her body. And then one night she suffered a deep venous thrombosis (blood clot) in her paralyzed leg and was rushed into surgery, where the clot

The children of
Cecilia DeMille
Harper, at C. B.'s
desk at his house,
March 1988. From
left: Peter Calvin,
Cecilia (Citsy) Presley
and Joseph (Jody)
Harper. On the table
at rear is a photograph
of C. B. at five (it is
reproduced on page
20 of this book).
Inside a glass bell on
the desk is a golden
ear of corn, a tribute
in 1952 to C. B.'s
drawing power at the
movie houses—from
the National
Association of
Popcorn
Manufacturers

was removed. Once again she began to recover and in the hospital started a book about her medical experience. More complications appeared, and surgery to remove an embolism from her throat was called for. After three months of hospitalization, Agnes's spirit began to flag.

She "wasn't half-well, she wasn't even free of immediate medical danger," Dr. Fred Plum, her attending physician, wrote. "But the malaise that threatened her spirit was potentially far more life-limiting than the disease that threatened her body." Agnes was sent home.

"There were reasons why I didn't despair," Agnes recalled. "One was the constant, vigilant love of my husband and son and sister. Every night my Walter served me dinner on a tray...and every morning...we had a very friendly and delicious forty-five minutes of talk....

"Every time I had said, 'I don't know what I'll do,' all he said was, 'Not for long; it won't last.'...And I held on to his faith....He never wavered.

" 'Walter,' I said quite soberly one morning....'I'm sorry for what I've done to your life. I am very, very sorry.' " She was moved to near tears when he replied quietly, "My dear, this has been the making of me."

For months she worked to accomplish the smallest feat—to move a foot a half-inch. Then she had a ballet barre put up in the back room of their apartment and practiced, "not pliés...but walking steps, forward and back, forward and back." The long road to some manner of independence had been embarked upon. On Thanksgiving her son Jonathan was married to a Jewish girl in a Jewish ceremony under a *chuppah*. The ritual wine glass was crushed beneath his foot, the toasts raised, the music begun.

"I wanted to stand up and feel my hands on [Jonathan's] shoulder, have him put his hand on my back, lead me. I was a dancer. I wanted to dance him proud. I had to yield my place." He took the bride's mother instead.

For one year she worked on her barre. Margaret was fighting too. She lived in Maryland, alone, her third husband, George B. Doughman, having died, her daughter living in another town. "She was gallant. She never made the slightest demand," Agnes remembered. "She used to call around six in the afternoon....We talked family news, gossip, political chit chat....She wanted to hear my voice at dusk, which is a very bad time."

On October 15, 1976, Agnes suffered a heart attack and again she fought her way back. She was proving to be more indomitable than her Uncle Ce. She wrote on almost a daily basis, and in 1978 published a brilliant memoir of her youth titled *Where the Wings Grow*. But the most important goal for her was to resume her place in the dance world. While she had been struggling for her life, Robert Joffrey, the American choreographer and dancer, had presented a "thunderingly successful" reconstruction of *Rodeo*. By 1979, Agnes was determined to return to the dance and proposed that together they produce her *Conversations About the Dance* which had been interrupted by her stroke. Though it was a risky undertaking, Joffrey agreed. They augmented the music by forty-five instruments and added excerpts from *Rodeo* and the first section of Jerome Robbins's *Interplay*. Agnes still could not hold anything safely in her hand or walk more than a few steps and had not even done that without a cane. The concert was to be held at the City Center Theater, which had a

Agnes deMille in 1976 in a photograph by Jack Mitchell

capacity of 2,932 seats, and she would have to talk clearly enough to be understood. And she was determined she would stand without her cane. The strain was tremendous and Walter was against her doing it, but she drove herself on. The golden night came.

"Bob Joffrey took my hand," she recalled, "and we stood. The stage manager signalled us and the barrier swished up and there was a rush of air. And there was absolute silence...and waiting.

"Applause, I guess. And then Bob seated me and I began to speak." She never lost her place or stumbled and when the curtain came down the entire audience rose on one count. Agnes could not walk forward without help and she could not bow. She stood up. "And the flowers came. Flowers and flowers." Since she could not hold them they were laid at her feet. She had made her way back.

As this book goes to press, Agnes deMille's eighty-third birthday will have come and gone. Age has not daunted her spirit any more than illness could. She has published two more books, *America Dances* (1980) and *Reprieve* (a journal of her illness, 1981).

In May 1987, she was interviewed for public television. "I'm not the success I meant to be," she said. "I just never forgave myself that....Living is a form of not being sure, of not knowing what is next, and the artist, before all others, never entirely knows. He guesses, and he may be wrong. 'Who am I?' he asks. And he devotes his entire career to answering." She paused thoughtfully. "I would like one word on my tombstone—*dancer*."

Beatrice would have been proud—and William—and Cecil.

226

NOTES/SOURCES

Full publishing information will be found in the bibliography. Works frequently cited are abbreviated as follows:

C.B.D.   Cecil B. DeMille, *The Autobiography of Cecil B. DeMille*
A.deM.   Agnes deMille
Speak   *Speak to Me, Dance with Me*
Wings   *Where the Wings Grow*
Dance   *Dance to the Piper*
Promenade   *And Promenade Home*
Reprieve   *Reprieve: A Memoir*
W.deM.   William deMille, *Hollywood Saga*
BYU   Brigham Young University Arts and Communications Archives
NYPL   New York Public Library, Manuscripts & Archives Division
PI   Personal Interview

The Lost City of Pharaoh DeMille, 1985

8 "were ignominiously," C.B.D., p. 253.
9 "that, both in," ibid., p. 252.
   "sent posthaste," ibid.
   "the mightiest," promotional copy.
   "They gave us," Peter L. Brosnan, *American West*, Sept./Oct. 1985.
   "(It gives bandit-proof," advertisement, Hellman Bank, c. 1923.
   "an invoice," *Los Angeles Examiner*, c. 1950.
   "Are you trying," ibid.
   "That was it," ibid.
   "Take the money," ibid.
   "Don't sell," C.B.D., p. 258.
10 *The final cost of the film was $1,475,836.93.
   "If, a thousand," ibid., p. 253.
11 "I don't think you," *American West*, Sept./Oct. 1985.
   "Well, this is it," ibid.
   *At this writing, they have not yet succeeded in raising the necessary funds.
   "August 12 my," C.B.D., p. 3.
   "But I cannot feel," ibid.

A Dynasty Begins, 1853–1893

13 "I was the only," A.deM., PBS broadcast, May 14, 1987.
   "A hundred and fifty," C.B.D., p. 3.
   *Cecil's second cousin was Sir Herbert Louis Samuel (1870–1963), first Viscount Samuel, Home Secretary (1916, 1931–32), leader of the Liberal Party (1931–35), first High Commissioner to Palestine (1920–25).
14 "slim, bewitching," ibid., p. 12.
15 "my English mother," A.deM., *Wings*, p. 83.
   "The Human Fiend," *Jennie*, Martin, vol. 2, p. 123.

"positively Chinese," C.B.D., p. 7.
"a decent respect," ibid.
*According to the genealogist Professor Louis P. deBoer, the deMille name, Flemish in origin, descended through the sequence deMild, deMelt, deMilt, deMil, deMill.
"in the late," C.B.D., p. 7.
*Adam deMil was acquitted by edict of Emperor Charles V (1643–90), but he was sentenced to pay a small fine and costs.
*In 1945, Cecil B. DeMille used "The Gilded Beaver" in the film *Unconquered* as the name of a colonial inn.
16 *William DeMill and his second wife, Margaret, had ten children; five died in childhood. The surviving children were Henry Churchill (1853), Margaret Mutter (1858), Anne Cambreling (1860), John Cambreling (1871), and Elizabeth Hoyt (1873). The name was then spelled DeMill. Henry added the last *e* upon his marriage to C. B.'s mother. The various other members of his family eventually followed his lead.
"visits to his," C.B.D., p. 8.
"went out at last," address of North Carolina Governor Z. B. Vance, Aug. 8, 1875.
"placid round of," ibid.
*The Southern Historical Society Papers, vol. 23, p. 189, lists Major *James* DeMill as commissary to Martin's brigade. C. B. claimed this was actually his grandfather, William, and town records (Greenville) verify that William was in Martin's brigade. General Martin was known as "Old One Wing" Martin because he had lost his right arm in the Mexican War.
*Two children were born to Margaret DeMill in Greenville; neither survived childhood.
"to knit his own," C.B.D., p. 8.
"the only available," ibid.
"one cent for every," ibid.
17 "went barefoot to," ibid., p. 10.
"a very happy year," ibid.
"thorough welding," ibid., p. 11.
*C. B. wrote in his *Autobiography* (p. 11), "I have tried to find the Society of New York for the Promotion of Religion and Learning, but it seems to have gone out of existence. I wanted to make some return on its investment in my father."
"It would break," ibid.
18 *C. B.'s middle name was his paternal great-grandmother's maiden name.
19 "as play reader," C.B.D., p. 15.
21 "the only vow," Gottlieb, p. 41.
*The play was subsequently and successfully produced at the Madison Square.
"an old pre-Revolutionary," C.B.D., p. 18.
"I had to get," ibid.
*Howard was the author of the successful

play *Saratoga* (1870), said to have changed American theatre managers' negative attitude toward native drama.
*To satisfy his passion for the literal, Belasco moved an Eighth Avenue theatrical boarding house, intact, on stage for *The Easiest Way* (1909) and put an exact replica of Child's restaurant on the stage for *The Governor's Lady* (1912).
22 "transfer the car to," *N.Y. Times*, Sept. 18, 1886.
*The heroine in *The Main Line* is presented with another dilemma when the "whistle of the night express is heard in the distance" (*N.Y. Times*, Sept. 18, 1886). She must now sacrifice the life of her lover for the hundreds of lives on the express; she switches his runaway car so that it will crash but will leave the track clear for the express. In the end, it is discovered that her lover got out of the car before the crash and the lovers are reunited.
"almost perfect illusion," ibid.
"*The Main Line* will," ibid.
"*The Main Line* is," *N.Y. World*, Dec. 26, 1890.
"... striding up and," Gottlieb, p. 41.
"smashing it," ibid.
"Henry excelled in," Winter, vol. 1, p. 374.
"set up a table," ibid., pp. 132–33.
23 "a tall, grave man," Atkinson, p. 42.
*Originally titled *Sir George*.
"I coax and cajole," Morris, p. 296.
"one sunny July," A.deM., unpublished manuscript, 1988.
24 "a blaze of notoriety," ibid.
"Do you wish," Winter, p. 363.
*Mrs. Carter (born Caroline Louise Dudley, 1862) became the star of some of Belasco's most successful plays, including the lavish spectacular *DuBarry*. In 1906, after a liaison of sixteen years with Belasco, Mrs. Carter, at the age of forty-four, married W. L. Payne, an actor considerably her junior. Belasco read about it in the newspapers. The shock was great and he refused ever again to see her and canceled her contract. She made a few films, but in essence this was the end of her career.
"I was almost worn," Winter, p. 363.
"The magnetism of her," Morris, *Curtain Time*, p. 296.
*Charles Frohman presented the first productions of *The Admirable Crichton* (1903) and *Peter Pan* (1904). He eventually either owned or controlled six theatres and managed twenty-eight stars and was considered the foremost producer of his time. He was drowned in the sinking of the *Lusitania* on May 7, 1915. He was said to have been the man who insisted the ship's orchestra keep playing as long as it was able.
25 "We soon found," ibid., p. 29.

"I was strongly tempted," Winter, pp. 373–74.

"About this time," ibid., p. 376.

"A deplorable lack," *The Herald*, Oct. 23, 1890.

"is cheap enough," N.Y. *Dramatic Mirror*, Oct. 30, 1890.

*Not to be confused with her namesake and future niece, the dancer and choreographer, Agnes George deMille.

26 "(one of the most," *Chicago Tribune*, Aug. 19, 1891.

"large white frame," C.B.D., p. 30.

"my dear Mr. George," The Henry George Institute.

27 "so well how he," ibid.

"the evenings, I think," C.B.D., p. 31.

"Mother brought Bill," ibid., p. 33.

Beatrice, 1893–1906

30 "Roads were blocked," Emanuel Einstein Memorial Library, article, "Season Royal," undated.

31 "pathetic small white," C.B.D., p. 41.

"and forced them," A.deM. *Wings*, pp. 53–54.

"made each of us boys," C.B.D., p. 41.

*Sixty years after his sister's death, C. B. was to write that he carried "a miniature of [Agnes] on [his] watch chain always" (C.B.D., p. 41).

"I . . . took my place," ibid., p. 42.

*William, as an adult, often included his grandmother Cecilia Samuel in family gatherings and brought her, Mark, and Beatrice's sister, Jennie, to California for visits with his family. C. B. appears to have been polite in his relationship to her, but little more, and was always to recall her early rejection of him and her displeasure at his being named for her.

*Beatrice held on to the school throughout her life. The main house was demolished in 1944 and rebuilt as a guest building for the Adams sanitarium. The original gatehouse across the road (which Beatrice had built) was still standing in 1987.

"Most managers believe," N.Y. *Dramatic Mirror*, June 10, 1912.

32*The theatre was under the management of Joseph Luckett, uncle of Nancy Davis Reagan. Edith Luckett Davis, Mrs. Reagan's mother, was, in fact, a child performer with her older brother's stock company in 1900, but she was not in Mrs. DeMille's play.

"The play is a unique," *The Washington Evening Star*, Feb. 13, 1900.

"This is the woman's," N.Y. *Dramatic Mirror*, June 10, 1912.

"great bunches of," ibid.

"Yes, yes," Anna George deMille, p. 234.

"the catafalque was," A.deM., *Wings*, p. 52.

"Poor people filed," Beer, p. 134.

33 "a Catholic, an," A.deM., *Wings*, p. 52.

("She was also a," ibid., pp. 52–53.

"upright and staunch," ibid., p. 52.

"worldliness and zest," ibid.

"to save train fare," ibid.

"quick, flashing adroit," ibid., p. 55.

"very sexy," ibid.

"completely smitten," ibid.

"Bill's inviolable," C.B.D., p. 45.

**The Governor's Vrouw* was written by H. Sydnor Harrison and Melville Cane. For this school production, music (composed by William deMille's classmate, future playwright John Erskine) was added.

"When we started," W.deM., p. 8.

34 "came out of the," ibid., p. 9.

*Arthur Schnitzler (1862–1931), the Austrian dramatist, had not yet become known to English-speaking audiences.

"on the 31st," C.B.D., p. 50.

*Constance Adams was born in East Orange, N.J., on April 27, 1873, the oldest of the five children (the others were John, Ellis, Rebecca, and Frederic III) of Frederic and Ella King Adams.

"In the whole," ibid., p. 51.

35*Sothern had originated and was to play again the title role.

"One night . . . [in]," ibid., p. 53.

36 "Sothern gave every," ibid., p. 52.

*C. B. added: "The way to direct crowds of extras is never to think of them as 'extras.' They are individuals, they are players, they are parts of the whole, with a function as important in its way as the function of the stars. They respond— and you can see the difference on the stage or screen" (C.B.D., p. 52).

"Bill deMille, that," A.deM., *Wings*, p. 54.

"who is in cahoots," N.Y. *Times*, c. 1902.

"notes addressed to her on," C.B.D., p. 35.

*Nesbit's diary would become a central piece of evidence and be read aloud in court in 1906, during Henry Thaw's trial for the murder of Stanford White.

"Mother had told Evelyn," ibid., p. 36.

"But I don't like," ibid., p. 36.

*Nesbit succinctly exclaimed, "Good God, Harry. What have you done!" (N.Y. *Times*, c. 1902). The sensational murder trial that followed and the public reading of Nesbit's diary caused the DeMilles some unpleasant publicity. The story of Evelyn Nesbit was eventually filmed as *The Girl in the Red Velvet Swing* (1955) and starred Joan Collins as Nesbit.

37 "There were some," A.deM., *Wings*, p. 54.

"Mother liked," ibid., p. 55.

"She, the beautiful," ibid., p. 56.

In Search of Adventure, 1906–1913

39 "was provincial and," Atkinson, p. 3.

"charm and a kind," ibid.

40 "Ibsen and Shaw," ibid.

"acted, sang, booked," ibid.

"Not long after," Pickford, p. 60.

42 "[Belasco] liked to talk," C.B.D., p. 62.

*During this period C. B. wrote: *Kit, The Man's the King, The Dullest*, alone; and with Bill *The Royal Mounted* and *Church Play*.

"the doctor deliver," ibid., p. 60.

He "often," ibid., p. 60.

43 "by David Belasco," play credits.

"among learned references," ibid.

"CECIL DE MILLE CHARGES," N.Y. *Times*, Oct. 1911.

"Probably he believed," C.B.D., p. 61.

"(I enjoyed the title," ibid., p. 64.

*Current antitrust laws prohibit such an arrangement today.

"natty with his high," ibid., p. 65.

44 "seated behind her desk," ibid.

"a big billboard," Lasky, p. 88.

"I had no," Lasky, p. 64.

*William deMille wrote David Belasco on July 25, 1911:

Oh, by the way, you remember that little girl, Mary Pickford, who played Betty in *The Warrens of Virginia*? I met her again a few weeks ago and the poor kid is actually thinking of taking up moving pictures seriously . . . it does seem a shame. After all, she can't be more than seventeen and I remember what faith you had in her future . . . and now she's throwing her whole career in the ashcan and burying herself in a cheap form of amusement. There will never be any real money in those galloping tintypes, and certainly no one can expect them to develop into anything which could . . . be called art. I pleaded with her not [to go into films] . . . but she says she knows what she is doing. So I suppose we'll have to say goodbye to little Mary Pickford. She'll never be heard of again, and I feel terribly sorry for her [NYPL].

"We used to daydream," Lasky, p. 90.

"(We all missed you," BYU.

45 "(Men with intellects," A.deM., *Wings*, p. 64.

"A lovely stretch of," Anna George deMille, p. 204.

"a little cabin-like," ibid.

*Anna George deMille's brother, Henry George, Jr., had inherited this house.

46 "That Mother and Father," A.deM., *Wings*, p. 20.

"Aunt Bettie de Mille Pitman," ibid., pp. 33–34.

47 "an unquestioned genius," ibid., pp. 75–76.

"had the wit of," ibid., pp. 56–57.

"There were, of course," ibid., pp. 75–76.

Cecil "had produced," W.deM., p. 35.

48 "disgust, [Cecil] took," C.B.D., p. 67.

"and his orderly," ibid.

"I'm pulling out," Lasky, p. 91.

"I told Sam I," ibid.

49 "To keep Cecil," ibid.

*C. B. and Lasky reported the sealing of this historic partnership in much the same manner. However, Sam Goldfish (later to be known as Sam Goldwyn) and a lawyer, Arthur Friend, were also present. Bill reported that Lasky and C. B.

had to be convinced by Friend, who had been the original film enthusiast. The story is told that after the historic luncheon they all went to a movie house to see *Bronco Billy*. After viewing the film, C. B. was reported to have said to Lasky, "I don't know anything about pictures, but if I can't do better than *that*, I ought to be shot at sunrise" (W.deM., p. 40).

Letter from William to Cecil, NYPL.
50 "He...suggest[ed]," W.deM., p. 46.
"one of the two," C.B.D., p. 69.
"she bundled up," ibid., p. 72.

A Strange New Medium, 1913–1915

51 "an Indian picture," Lasky, p. 92.
"Cecil seemed to have," ibid., p. 93.
52 "We should have been," C.B.D., p. 77.
"The train was beginning," ibid., p. 78.
"At the end of the railroad," ibid.
*The American Biograph and Mutoscope Company, in a small building at 1845 Alessandro Street.
"yellowish heat-beaten," ibid., pp. 79–80.
*The actual address of the studio was 6284 Selma Avenue.
"Stalls were turned into," Lasky, p. 94.
*Contrary to future claims that *The Squaw Man* was the first American feature film, Hobart Bosworth's *The Sea Wolf* was shown at Grauman's Imperial Theater in San Francisco on October 5, 1913 (nearly three months before the start of principal photography on *The Squaw Man*). Bosworth had already produced three more feature-length films: *Martin Eden*, *John Barleycorn*, and *Valley of the Moon*.
"word...vaguely," Brownlow, p. 34.
*The word was used in such a derogatory manner in the early days of film that the industry referred to it in quotes—and then not too often. They liked it known that they made *pictures* or *films*, not "movies."
"the wolf would," C.B.D., p. 83.
53 *Sheba played a role in *The Squaw Man* and was then given to the San Diego Zoo.
"fresh flowers in January," ibid., p. 86.
"unwound, thrown in a," C.B.D., p. 85.
"homeward in the," ibid., p. 87.
54 "ready to shoot," ibid.
"We carried [our lunch]," Lasky, p. 96.
"Cecil gave a signal," ibid.
"spent all Sam," ibid., p. 98.
"Cecil went into," ibid., p. 99.
55 "and a musical," W.deM., p. 58, 59, 61.
"As the picture ended," ibid., p.59.
"Dearest Boy: —" (July 7, 1914, letter), DeMille Estate.
"Dearest Boy: —" (July 13, 1914, letter), ibid.
"It seems that," BYU.
56 "The hills were," NYPL.
"Perhaps," A.deM., *Dance*, p. 5.
"After a chaste," W.deM., p. 66.
"a solidly-built person," ibid., p. 67.

In "his nine months," ibid., p. 71.
"Hello, Bill," ibid., p. 67.
"Costumed, booted," ibid., p. 68.
"Because my attention," ibid., p. 70.
*C. B. had used Constance and Cecilia in *The Squaw Man*. Agnes deMille remembered the strong impression it made upon her when she was taken to the movie theatre "to see my cousin Cecilia abducted by the Indians, while my handsome aunt was carried off in a backbend over an Indian saddlebow, her mane of brown hair sweeping the sagebrush" (A.deM., *Dance*, p. 7).
"We're in a hurry," W.deM., p. 81.
"to write entirely," W.deM., p. 101.
"Sam, I'm only," NYPL.
58 "...worried that she," C.B.D., p. 159.
"sent her a check," ibid.
60 "I was unshakable," ibid.
"She liked it;" ibid.
"Mother and Brother had," N.Y. *Dramatic Mirror*, Aug. 4, 1917.
"wild destructive," ibid.
"Hollywood [in 1915] was," A.deM., *Dance*, pp. 8–10.
61 "a dear little," ibid.
"was a shambling," ibid.
"came home to dinner," ibid.
"total and," ibid., p. 41.
"before his mother," ibid., p. 41.
*This passage from *Dance to the Piper* (Agnes deMille) was also quoted by C. B. in his *Autobiography*. Most revealing is the fact that he chose to add lines which are not in Ms. deMille's book and attributed them to her. The addition reads: "He always listened...at the praise or condemnation of his mother, his heart jumped. She remained critical, hard to please, and enormously proud of her extraordinary son" (C.B.D., p. 161).
"seldom came home," A.deM., *Dance*, p. 38.
"like a Pasha at," ibid., p. 40.
"and asked for a few," C.B.D., pp. 161–62.
"I knew they," *Photoplay*, No. 5, Oct. 1923, pp. 50–51, 127–28.

The Early Silent Years, 1915–1918

63 "She remains the dominant," BYU.
"enormous ambition," Higashi, p. 2.
*C. B.'s film backgrounds and genres varied: Westerns (*The Squaw Man*, *The Virginian*, *The Rose of the Rancho*, *The Girl of the Golden West*, *The Trail of the Lonesome Pine*, *Romance of the Redwoods*); war films (*The Warrens of Virginia*, *The Captive*, *The Little American*, *Till I Come Back to You*); spectacle (*Joan the Woman*, *The Woman God Forgot*); melodrama (*The Call of the North*, *What's His Name?*, *The Unafraid*, *The Arab*, *Kindling*, *Carmen*, *Temptation*, *The Heart of Nora Flynn*, *Maria Rosa*, *The Whispering Chorus*, *The Cheat*, *The Devil Stone*); society dramas (*The Man From Home*, *The Wild Goose Chase*, *The Golden

Chance, *The Dream Girl*, *Old Wives for New*, *We Can't Have Everything*); and comedies (*Chimmie Fadden*, *Chimmie Fadden Out West*)—thirty-two films in all, made between the winter of 1914 and the autumn of 1918.
64 "spectacle as the," ibid., p. 24.
The Cheat (original story by Hector Turnbull, scenario by Turnbull and Jeanie Macpherson) was remade twice as a sound film in France, where C. B.'s original silent version has always been considered a classic. It was also dramatized for the stage and adapted as the libretto for an opera premiered at the Metropolitan.
*Sessue Hayakawa, who starred in *The Cheat*, also portrayed the same role in *Forfaiture*, the 1937 French remake of the film. Turnbull's original story had the character Japanese, but as Japan was a necessary ally in 1914, Hayakawa's villainous Oriental became Burmese.
*Few Orientals were included in society circles in 1915. William deMille was related through marriage to Dr. Jokichi Takamine, a distinguished Japanese (Anna George deMille's sister-in-law's sister was Lady Caroline Takamine, his wife). The Takamines owned a beautiful home near Merriewold, and the mixed family was part of the Merriewold social set of which C. B. had been a fringe member before going to California.
*Several years later when the Film Censorship Board was set up, the production code prohibited "branding of humans on screen," a rule that owed its inclusion directly to *The Cheat*.
"DeMille avoids all...," Pacific Film Archives, Sept. 9, 1972.
*Fannie Ward had appeared in *The Marriage of Kitty* before *The Cheat*. She is perhaps most famous today for having been the inspiration for the novel and film *Mr. Skeffington* (the latter starring Bette Davis as Mrs. Skeffington, the woman who refuses to age).
"took hours to fix," ibid.
"You have made," BYU.
"sexually charged content," ibid.
*The South found the integration of an Oriental into society in *The Cheat* a threat to black and white segregation. For that reason, it was not released in Mississippi, Alabama, and Georgia, and perhaps one or two other of the Southern states.
65 "as always," C.B.D., p. 150.
"There is a new force," *The Moving Picture World*, Jan. 8, 1916.
"as well as his," ibid.
"abnormal morbidity," Brownlow, p. 180.
"It lost a great," ibid.
"DeMille changed," ibid.
66 "Europe really had," Lasky, p. 110.
"These countries," ibid.
"There were two," ibid., p. 111.
"with real Springfield," ibid.
67 *In 1915, Geraldine Farrar was perhaps the most famous theatrical figure in Amer-

ica. "She was adulated...by people of all ages and kinds. Princes of Europe were at her feet. American teen-agers swarmed around her whenever she appeared, copied her style, gloried in being nicknamed 'Gerry-flappers' "(C.B.D., p. 140).

"recently overtaxed," Lasky, p. 117.

"a private railroad car," ibid.

"cut her teeth," ibid.

"[Cecil] outlined," Farrar, p. 168.

*In addition to *Maria Rosa* and *Carmen*, C. B. directed Farrar in *Temptation, The Devil Stone* (from an original story by Beatrice DeMille), and two spectacles, *Joan the Woman* and *The Woman God Forgot*.

68 "I asked [Cecil]," ibid.

*Farrar had also played Micaela in the Metropolitan Opera's 1908 production of *Carmen*.

"My biggest," ibid.

*Charles Chaplin wrote: "I was so impressed with [DeMille's] *Carmen* that I made a two-reel burlesque of it" (Chaplin, p. 185).

69 "a lovely, petite," C.B.D., p. 113.

*Macpherson always claimed she was a descendant of Charles Edward Stuart (Bonnie Prince Charles), the Royal Scottish heir of the Highlands uprisings of 1745, who was an unsuccessful claimant to the English throne.

*It has been suggested that a love letter written by Macpherson to Griffith was the cause of the breakup in 1911 of Griffith's marriage to his first wife. Macpherson appeared in six of Griffith's films.

"I want a job," Higham, p. 38.

70 "Kindly vacate," ibid.

"Go chase yourself," ibid.

Joan the Woman was later cut to 115 minutes.

71 "In the gory fight," Farrar, p. 175.

"The Sunday the battle," A.deM., *Dance*, pp. 20–21.

*Some of the footage from *Joan the Woman* was also used (by special arrangement) by Sarah Bernhardt for her film *Mères Françaises* (*Mothers of France*), released in 1917.

72*One critic wrote: "There is an air of distinction and class about the entire offering which places it in the front rank of big productions....It is certainly an impressive spectacle...." (*N.Y. Times*, Jan. 4, 1917).

"to tell an absorbing," C.B.D., p. 170.

"could recharge," C.B.D., p. 163.

*C. B.'s granddaughter, Cecilia Presley (Cecilia Junior), recalls her mother telling her, "People would ask, 'Where has your father gone?' I'd say to Paradise. And they'd say, 'Oh, I'm so sorry, I didn't know' " (Cecilia Presley, PI).

"She never chose to," ibid.

"right through it," ibid.

"When they [the," ibid.

73 "Cecil was a student," ibid.

"The colored Cossack," A.deM., unpub-

lished manuscript, 1988.

"After dinner," Cecilia Presley, PI.

"ready for all eventualities," A.deM., *Dance*, p. 38.

74 "up on the hill," ibid.

"[On Christmas] Cecil," ibid., pp. 39–40.

"moved through this," ibid., pp. 37, 38.

"kept the place," ibid.

"beautiful, curly-haired," Cecilia Presley, PI.

"put a wicked wedge," ibid.

"He came from," Katherine DeMille Quinn, PI.

"after burning up all," Richard DeMille, PI.

*Katherine Lester DeMille's father, Edward Lester, according to another family member, "was from a long line of English ministers and he was born in Scotland. He was a very handsome man and became a painter in London, then emigrated to Vancouver, where he was a schoolteacher and was killed with the Royal Air Force during World War I. Her mother's father was a Swiss architect [from the Italian region]. His name was Colanni. Her mother's mother, however, was German, and Katherine's mother was sent to school in Germany, where she grew up. She went to London as a nursemaid and there met Edward Lester" (Katherine DeMille Quinn, PI).

"Katherine's father," Cecilia Presley, PI.

75 "She pinned a note," ibid.

"Though it was so," Katherine DeMille Quinn, PI.

"A woman wanted to," ibid.

"Everyone fell in love," Cecilia Presley, PI.

"I remember the formality," Katherine DeMille Quinn, PI.

76 "When I first came," ibid.

77 "he couldn't very well," Cecilia Presley, PI.

"the problems of mankind," A.deM., *Dance*, p. 27.

"grew accustomed to," ibid., p. 27.

"Having known one," ibid., p. 28.

"My relation varied," A.deM., PBS Broadcast, May 14, 1987.

78 "Resting [Anna]," ibid.

"I lived in debt," A.deM., *Dance*, pp. 25–27.

"up on the hill," A.deM., *Dance*, p. 38.

79*His first directorial job was the filming of *Anton the Terrible*, also in 1915.

"I wanted to launch," W.deM., pp. 162–63, 165.

"considerably for their," *Motion Picture Directory*, p. 41.

"Father didn't care," A.deM., *Dance*, p. 34.

Miss Lulu Bett is in the archives of The Museum of Modern Art, *The Volga Boatman* at the University of Southern California. A few of William deMille's silent films were given to the Moscow Film Archive in the 1930s and presumably are still there.

"The sense of observation," Brownlow, p. 187.

"It retains its magic," ibid.

80 "This beautiful [film]," Pacific Film Archives, Oct. 7, 1984.

*When Sam Goldfish ran *The Warrens of Virginia* in a New York projection room, he wired C. B.: "CECIL, YOU HAVE RUINED US, IF YOU ARE GOING TO SHOW HALF AN ACTOR ON THE SCREEN THE EXHIBITORS WILL PAY ONLY HALF PRICE FOR THE PICTURE." C. B. telegraphed back: "SAM IF YOU AND THE EXHIBITORS DON'T KNOW REMBRANDT LIGHTING WHEN YOU SEE IT DON'T BLAME ME, CECIL." To which Goldfish replied: "REMBRANDT LIGHTING WONDERFUL IDEA. FOR THAT THE EXHIBITORS WILL PAY DOUBLE. SAM."

81 "the subtle and intelligent," A.deM., *Dance*, p. 41.

"The only thing that," ibid.

The Foundation and the Superstructure of the Works of God and the Works of Man, by Richard Mead DeMille.

"(I think that she," ibid.

82*Cecilia, when she was a few years older, was told by C. B. that Richard was William deMille's son and, therefore, her cousin as well as her adopted brother, but she was sworn to secrecy.

*Her obituary in the *Los Angeles Times*, May 3, 1930, called her "One of the three best scenario writers in Hollywood, before talking pictures."

"I don't want people," *Los Angeles Herald*, April 1930 (day illegible).

"one of the sad," Katherine DeMille Quinn, PI.

"I remember sailing," Richard DeMille, PI.

Carrying the Torch, 1918–1928

83 "not entirely inexperienced," W.deM., pp. 238, 239.

"Loosened marriage bonds," Ruth Perlmutter, *Film Comment*, Jan.–Feb. 1976, pp. 24–28.

"missionary zeal," ibid.

"hit sex hard," ibid.

84 "A typical DeMille," *Photoplay*, Dec. 1919.

"gold cloth and lace," *Variety*, Feb. 7, 1919.

"sleeveless, backless, transparent," title for *Why Change Your Wife?*

"DeMille's frivolous," Higashi, p. 32.

"seductive, playful," title for *Why Change Your Wife?*

"the marital misadventures," Higashi, p. 32.

*Swanson and Beery divorced one year later.

*Swanson was not starred in her first films with C. B. "She received the same billing as any other member of the cast," he later wrote. "She also received...a relatively small salary." With her third film, *Male and Female*, she gained star billing but under the title and in smaller print than "Cecil B. DeMille Presents" (C.B.D., p. 220).

"I first noticed her," ibid.

"When I drove up to," Swanson, pp. 102–3.

85 *The Pinkerton men stood by during shooting and at the end of the work day "carried [the] jewelry away" (Swanson, p. 104).

"certainly not!" ibid., p. 105.

"Working for Mr. DeMille," ibid., p. 110.

"There's nothing wrong," ibid.

"Hattie told me," ibid., p. 112.

"There wasn't a woman," Cecilia Presley, PI.

*C. B. referred to his secretary Gladys Rosson as "Hollywood's first stand-in.... I called [her] away from her desk and burned her at the stake while we were setting up the scene in preparation for Miss Farrar['s close-up]...of course, a dummy was substituted for the actual burning" (C.B.D., p. 174).

87 "Gladys was patient," C.B.D., p. 96.

"Grandmother was," Cecilia Presley, PI.

*Richard Rosson (1894–1953) directed low-budget silent and sound films, none very distinguished. Arthur Rosson (1889–1960), the oldest Rosson brother, entered films as a stunt man and bit actor for C. B. He did some screenwriting and directed a few low-budget films. In 1937, he became C. B.'s associate director and made eight films with him in this capacity. Harold (Hal) Rosson (born 1895) was C. B.'s lighting camera operator, but went on to become one of the most celebrated cameramen in the industry. He shared the Academy Award for *The Garden of Allah* (color cinematography). Numbered among his nearly one hundred film credits were *Red Dust*, *Treasure Island*, *Captains Courageous*, *The Wizard of Oz*, *On The Town*, *The Asphalt Jungle*, *The Red Badge of Courage*, and *Singing in the Rain*. He was Jean Harlow's last husband (1933–35) and widower.

*In *I Blow My Horn*, Jesse Lasky wrote: "The publicity and sales departments made strong objection to the [original] title *The Admirable Crichton*. They said the public...would confuse [the word *admirable*] with 'admiral' and stay away from theatres showing it, under the impression that it was a sea picture" (p. 140). The final title, *Male and Female*, was C. B.'s invention. "I guess the sales department and the public will understand that!" he told Lasky.

"sex, sadism and," Ruth Perlmutter, *Film Comment*, Jan.–Feb. 1976, pp. 24–28.

"until the very," Swanson, p. 123.

*William deMille wrote:

It was...during the production of *Male and Female* that [C. B.] started his series of "fade-backs" to ancient times....

The public liked this so well that for a time C. B. made it a part of his formula ...[so that] he could indulge his taste and that of his audience for spectacle, and still tie it into his story by analogy [W.deM., p. 240].

*Class barriers prevail in C. B.'s adaptation. The last shot "irises in" on Crichton and Lady Mary's maid following the ship-wreck, now happily married and living in America.

"...Mr. DeMille said I," Swanson, p. 123.

88 *Swanson wore a "gown made entirely of pearls and white beads—enough to fill a bushel basket—and [a] towering headdress...made of white peacock feathers" (Swanson, p. 123). Attached to the dress was a long train. The sheer weight of the costume added more danger to the shooting of the scene. Additionally, she wore two-inch cork lifts on her shoes "so maneuverability was a serious problem" (ibid., p. 124).

"There were two," ibid.

89 "That's it!" ibid.

"looked marvelous," ibid., p. 125.

"All right," ibid.

"How lovely," ibid., p. 126.

*According to Agnes deMille, "The slave girl dancing in front of the king's throne before Gloria Swanson's superb entrance borne in on a palanquin by six Nubians was a Denishawn dancer who later became well known—Martha Graham" (A.deM., unpublished manuscript, 1988).

90 "filled with automatic," Lasky, p. 100.

*When Pickford went to work for Zukor in 1912, she was making $500 a week. Four years later, she was earning an astonishing $10,000 weekly and a yearly $300,000 bonus. In late 1917, she broke her contract to sign with First National for $350,000 a picture and made six films in the year that followed. The two films she made for C. B. in 1917, *A Romance of the Redwoods* and *The Late American*, were made under the terms of her contract with Zukor.

92 "The matter of," W.deM., p. 178.

*The name was changed to Paramount Famous Lasky Corporation in 1927 and in 1930 to Paramount Publix Corporation, which went bankrupt in 1933. It was reorganized in 1935 as Paramount Pictures, Inc., and became one of Hollywood's major studios.

"I had tremendous," Lasky, p. 123.

*Goldfish was to divorce Blanche Lasky a year after the break with Lasky.

"In the early years," Cecilia Presley, PI.

"one of the bitterest," C.B.D., p. 178.

"that the day might," ibid., p. 229.

"youthful and brilliant," ibid.

*Judge Adams and his second wife (a cousin to Constance's mother who bore the same name as her predecessor) had moved out to California a few years earlier.

*Four writers had collaborated on this script about a farm wife who steals from the church treasury to buy a dress: Jeanie Macpherson, Beulah Marie Dix, Elmer Harris, and Lorna Moon. Moon's writing assignment coincided with her pregnancy and was followed by the birth of Richard DeMille.

93 "(a tale of the," ad copy.

"After *Male and Female*," Chaplin, p. 185.

"his intuitive ability," Robinson, p. 87.

"the wish-dreams," ibid.

"dope, blackmail and," C.B.D., p. 237.

"a sickness in," ibid., pp. 237–38

"a citadel of sin," ibid., p. 239.

"it was necessary," ibid.

"Here was a theme," ibid., p. 249.

94 "scattered situations," Jeanie Macpherson, premiere program, *The Ten Commandments*, Dec. 1923.

"the mosaic," ibid.

"namely that if you," ibid.

"Egypt. The days," ibid.

95 *Dan becomes rich through graft and as a contractor builds a cathedral using one part cement to twelve parts of sand. When his mother prays there the cathedral collapses and buries her in the ruins. Dan takes a Eurasian mistress from whom he contracts leprosy and is eventually killed in a storm at sea. Mary is saved by John (the good brother) and through prayer regains purity.

"I AM VERY," C.B.D., p. 257.

"...AS AN...," ibid.

*C. B. was forfeiting about $100,000 due to him for the making of the film, above his $6,500 weekly salary. C. B. also had huge earnings from his share in the company.

"Cecil...began pouring," Lasky, p. 168.

"What do they," ibid.

*The film's prestige grew with the years. In 1971, when it was shown in a DeMille retrospective, Ronald Haver wrote: "The prologue, detailing the Israelites' flight from Egypt, is remarkably dynamic. Lavishly set and costumed, amazingly well-designed and photographed, this section of the film holds up surprisingly well. The scenes, originally in Technicolor, of the desert crossing, the parting of the Red Sea and the subsequent destruction of the pursuing Egyptians have never been done as well, not even in DeMille's own 1956 re-make. The impact of the prologue accounts in large part for the slightly anticlimactic aspects of the modern story. An uneasy mixture of religion, symbolism, leprosy and Divine Intervention, it is none the less fascinating as an excellent example of DeMille's work as well as what this nation was responding to in the mid-Twenties" (Program no. 13, 1971, Academy of Motion Picture Arts and Sciences).

98 *This was designer Edith Head's first major assignment and taking Macpherson's script literally (life-sized candyland and chocolate-bar women were called for), she ordered lollipop wigs, peppermint-stick fingernails, and chocolate-drop necklaces. The high-powered klieg lights began to melt the confections and the orgiastic scene that followed was set into motion. C. B., at first horrified, kept the camera rolling. Head also had been Agnes and Margaret deMille's art teacher at the Hollywood School for Girls.

"DeMille...had," Head, p. 9.

"This rapidly expanding," Lasky, p. 169.

"In July, D.W.," C.B.D., p. 263.

99 "…WE OBJECT TO," ibid., p. 264.
*Leisen became a leading director in the 1930s with films such as *Death Takes a Holiday* (1934) and *Easy Living* (1937) but was at his peak in the 1940s with *Frenchman's Creek* (1940), *Lady in the Dark* (1944), *To Each His Own* (1946), and *Golden Earrings* (1947).
"His contract was," Lasky, p. 169.
"We did not sail," C.B.D., p. 264.
"DEAREST CHIEF," Western Union, Oct. 9, 1925, DeMille Archives, BYU.
"MISS JEANIE MACPHERSON," ibid.
100 "C. B. was very," Chierichetti, p. 39.
101 "the nice Lubitschean," ibid., p. 271.
*Ernst Lubitsch was at his height as a director of sophisticated romantic stories. "The Lubitsch touch" was a famous quote of the time.
"had no nuances," ibid., p. 28.
"out to challenge," C.B.D., p. 273.
*The writers were Denison Clift, Clifford Howard, and Jack Jungmeyer. In the end, Jeanie Macpherson received solo credit for the scenario.
"when the *Seaward*," ibid., pp. 278–79.
102 "Katherine is a 'dark," Richard DeMille, PI.
"I was expelled," ibid.
*Katherine also attended the Hollywood School for Girls in the seventh and eighth grades but was not there at the same time as her younger adopted brother, Richard, or Agnes and Margaret.
103 "John was," Cecilia Presley, PI.
"Well, even at five," Katherine DeMille Quinn, PI.
"There were no," Chierichetti, p. 41.
"Was there [on," Katherine DeMille Quinn, PI.
104 "All through the," C.B.D., p. 279.
"to see Christ," Chierichetti, p. 42.
"had a fervid attachment," A.deM., *Dance*, p. 39.
"imprisoned in someone," A.deM., PBS broadcast, May 14, 1987.
"at best exhibitionist," A.deM., *Dance*, pp. 70–71.
105 "naked in feathers," ibid., p. 52.
"He said my knees," ibid., p. 53.
"abnormally short," ibid., p. 57.
"broad and short," ibid.
"What I did not," ibid.
"Why did I not," ibid., p. 58.
"Pop was too," ibid., p. 72.
"(using a trip," ibid., p. 85.
106 "They were never asked," ibid., p. 85.
*Agnes was to meet Rebecca West years later when a grown woman living in England, and the two became quite good friends.
"mostly to Chopin," A.deM., *Dance*, p. 91.
"they had stood," ibid., p. 98.
107 "a desperate pilgrimage," ibid., p. 99.
"dragged at the," ibid.
"The trip was so," ibid.
"You know, Agnes," A.deM., PBS broadcast, May 14, 1987.
"got right on their," *The New Yorker*, Oct. 14, 1946.

"a gentleman," A.deM., PBS broadcast, May 14, 1987.
"loving drudgery," ibid., p. 107.
108 "there was some," W.deM., pp. 268–69.

They Talk, 1928–1932

110 "racket squad," Lasky, p. 216.
111 "with thanks. He," Bickford, p. 167.
"Which is it to be—," ibid., p. 168.
"glittering black," ibid., p. 169.
"a small blue," ibid.
"Exclusive of," ibid., pp. 171–72.
"Russian blouse," ibid., p. 173.
"as guest of," ibid., p. 174.
"marched," ibid.
"He always seemed," ibid.
112 "The big playroom," ibid., pp. 177–79.
"fully-clothed," ibid.
"was innocent," ibid.
"Ascended a platform," ibid., p. 192.
"a commendably," ibid.
"He had been," ibid.
"a genuine respect," ibid., p. 212.
"Working with that," Chierichetti, p. 32.
113 "Those are DeMille," Bickford, p. 216.
"It's arithmetical," Chierichetti, p. 26.
"I could not say," C.B.D., pp. 295–96.
"who came out," Cecilia Presley, PI.
114 "the story of a," C.B.D., p. 300.
"a horrid fate for," ibid., p. 301.
"Everybody said, 'Cecil,' " Katherine DeMille Quinn, PI.
"hell. Metro," Chierichetti, pp. 44–45.
115 "humbly, hat-in-hand," Higham, C.B.D., p. 213.
"a pleasant husky," A.deM., *Dance*, p. 93.
*Montgomery appeared in many American and English films, most notably *Little Women* (1933), *The Mystery of Edwin Drood* (1935), and *The Cat and the Canary* (1939). He tested for Ashley Wilkes in *Gone With the Wind* but lost the part to Leslie Howard. He also appeared opposite Vivien Leigh in her test for Scarlett O'Hara (playing Wilkes).
"tears of excitement," ibid., p. 94.
"a very great," ibid.
"a broken woman," ibid., p. 102.
"usually performed," ibid., p. 101.
116 "while the dressing," ibid., p. 104.
"All I know about," ibid., p. 105.
"It smelled rather high," ibid., p. 111.
"Three hundred," ibid., p. 112.
"the very ends," ibid., p. 113.
"blue Indians," ibid., p. 118.
"who always," ibid.
"Here is undoubtedly," ibid.
"She leaves you with," ibid.
"WELCOME, MY DAUGHTER," ibid., p. 117.
117 "let off steam," ibid., p. 120.
"pugnacious, stubborn," ibid., p. 134.
118 "I wished to be," ibid., p. 136.
"On the arm of Cecil," ibid., p. 138.
"If I were going," ibid.
119*Twelve years later Agnes was to create her striking choreography under Hammerstein's auspices for *Oklahoma!*
"of course," ibid., p. 139.

"DE MILLE GIRL MAKES GOOD," ibid., p. 139.
"exploitation on a," ibid., p. 140.
"Now is the time," ibid., p. 141.
"Father indicated that," ibid., p. 142.
"unscrupulous European," ibid.
120 "What shall I do," ibid.
"remarked quietly," ibid., p. 143.
"put out the light," ibid.
"Politically a shade," Lasky, Jr., p. 137.
"sheer brain power," C.B.D., p. 326.
"presented the president," Lasky, Jr., p. 137.
"a story of the," C.B.D., p. 323.
121 "After setting Rome," Higashi, p. 91.
*A prologue, written by Dudley Nichols, was added to the film when it was re-released in 1943, during World War II, which interspersed scenes of Rome's contemporary bombardment with scenes of the ancient city ablaze during Nero's reign.
122 "daringly for a," Higham, *Laughton*, p. 36.
"an Olympic-sized," ibid.
*The office of film censorship fought the inclusion of this scene, but C. B. won out in the end and the controversial scene remained. C. B. had claimed that the dance showed by contrast "the greater strength and purity of Mercia's faith" (C.B.D., p. 323).
"these cats don't," ibid.
"up they went," ibid.
"We've just used up," Chierichetti, p. 50.
"scribbled on little," C.B.D., p. 325.

The Growth of the Legend, 1932–1941

123 "God. That's what," Lasky, Jr., p. 132.
124 "Golden opportunities do," "Films in Review" article by George Gelzer, Jan., 1956.
"She married me," A.deM., *Speak*, p. 11.
"and had become," A.deM., *Dance*, p. 179.
"This is the greatest," ibid.
125 "you could be a," ibid.
"embarked on a," A.deM., *Dance*, p. 179.
"a young friendly drudge," ibid, p. 181.
"for a fixed," ibid., p. 181.
"The house reeked," ibid., p. 195.
"down precipitous," ibid., p. 183.
"The floor was of," ibid.
126 "There it was:," A.deM., *Speak*, p. 33.
*His name was actually Percy Thorpe, Agnes said later. She had changed it to Sharpe to avoid any possible lawsuit (A.deM., unpublished manuscript, 1988).
"a tall bony," ibid., p. 68.
"a huge black tomcat," ibid., p. 33.
"He is very," ibid., p. 33.
"I danced," ibid., pp. 35–36.
"He is half-mad," ibid., pp. 40–41.
127 "the absolute essence," A.deM., *Dance*, p. 213.
"a good evocation," ibid.
"to study," ibid., p. 214.
"for the first time," ibid.

*Arnold Dolmetsch (1858–1940) was a British musician of Belgian origin, known for his interest in early music and early musical instruments. He established workshops at Haslemere for students to study pre-Baroque music, dance forms, and instruments. The Haslemere Festival is still a celebrated event in the musical world (A.deM., *Dance*, p. 214).

"a young lady who," A.deM., *Speak*, p. 111.

"Sharpe took in," ibid., p. 113.

"one-half day," ibid., p. 116.

"repel them," ibid.

"Queen Anne beauties," ibid.

128 "nicely successful and," A.deM., *Dance*, p. 200.

"ate three string," ibid., p. 201.

"It was Mim," ibid.

"the black weakness," ibid., p. 202.

"the breath belt," ibid.

"Sow some," A.deM., *Speak*, p. 137.

129 "met [her] like," ibid., p. 158.

"lovely new negligee," ibid.

"He had no idea," ibid., pp. 158–59.

"a bit frantic," ibid., p. 160.

"Hardly anything," ibid., p. 161.

"to shoot the works," ibid.

"the next day," ibid., pp. 161–62.

"mere excuse," ibid., p. 165.

"quiet and deferential," ibid., p. 164.

"finely boned and," ibid.

*Cole Porter's tragic fall from a horse in which both legs were crushed did not occur until 1937, so Agnes could not have been describing a disability but rather a mannerism. From 1937 until 1942, Porter submitted to a total of thirty-one operations, but his pain and disability were never to be alleviated.

130 "Gertie and Doug," ibid., p. 169.

"stopped the show," ibid., pp. 177–78.

"I'm an outsider...," ibid., p. 191.

"the dances got," ibid., p. 193.

Georgia Sand was removed from the show.

"gloomy impression," ibid., p. 198.

"disagreeable, stubborn," ibid., p. 193.

"a fake and revolting," ibid., p. 202.

131 "a large front," ibid., p. 213.

"source of strength," ibid., p. 216.

"delightful," ibid., p. 217.

"Thick, heavy, throat-wrecking," ibid., p. 222.

"She can't dance," ibid., p. 227.

"There will be," ibid., p. 215.

"When Uncle Ce's," ibid., p. 250.

"Godspeed," ibid., p. 250.

"gave him a growing," ibid.

132 "C. B. never got," Chierichetti, p. 51.

"He shot it all," ibid.

"to the evil of," C.B.D., p. 326.

"the uncontaminated," ibid.

"very businesslike rats," ibid., p. 327.

133 "to dance naked," A.deM., *Speak*, p. 250.

"his quizzical," A.deM., *Speak*, p. 255.

"Lift your skirts," ibid.

"dance dirty," ibid., p. 258.

"something mysterious," ibid.

"to rehearse," ibid., p. 262.

"outwardly friendly," ibid., p. 261.

"Uncle Ce keeps," ibid., pp. 261–62.

136 "I've made the," ibid., p. 266.

"a great dark," ibid.

"a strangely subdued," ibid.

"I was...rendered," ibid., p. 267.

"you mustn't mind me," ibid.

"Twice the jeweled collar," ibid., p. 269.

"Oh, no!," ibid.

"'Boy! If we," ibid.

"That dance," ibid., p. 270.

"left his house," ibid., p. 271.

*When Agnes published her first memoirs, *Dance to the Piper*, in 1952, she complied with C. B.'s request that she delete mention of this *Cleopatra* episode in her life. She did include it in *Speak to Me, Dance with Me*, published in 1973, after C. B.'s death.

"had offered practical," ibid., p. 274.

"shaping influence," ibid., p. 275.

"I know," ibid., pp. 275–76.

137 "rare skill in the," *Variety*, Aug. 21, 1934.

"Of course, it was," *The New Yorker*, Sept. 14, 1946.

"I understood," Katherine DeMille Quinn, PI.

"With Father," ibid.

"I want to talk," ibid.

"a friendly," ibid.

138 "telescoping history," C.B.D., p. 344.

"I purposely," Katherine DeMille Quinn, PI.

"One simply didn't," ibid.

139 "As a picture it," *Time*, Sept. 2, 1935.

"The trouble with," Zierold, p. 177.

Hollywood Saga (1939, Dutton).

140 "no peer in," *N.Y. Times*, Aug. 22, 1935.

"that pulls an," ibid.

"dashing pirate of," ibid.

"It's like the good," *Motion Picture Magazine*, Nov. 1932.

"To insure against," Lasky, Jr., p. 134.

*Frank Calvin worked as technical adviser on *Union Pacific*.

"Know what this," ibid., pp. 151–52.

"She always wore," ibid., p. 157.

142 "Shut up, Jeanie," Lasky, Jr., pp. 154–55.

"to retrieve," ibid.

"waved away," ibid.

"If that woman," ibid., p. 156.

"Our time was his," ibid., p. 163.

143 "I'm Cheyenne," Quinn, p. 231.

"Napoleon," ibid.

"She was dark-haired," ibid., p. 240.

144 "Kid, I just," ibid., pp. 244–45.

"I've tested several," ibid., p. 262.

"Goddamit!" ibid.

"After all," ibid.

"I played," Anthony Quinn, PI.

"Why should I read," Quinn, p. 263.

"away from her," ibid., p. 270.

145 "I wanted her," ibid.

"Remember, Tony," Anthony Quinn, PI.

"Katie's mother had," Quinn, pp. 273–75.

"The look on," ibid., p. 278.

"drove over those," ibid.

"To a poor boy," ibid.

146 "the bride had," *Kansas City Star*, Jan. 22, 1938.

*This ballet dealt with the Devil tricking three virgins into going to hell. This was later to be expanded into deMille's comedy ballet *Three Virgins and a Devil*, presented in New York in 1941 by the Ballet Theatre to excellent reviews. The scenario is the only written work of Reed's to have survived.

147 "champagne and birthday cake," A.deM., *Speak*, p. 292.

"singing at the top," ibid., p. 293.

"little new," ibid., pp. 321, 323.

"I ordered," ibid., p. 324.

"extraordinarily well," ibid., p. 323.

"The press were," ibid., p. 323.

"Ag, I've begun," ibid., p. 330.

"Will I be here," ibid., p. 360.

"Ramon, I'll stay," ibid., pp. 365–66.

"cabled a great sheaf," ibid., p. 367.

"The play scene," Houseman, *Run-Through*, p. 227.

"That night the," ibid.

149 "The book is not," Richard DeMille, PI.

"was somewhat taken," A.deM., *Dance*, p. 247.

Hooray for What opened at the Winter Garden in New York on December 1, 1937, starring Ed Wynn, book by Howard Lindsay and Russel Crouse, lyrics by Yip Harburg, music by Harold Arlen. It contained one hit song, "Down with Love." Though the critics called it a cross between an "old-fashioned melodrama and pretentious satire" (*Time*, Dec. 13, 1939), Wynn's singular talent and popularity were responsible for the show's 200-performance run.

*Mary Hunter was known at the time for her role as Marge on the nightly radio show "Easy Aces."

"a gigantic," ibid., p. 251.

*Fokine presented a new *Sylphides* and *Carnaval*; Dolin restaged *Giselle* and *Swan Lake*; Loring composed *The Great American Goof*; Tudor supplied three finished works—*Lilac Garden*, *Dark Elegies*, and *Judgment of Paris*; Andrée Howard staged her *Death and the Maiden* and *Lady into Fox*. Agnes danced only one ballet that season, Tudor's *Judgment of Paris*.

151 "exotic work for," ibid., p. 255.

"It was danced," ibid., p. 257.

152 "all nearly dead," ibid., p. 260.

"at night," ibid., p. 265.

"Youth gone," ibid., p. 234.

"the famous DeMille," *Motion Picture Herald*, April 29, 1939.

"his special art," ibid.

"We were giving," Lasky, Jr., p. 195.

A Twentieth-Century Success, 1941—1946

155 *According to records at the Writers' Guild of America West (dated October 21, 1941), Alan LeMay, Charles Bennett, and Jesse Lasky, Jr., were credited with the screenplay. However, Jeanie Macpherson is credited with having contributed "more than 10% of the value of the

completed screenplay" to the screenplay's construction ("plot material developed and converted into [final screenplay]") (Writers' Guild, Oct. 21, 1941). She did not, however, receive mention in the released film credits of the picture.
"I want to smell," Lasky, Jr., p. 216.
"whacking at each," ibid., pp. 219–20.
156 "would galvanize," ibid., p. 219.
"we just haven't," ibid.
"scarf tucked," ibid., p. 220.
"The first," ibid.
"this ink-throwing," ibid., p. 221.
"in stunned silence," ibid.
"DeMille looked," ibid.
157 "Now, for the first," C.B.D., p. 374.
"somehow escaped," ibid., p. 371.
"The film industry," N.Y. Herald Tribune, March 19, 1942.
158 "so involved and," The New Yorker, April 4, 1942.
"celebration of the," ibid.
"every bit a," N.Y. Herald Tribune, March 19, 1942.
"one man's protest," N.Y. Times, June 16, 1942.
"until France is," ibid.
"had no sex appeal," A.deM., Promenade, p. 7.
"mare's nest on," ibid., p. 8.
"a real burden," ibid.
"Wear your," ibid., p. 14.
"purchased with," ibid.
159 "pulled from a lake," ibid.
"a nice combination," ibid.
"chattering," ibid., p. 15.
"a savage wit," ibid., p. 16.
"Draining great pots," A.deM., Dance, p. 267.
"who dresses and," ibid., p. 275.
"Whom do you," ibid., p. 272.
"propped up with," ibid., p. 275.
"Couldn't we do a," ibid.
"You be arrogant," ibid., p. 274.
160 "over buttered scones," ibid., p. 275.
"It scarcely deviated," ibid.
"I really think," A.deM., PBS broadcast, May 14, 1987.
"If you don't like," ibid.
"chewing gum, squinting," ibid.
"The movements of the," Terry, p. 252.
"roaring," ibid.
"and turned on," A.deM., PBS broadcast, May 14, 1987.
"I don't really," Peter Buckley, Horizon, Sept. 1980.
163 "like four young," The New Yorker, Sept. 14, 1946.
"Well, you couldn't," Rodgers, p. 217.
*After Oklahoma!, Rodgers did one more show with Hart, a revival of A Connecticut Yankee. Hart died on November 22, 1943, a few days after the show's New York opening.
"WE THINK YOUR WORK," Fordin, p. 194.
165 "No gags, no girls," ibid., p. 198.
"a sentimental look," Boardman, p. 534.
"took to the," ibid., p. 197.

166 "with the most," A.deM., Dance, p. 321.
"The orchestra played," ibid.
"I was like a," ibid., p. 324.
"We live in the," ibid., p. 326.
"but Rouben retaliated," Rodgers, p. 223.
167 "The wrecking crew," A.deM., Dance, p. 328.
"first-night hounds," ibid.
"There's hell ahead," ibid., p. 327.
"the matinee went," ibid., p. 331.
"if he lost," ibid., p. 332.
"The curtain went," ibid., pp. 332–33.
168 "to express moods," Boardman, p. 536.
"the current year," A.deM., Promenade, p. 35.
"Laurence, I'm not," A.deM., PBS broadcast, May 14, 1987.
*Oklahoma! was to run for five years and nine weeks in New York City. A traveling American road company played almost without interruption for nine and a half years. It ran three and a half years in London and had half a dozen or more foreign companies. The film was released in 1955. A $5,000 investment in Oklahoma! realized $1,500,000 in profit. Agnes earned less than $5,000 in the first three years of the show's run. The Theatre Guild then voted in 1947 to accord her ½% royalty.
"I can pay," A.deM., Dance, p. 334.
169 "And!," A.deM., Promenade, p. 46.
"One does not," ibid.
"like a vise," ibid.
"proceeded with propriety," ibid.
"Grandfather once," Cecilia Presley, PI.
"troubled, rebellious," Katherine DeMille Quinn, PI.
"I thought everybody's," Richard DeMille, PI.
*John Blount DeMille was to have two more children. His offspring were: Allan Blount DeMille, born May 22, 1938; John Frederick DeMille, born November 11, 1942; Dianne Constance DeMille, born July 26, 1948; and Christopher DeMille, born February 27, 1961, the son of John's second wife, Cynthia.
"third-rate gangsters," Quinn, p. 287.
"who were always," ibid.
174*In 1945, the Quinns' living children were Christina Frances Quinn, born December 1, 1941; Kathleen Lester Quinn, born November 12, 1942; and Duncan Christopher Quinn, born August 3, 1945. A fourth child, Valentina Andrea Quinn, was born December 26, 1952 (Quinn, PI).
"[DeMille] considered his," Anthony Quinn, PI.
"Grandfather wanted," Cecilia Presley, PI.
"Katie would read," Quinn, p. 25.
"Grandfather turned," Cecilia Presley, PI.
"One of Grandfather," ibid.
175*The passage in 1947 of the Taft-Hartley Act assured that no one could be denied the right to work for refusal to pay a political assessment such as AFRA (American Federation of Radio Artists)

had demanded two years earlier of its members.
"DeMille never," Chierichetti, p. 254.
"was to work," C.B.D., p. 389.
"to the birth," ibid., p. 391.
"I was familiar," ibid.
176 "consulting 2,500," Unconquered script, Jan. 1948.
"special DeMille brand," Lasky, Jr., p. 250.
"We [the writers]," Lasky, Jr., p. 251.
"Cut the price," Koury, p. 168.
"He suggested," ibid.
"Just about as," N.Y. Times, Oct. 19, 1947.
"as viciously," ibid.
"sensationalized history," ibid., Nov. 26, 1947.
"DeMille pictures," ibid., Oct. 13, 1947.
177 "Oh, What a Beautiful Mornin' ," "People Will Say We're in Love," "Oklahoma!," and "The Surrey with the Fringe on Top" were the four songs in the top ten.
"was just another," Boardman, p. 538.
178 "once a goddess," ibid.
"in a blinding," ibid.
"Kurt Weill," A.deM., Promenade, pp. 77–78.
"the gentle-voiced," ibid.
"used to score," ibid.
"the Sugarplum Fairy," ibid., pp. 79–80.
"Version V," ibid., p. 113.
"Two triumphs...," Boardman, p. 539.
179 "Our little shows," A.deM., Promenade, p. 143.
"a gay and bawdy," ibid., p. 157.
"although only one-third," ibid.
"an engaging comedy," Terry, p. 300.
"[Anton] Pat Dolin," A.deM., Promenade, p. 167.
*Dolin was an Irishman. His real name was Patrick and those close to him called him "Pat."
"pure Gainsborough," ibid., p. 173.
180 "I should say," ibid., p. 174.
"beside the bed," ibid., p. 176.
"Every worker," ibid., pp. 179–80.
"I can name mine," ibid., pp. 179–80, 182, 185.
181 "lived from moment," ibid., p. 194.
"in order to do," ibid., p. 197.
"impassioned, tuneful," Boardman, p. 43.
"superficial, somewhat," ibid.
"a rushing," The New Yorker, Sept. 14, 1946.
"No. No. No," A.deM., Promenade, p. 196.
"How the hell," ibid.
"whipped up a happy," ibid., p. 197.
182 "Oh, my God," ibid., p. 198.
"all very Fourth," ibid.
"Vilification was," ibid., p. 200.
"[The ballet]," ibid., p. 201.
"no one breathed," ibid., p. 202.
"Goddamit!" ibid.
"Darling, it," ibid.
183 "sings first with," Fordin, p. 221.
*This developed into the famous seven-minute "Soliloquy" from Carousel.
"zit, zat," ibid.
"I want it," ibid.
"Remembering the," ibid., p. 231.

"*Carousel* was a," A.deM., *Promenade*, p. 243.

185 "struggled and strained," ibid.
"Well," Rodgers said, ibid., p. 248.
Carousel played 890 performances on Broadway, opened at the Drury Lane, London, June 7, 1950, and remained for 566 performances. It toured worldwide and was filmed in 1956 by Twentieth Century-Fox with Gordon MacRae and Shirley Jones.
*Released in the United States as *My Heart Goes Crazy*.
"far, far, worse," ibid., p. 266.
"The songs were," ibid.
"while twenty girls," ibid., p. 267.
186 "Your evening paper," ibid., p. 271.
"We're having," ibid., p. 279.
"There were," C.B.D., p. 113.
187 "He once told," Cecilia Presley, PI.

A Display of Endurance, 1946–1959

191 "make Brigadoon and," *Brigadoon*, book by Alan Jay Lerner.
"something like a," Rodgers, p. 251.
"a smooth interflow," ibid.
"when I first," A.deM., unpublished manuscript, 1988.
192 "she found them," Fordin, p. 253.
"Oscar, you're," ibid.
"Oscar, what is," ibid., p. 254.
"was giving me," A.deM., unpublished manuscript, 1988.
"Agnes is supreme," Rodgers, p. 251.
"It was not," ibid.
"Now you'll learn," ibid.
193 "An out-and-out," *N.Y. Post*, Oct. 11, 1947.
"Rodgers and," *N.Y. Times*, Oct. 11, 1947.
"When I was," Peter Buckley, "The Fiery deMille," *Horizon*, Sept. 1980.
194*Agnes was also to write *Lizzie Borden: Dance of Death* (1968).
195 "a towering amazon," Boardman, p. 565.
"splashily mounted," ibid.
"I have been," Koury, p. 168.
"The chemicals," ibid., pp. 167–68.
196*Condon later became the best-selling author of *The Manchurian Candidate* (1959).
"to flood the," Head, p. 86.
"for producing a," ibid.
"catching feathers," ibid.
"Of course," ibid., p. 88.
"I always had," ibid.
"He never did," ibid., p. 81.
197 "with its stained," ibid., p. 83.
"He would flick," ibid.
"the greatest," *N.Y. Times*, Nov. 14, 1949.
"a woman in," *Bible*, Judg. 16:4.
"unleashes a," Lasky, Jr., p. 258.
"The woman scorned," ibid., pp. 258–59.
"in the small," Koury, p. 15.
"progress from," ibid.
200 "At the far," ibid., p. 16.
"He felt he," ibid., p. 233.
"You have got," ibid.
"When Samson," ibid., p. 232.

"Beautiful, yes," Head, pp. 81–82.
"We ran into," ibid., p. 82.
"I have always," ibid., p. 85.
201 "Mr. DeMille took," Swanson, p. 499.
"Well, that's it," Lasky, Jr., p. 265.
"Just like that," ibid.
202 "Great films are," Selznick, *N.Y. Times*, April 25, 1948.
"idealism worthy," ibid.
"Cecil B.," ibid.
203*Dated September 16, 1953.
"the idea of," ibid.
204*North sued C. B. and Paramount for his share of the profits, which by 1958 he had not yet received, although *The Greatest Show on Earth* had recouped nearly four times its original cost.
"This is not," *Los Angeles Times*, July 24, 1949.
"DeMille's antics," Koury, p. 247.
"When Jody says," ibid., p. 248.
"Once upon a time," ibid.
205 "a stalking figure," ibid., p. 257.
"It's 101," ibid., p. 258.
"It's a lot," ibid., p. 278.
"all the wonders," *The New Yorker*, Nov. 19, 1952.
206*Academy Awards were presented to Victor Milner (*Cleopatra*), Cinematography, 1934; Art Direction, Hans Dreier, Walter Tyler, Sam Comer, Ray Moyer (*Samson and Delilah*), 1950; Costume Design, Edith Head, Dorothy Jenkins, Elois Jenssen, Gile Steele, Gwen Wakeling (*Samson and Delilah*), 1950.
"I wish to," Academy of Motion Picture Arts and Sciences Archives.
"They've given me," Philip Jenkinson, BBC broadcast, Aug. 1981.
*Gary Cooper won Best Actor for *High Noon*, Shirley Booth won Best Actress for *Come Back, Little Sheba*, and Gloria Grahame, Best Supporting Actress, not for *The Greatest Show on Earth*, but for *The Bad and the Beautiful*. Ironically, John Ford won Best Director for *The Quiet Man*, and though only three writers received final credit, the award for Best Motion Picture Story went to *The Greatest Show on Earth*.
"Why make a," Cecilia Presley, PI.
"Katie and I sat," Quinn, pp. 291–92.
"Really, Tony," ibid., p. 293.
207 "almost choked the," ibid., p. 295.
"I hated the atmosphere," Anthony Quinn, PI.
"The world needs," C.B.D., p. 411.
"COME WADE," Lasky, Jr., p. 282.
*The other three writers on *The Ten Commandments* were Aeneas MacKenzie, Jack Gariss, and Fredric M. Frank.
"My choice was," C.B.D., p. 415.
208 "Brynner the story," ibid., p. 416.
"a rather bogus," Lasky, Jr., p. 300.
"a deep sense," ibid., p. 301.
"as much from," ibid.
"suddenly he was," ibid., p. 302.
"Packing, Jesse?" ibid.
"You're—walking," ibid., p. 303.
"Max Jacobson," Cecilia Presley, PI.

209*Dekker died in a bizarre suicide by self-strangulation. Since he was known to be on drugs dispensed by Jacobson, his death led to the trial and revocation of Max Jacobson's license to practice medicine.
"Good old pals," ibid.
"On the Egyptian," C.B.D., p. 421.
"his old friend," ibid., p. 428.
210 "I was spending," Westmore, p. 164.
"I sensed that," ibid., p. 165.
"Suddenly," ibid.
"He strode off," ibid., pp. 165–66.
214 "Something's happened," ibid., p. 166.
"He's alive, Frank," ibid., p. 167.
"was slumped in," ibid.
"What happened," ibid.
"That's all right," ibid.
"madly in love," ibid., p. 168.
"a little pointed," ibid.
"A beat-up," ibid., p. 170.
"We talked a bit about," ibid.
"In the city," Philip Jenkenson, BBC documentary, Aug. 1981.
215 "Who do you," ibid.
"Not that I," ibid.
"raw pain," Anthony Quinn, PI.
"I took the picture," ibid.
216 "In the Midrash," *Wisdom*, Oct. 1956.
217 "Against the advice," C.B.D., p. 439.
"We have a lot," Higham, p. 312.
"He was dressed," Anthony Quinn, PI.

The Dynasty Continues

219 "On the side," "Small World," CBS, Dec. 6, 1959.
"Grandfather refused," Cecilia Presley, PI.
220 "There was a picture," "Small World," CBS, Dec. 6, 1959.
"rollicking, boom-or-bust," Boardman, p. 581.
221*The story was to be greatly rewritten for the film version made in 1969 starring Lee Marvin, Clint Eastwood, and Jean Seberg.
*A song from the original score, which was to become a Porter classic, "From This Moment On," had been deleted in Philadelphia.
"the airy grace," ibid.
"During the forties," *Horizon*, Sept. 1980.
222 "modern morality," Terry, p. 248.
"At 5:50 P.M.," A.deM., *Reprieve*, p. 15.
224 "Nothing had seemed," ibid., pp. 19–20.
"Shortly before the," ibid., p. 51.
" 'Mag, this should,' " ibid., pp. 51–52.
"wasn't half-well," ibid., pp. 151–52.
"There were reasons," ibid., pp. 159–60.
"Walter,' I said," ibid., p. 160.
"not pliés...but," ibid., p. 179.
225 "I wanted to stand," ibid., p. 211.
"She was gallant," ibid., p. 243.
"thunderingly successful," ibid., p. 272.
226 "Bob Joffrey," ibid., p. 285.
"And the flowers," ibid., p. 287.
"I'm not the," A.deM., PBS broadcast, May 14, 1987.

PLAYS, FILMS, CHOREOGRAPHY, BOOKS

Henry DeMille

PLAYWRIGHT

John Delmer's Daughters; or, Duty. Madison Square Theatre, New York, December 10, 1883

The Main Line, or Rawson's Y: An Idyl of the Railroad. With Charles Barnard. Lyceum Theatre, New York, September 18, 1886, rewritten 1891 as *The Danger Signal*

The Wife. With David Belasco. Lyceum Theatre, New York, November 1, 1887

Lord Chumley. With David Belasco. Lyceum Theatre, New York, August 20, 1888

The Charity Ball. With David Belasco. Lyceum Theatre, New York, November 19, 1889

Men and Women. With David Belasco. Proctor's Twenty-third Street Theatre, New York, October 21, 1890

The Lost Paradise. Adapted from Ludwig Fulda's *Das verlorene Paradies.* Proctor's Twenty-third Street Theatre, New York, November 16, 1891

The Promised Land. Unfinished (see page 31)

William deMille

PLAYWRIGHT, ESSAYIST

A Mixed Foursome. January 21, 1900

The Forest Ring. December 20, 1900, with Charles Barnard

The Marriage of Guinnette. Private performance, March 1, 1901

Forest Flower. March 6, 1902, *Smart Set*, June 7, 1902

The Staiseling. Smart Set, November 1902

The Higher Law. Life, January 21, 1904

As It Was in the Beginning. Life, February 11, 1904

Old Mother Hubbard. Smart Set, April 1904

Diary of a Play. Skit, *Life*, May 5, 1904

Strongheart. December 29, 1904

The Martyrs. Smart Set, February 1906

The Land of the Free. April 2, 1906

Son of the Wind. 1906, with Cecil B. DeMille

Jefferson Play. Satire written for dinner for Single Tax, April 18, 1907

Classmates. Springfield, August 26, 1907; New York, August 29, 1907, with Margaret Turnbull

The Warrens of Virginia. Philadelphia, November 19, 1907; New York, December 3, 1907, production under the supervision of Mr. Belasco

The Royal Mounted. Plainfield, N.J., March 12, 1908; New York, April 6, 1908, with Cecil B. DeMille

The Rubber Plant. Life, January 22, 1911

The Land of the Free. 3 acts, New Haven, September 18, 1910

The Man Higher Up. Sketch, Columbia Lit., April 1911

The Woman. Washington, D.C., April 17, 1911; New York, September 19, 1911

Rolls. Skit, 12th Night Revel, January 6, 1912; Proctor's Fifth Ave., February 5, 1912

The Unwritten Agreement. Essay

The Ogdens, with May Turnbull

The Stork. Skit, Lambs' Gambol, February 4, 1912

Number 13 West. Farce,

After Five, with Cecil B. DeMille, 1912

Fifty Years from Now. Lyceum Benefit, March 18, 1912; Princess, April 12, 1913

Church Play. March 6, 1913, with Cecil B. DeMille

Christmas Spirit. Children's play, John Martin's book, January 1913

Votes for Fairies. Children's play, John Martin's book, February 1913

The Squealer. Union Hall, March 17, 1913

The Ride to Hell. Written August 1913

Poor Old Jim. Odeon, 145th St., September 15, 1913

FILM SCREENWRITER (See also FILM DIRECTOR)

The Warrens of Virginia. Presented by Jesse L. Lasky in association with David Belasco, released by Paramount Pictures, February 15, 1915. Director and Producer: Cecil B. DeMille

Carmen. Produced by Jesse L. Lasky Feature Play Company, released by Paramount Pictures, October 31, 1915. Director and Producer: Cecil B. DeMille

Maria Rosa. Produced by Jesse L. Lasky Feature Play Company, released by Paramount Pictures, May 7, 1916. Director and Producer: Cecil B. DeMille

The Soul of Kura San. Produced by Jesse L. Lasky Feature Play Company, released on the Paramount Program, November 2, 1916. Director: E. J. LeSaint. Producer: Jesse L. Lasky. Scenario by William C. deMille

We Can't Have Everything. Produced by Artcraft Pictures, released by Famous Players-Lasky on the Paramount Program, July 7, 1918. Director and Producer: Cecil B. DeMille

Why Change Your Wife? Produced by Artcraft Pictures, released by Famous Players-Lasky on the Paramount Program, May 2, 1920. Director and Producer: Cecil B. DeMille. Scenario by Olga Printzlau and Sada Cowan, from the story by William deMille

Captain Fury. Hal Roach, 1939. Director: Hal Roach. With Grover Jones and Jack Jevne

FILM DIRECTOR

Anton, the Terrible. Produced by Jesse L. Lasky Feature Play Company, released by Paramount Pictures, 1915

The Ragamuffin. Produced by Jesse L. Lasky Feature Play Company, released by Paramount Pictures, January 20, 1916. Scenario

by William C. deMille. Refilmed in 1925 by William C. deMille as *The Splendid Crime*

The Sowers. Produced by William C. deMille, presented by Jesse L. Lasky, released by Paramount Pictures, March 30, 1916. Producer: William C. deMille

The Clown. Produced by Jesse L. Lasky Feature Play Company, released by Paramount Pictures, June 7, 1916. Producer: William C. deMille

The Black List. Produced by Jesse L. Lasky Feature Play Company, released by Paramount Pictures, 1916

The Heir of the Hoorah. Presented by Jesse L. Lasky Feature Play Company, released by Paramount Pictures, 1916. Scenario by William C. deMille

Hashimuro Togo. Presented by Jesse L. Lasky Feature Play Company, released by Paramount Pictures, 1917. Scenario by William C. deMille

The Ghost House. Presented by Jesse L. Lasky Feature Play Company, released by Paramount Pictures, 1917

The Secret Game. Produced by Jesse L. Lasky under the direction of William C. deMille, presented by Jesse L. Lasky, released by Paramount Pictures, December 1917.

One More American. Presented by Jesse L. Lasky, released by Paramount Pictures, February 25, 1918. Producer: William C. deMille. Scenario by William C. deMille

The Honor of His House. A Jesse L. Lasky Production, distributed by Paramount Pictures, April 1, 1918

Yellow Tickets. A Jesse L. Lasky Production, distributed by Paramount Pictures, 1918

The Widow's Might. A Jesse L. Lasky Production, distributed by Paramount Pictures, 1918

Mirandy Smiles. A Jesse L. Lasky Production, distributed by Paramount Pictures, 1918

The Mystery Girl. Presented by Jesse L. Lasky, distributed by Paramount Pictures, released December 27, 1918. Producer: Jesse L. Lasky

Peg o' My Heart. Filmed in 1919 for Paramount-Artcraft but never released as the play's author claimed the screen rights had been sold by his producer, Oliver Morosco, without his consent

The Tree of Knowledge. Presented by Paramount-Artcraft, released January 1920

The Prince Chap. Presented by Jesse L. Lasky, released by Paramount-Artcraft, 1920. Producer: William C. deMille

Jack Straw. Presented by Jesse L. Lasky, distributed by Paramount-Artcraft, released 1920. Producer: William C. deMille

The Last Romance. Presented by Famous Players-Lasky, distributed by Paramount Pictures, 1920. Producer: William C. deMille

Midsummer Madness. A William deMille Production, Famous Players-Lasky, released by Paramount Pictures, December 18, 1920. Scenario by William C. deMille

What Every Woman Knows. Presented by Famous Players-Lasky, distributed by Paramount Pictures, released April 24, 1921 (premiered in New York March 12, 1921). Producer: Jesse L. Lasky

After the Show. Presented by Jesse L. Lasky, Famous Players-Lasky, distributed by Paramount Pictures, October 30, 1921. Producer: Jesse L. Lasky

Conrad in Quest of His Youth. Presented by Famous Players-Lasky, distributed by Paramount Pictures, November 1921. Producer: William C. deMille

Miss Lulu Bett. Presented by Famous Players-Lasky, distributed by Paramount Pictures, released January 1, 1922 (premiered in Los Angeles, November 13, 1921). Producer: Adolph Zukor

Bought and Paid For. Presented by Adolph Zukor, Famous Players-Lasky, distributed by Paramount Pictures, released April 16, 1922

Nice People. Presented by Adolph Zukor, Famous Players-Lasky, distributed by Paramount Pictures, released September 4, 1922

Clarence. Presented by Adolph Zukor, Famous Players-Lasky, distributed by Paramount Pictures, released November 19, 1922

The World's Applause. Presented by Adolph Zukor, Famous Players-Lasky, distributed by Paramount Pictures, released January 29, 1923

Grumpy. Presented by Adolph Zukor, Famous Players-Lasky, distributed by Paramount Pictures, released April 8, 1923

The Marriage Maker. Presented by Adolph Zukor, Famous Players-Lasky, distributed by Paramount Pictures, released 1923

Only 38. Presented by Adolph Zukor, Famous Players-Lasky, distributed by Paramount Pictures, released June 17, 1923

Don't Call It Love. Presented by Adolph Zukor, Famous Players-Lasky, distributed by Paramount Pictures, released January 6, 1924

Icebound. A William deMille Production, presented by Adolph Zukor and Jesse L. Lasky, distributed by Paramount Pictures, released March 20, 1924

Bedroom Window. A William deMille Production, presented by Adolph Zukor and Jesse L. Lasky, Famous Players-Lasky, distributed by Paramount Pictures, released June 15, 1924

The Fast Set. A William C. deMille Production, Paramount Pictures, November 1924

Locked Doors. A William deMille Production, presented by Adolph Zukor and Jesse L. Lasky, Famous Players-Lasky, distributed by Paramount Pictures, released January 5, 1925

Men and Women. Presented by Adolph Zukor and Jesse L. Lasky, Famous Players-Lasky, distributed by Paramount Pictures, released March 23, 1925

Lost—A Wife. Famous Players-Lasky, released June 1925

New Brooms. A William deMille Production, presented by Famous Players-Lasky, released November 1925

The Splendid Crime. Presented by Adolph Zukor and Jesse L. Lasky, Famous Players-Lasky, distributed by Paramount Pictures, released January 4, 1926

The Runaway. Presented by Famous Players-Lasky, April 1926

For Alimony Only. A William deMille Production, presented by John C. Finn, distributed by Producers Distributing Corporation, September 20, 1926. Producer: William C. deMille

The Little Adventuress. A William C. deMille production, distributed by Producers Distributing Corporation, 1927

Tenth Avenue. A William C. deMille Production, Pathé release, October 7, 1928

Craig's Wife. Pathé production and release, December 2, 1928

The Doctor's Secret. Paramount production and release, February 1929

The Idle Rich. Metro-Goldwyn-Mayer Production, June 1929

The Man Higher Up. Metro-Goldwyn-Mayer Production, 1929. Scenario by William C. deMille, based on his own play of the same title

This Mad World. Metro-Goldwyn-Mayer Production, released April 12, 1930

Passion Flower. Metro-Goldwyn-Mayer Production, released by M-G-M, December 6, 1930

Two Kinds of Women. A Paramount Pictures Production, released by Paramount, June 15, 1932

His Double Life. A Paramount release, December 1933, with Arthur Hopkins

The Great Adventure. A Paramount release, 1934, with Arthur Hopkins

Cecil B. DeMille

ACTOR

The Fan. 1899
Put to the Test. 1899
Le père prodigue. 1900
Mas'r Van. 1900
A Repentance. 1900
The Coxcomb. 1900
Hearts are Trump. 1900
To Have and to Hold. 1901
Are You a Mason? 1901
Alice of Old Vincennes. 1901
His Grace the Janitor. 1902
Mistakes Will Happen. 1903
Nell Gwynne. 1903
Lord Chumley. 1903, 1905
If I Were King. 1903
Hamlet. 1903
A Gentleman of France. 1903
The Missourians. 1904
Lord Chumley. 1905
My Wife's Husbands. 1905
The Prince Chap. 1905
Summer stock in Elitch Gardens, Denver:
  A Japanese Nightingale, The Maneuvers of Jane, Hearts Courageous, As You Like It, Mice and Men, Dorothy Vernon of Haddon Hall, Tess of the D'Urbervilles, The Taming of the Shrew, Ingomar, Madame Sans Gêne, When Knighthood Was in Flower, Under Two Flags
The Warrens of Virginia, 1907
The Wishing Ring. 1909

PRODUCER, DIRECTOR

The Land of the Free. 1910, producer
The Stampede. 1910, producer and writer, with Lillian Buckingham
Speed. 1911, producer
The Marriage-Not. 1912, director
Cheer Up. 1912, producer
Standard Opera Company, stage manager and director, 1906:
  The Bohemian Girl (also played role of Florestein), *Martha, The Chimes of Normandy, The Mikado*

PLAYWRIGHT

Son of the Winds. 1906, with William deMille
Kit. 1907
The Man's the King. 1907
The Royal Mounted. 1908, with William deMille
The Duelist. 1908
The Stampede. 1910, producer and writer, with Lillian Buckingham
The Return of Peter Grimm. 1910, with David Belasco
California. 1911
After Five. 1912, with William deMille
The Antique Girl. 1912, with William Le Baron
In the Barracks. 1912, with Grant Stewart
Church Play. 1913, with William deMille
The Reckless Age. 1913
The Water Cure. 1913, with Mary Roberts Rinehart

FILM DIRECTOR AND PRODUCER

The Squaw Man. Released by Jesse L. Lasky Feature Play Company, February 15, 1914. Director and Producer: with Oscar Apfel
The Call of the North. Released by Jesse L. Lasky Feature Play Company, August 15, 1914
The Virginian. Produced by Jesse L. Lasky Feature Play Company, Released by Paramount Pictures, September 7, 1914
What's His Name. Produced by Jesse L. Lasky Feature Play Company, released by Paramount Pictures, October 22, 1914
The Man from Home. Produced by Jesse L. Lasky Feature Play Company, released by Paramount Pictures, November 9, 1914
Rose of the Rancho. Produced by Jesse L. Lasky Feature Play Company, released by Paramount Pictures, November 15, 1914
The Girl of the Golden West. Presented by Jesse L. Lasky Feature Play Company in association with David Belasco, released by Paramount Pictures, January 4, 1915
The Warrens of Virginia. Presented by Jesse L. Lasky in association with David Belasco, released by Paramount Pictures, February 15, 1915
The Unafraid. Produced by Jesse L. Lasky Feature Play Company, released by Paramount Pictures, April 1, 1915
The Captive. Produced by Jesse L. Lasky Feature Play Company, released by Paramount Pictures, April 22, 1915
The Wild Goose Chase. Produced by Jesse L. Lasky Feature Play Company, released by Paramount Pictures, May 27, 1915

The Arab. Produced by Jesse L. Lasky Feature Play Company, released by Paramount Pictures, June 14, 1915

Chimmie Fadden. Produced by Jesse L. Lasky Feature Play Company, released by Paramount Pictures, June 28, 1915

Kindling. Produced by Jesse L. Lasky Feature Play Company, released by Paramount Pictures, July 22, 1915

Carmen. Produced by Jesse L. Lasky Feature Play Company, released by Paramount Pictures, October 31, 1915

Chimmie Fadden Out West. Produced by Jesse L. Lasky Feature Play Company, released by Paramount Pictures, November 21, 1915

The Cheat. Produced by Jesse L. Lasky Feature Play Company, released by Paramount Pictures, December 12, 1915

The Golden Chance. Produced by Jesse L. Lasky Feature Play Company, released by Paramount Pictures, December 30, 1915

Temptation. Produced by Jesse L. Lasky Feature Play Company, released by Paramount Pictures, January 3, 1916

The Trail of the Lonesome Pine. Produced by Jesse L. Lasky Feature Play Company, released by Paramount Pictures, February 14, 1916

The Heart of Nora Flynn. Produced by Jesse L. Lasky Feature Play Company, released by Paramount Pictures, April 23, 1916

Maria Rosa. Produced by Jesse L. Lasky Feature Play Company, released by Paramount Pictures, May 7, 1916

The Dream Girl. Produced by Jesse L. Lasky Feature Play Company, released by Paramount Pictures, July 27, 1916

Joan the Woman. Exploited by the Cardinal Film Co., released by Paramount Pictures, December 1916

Romance of the Redwoods. Produced by Artcraft Pictures, released by Paramount Pictures, May 14, 1917

The Little American. Produced by Artcraft Pictures, released by Paramount Pictures, July 12, 1917

The Woman God Forgot. Produced by Artcraft Pictures, released by Paramount Pictures, November 8, 1917

The Devil Stone. Produced by Artcraft Pictures, released by Paramount Pictures, December 31, 1917

The Whispering Chorus. Produced by Artcraft Pictures, released by Famous Players-Lasky on the Paramount Program, March 28, 1918

Old Wives for New. Produced by Artcraft Pictures, released by Famous Players-Lasky on the Paramount Program, May 1918

We Can't Have Everything. Produced by Artcraft Pictures, released by Famous Players-Lasky on the Paramount Program, July 7, 1918

Till I Come Back to You. Produced by Artcraft Pictures, released by Famous Players-Lasky on the Paramount Program, September 1, 1918

The Squaw Man. Produced by Artcraft Pictures, released by Famous Players-Lasky on the Paramount Program, December 15, 1918. Remake of DeMille's first film

Don't Change Your Husband. Produced by Artcraft Pictures, released by Famous Players-Lasky on the Paramount Program, January 26, 1919

For Better, for Worse. Produced by Artcraft Pictures, released by Famous Players-Lasky on the Paramount Program, May 4, 1919

Male and Female. Produced by Artcraft Pictures, released by Famous Players-Lasky on the Paramount Program, November 30, 1919

Why Change Your Wife? Produced by Artcraft Pictures, released by Famous Players-Lasky on the Paramount Program, May 2, 1920

Something to Think About. Presented by Jesse L. Lasky for Artcraft Pictures, released by Famous Players-Lasky on the Paramount Program, October 24, 1920

Forbidden Fruit. Released by Famous Players-Lasky on the Paramount Program, February 12, 1921. Remake of *The Golden Chance* (1915)

The Affairs of Anatol. Released by Famous Players-Lasky as a DeMille-Paramount special, September 18, 1921

Fool's Paradise. Released by Famous Players-Lasky on the Paramount Program, December 9, 1921

Saturday Night. Released by Famous Players-Lasky on the Paramount Program, January 29, 1922

Manslaughter. Released by Famous Players-Lasky on the Paramount Program, September 29, 1922

Adam's Rib. Released by Famous Players-Lasky on the Paramount Program, March 4, 1923

The Ten Commandments. Released by Famous Players-Lasky as a DeMille-Paramount special, November 23, 1923

Triumph. Presented by Adolph Zukor and Jesse L. Lasky, released by Famous Players-Lasky on the Paramount Program, April 27, 1924

Feet of Clay. Presented by Adolph Zukor and Jesse L. Lasky, released by Famous Players-Lasky on the Paramount Program, September 28, 1924

The Golden Bed. Presented by Adolph Zukor and Jesse L. Lasky, released by Famous Players-Lasky on the Paramount Program, January, 1925

The Road to Yesterday. Filmed at the DeMille Studio, released by Producers Distributing Corporation, November 15, 1925

The Volga Boatman. Filmed at the DeMille Studio, released by Producers Distributing Corporation, May 23, 1926

The King of Kings. Filmed at the DeMille Studio, produced by Cinema Corporation of America, released by Pathé Exchange, April 19, 1927

The Godless Girl. Filmed at the DeMille Studio, released by Pathé Exchange, March 31, 1929

Dynamite. Released by Metro-Goldwyn-Mayer Distributing Corporation, December 13, 1929

Madam Satan. Released by Metro-Goldwyn-Mayer, October 5, 1930

The Squaw Man (Entitled in England, *The White Man*). Released by Metro-Goldwyn-Mayer, September 19, 1931. Remake of the 1914 and 1918 silent versions

The Sign of the Cross. Released by Paramount Publix, December 3, 1932

This Day and Age. Released by Paramount Productions, August 25, 1933

Four Frightened People. Released by Paramount Productions, January 27, 1934

Cleopatra. Presented by Adolph Zukor, released by Paramount Productions, July 25, 1934

The Crusades. Presented by Adolph Zukor, released by Paramount Productions, August 21, 1935

The Plainsman. Presented by Adolph Zukor, released by Paramount Pictures, January 1, 1937

The Buccaneer. Presented by Adolph Zukor, released by Paramount Pictures, February 4, 1938

Union Pacific. Released by Paramount Pictures, April 28, 1939

North West Mounted Police. Released by Paramount Pictures, October 22, 1940

Reap the Wild Wind. Released by Paramount Pictures, March 19, 1942

The Story of Dr. Wassell. Released by Paramount Pictures, April 26, 1944

Unconquered. Released by Paramount Pictures, September 24, 1947

Samson and Delilah. Released by Paramount Pictures, October 21, 1949

The Greatest Show on Earth. Released by Paramount Pictures, July 1, 1952

The Ten Commandments. Released by Paramount Pictures, October 5, 1956

Katherine DeMille

MOVIE ROLES

Madam Satan. Released by Metro-Goldwyn-Mayer Distributing Company, October 5, 1930. Directed and produced by Cecil B. DeMille

Viva Villa. M-G-M (David O. Selznick), 1934

The Trumpet Blows. Produced and released by Paramount Pictures, April 1934

Belle of the Nineties. Paramount Pictures (William Le Baron), 1934

All the King's Horses. Paramount Pictures, 1935

Call of the Wild. TCF (Darryl F. Zanuck), 1935

The Crusades. Presented by Adolph Zukor; released by Paramount Productions, August 21, 1935. Directed and produced by Cecil B. DeMille

Drift Fence. Harold Hurley Production, released by Paramount Pictures, March 1936

Sky Parade. Harold Hurley Production, released by Paramount Pictures, April 1936

Ramona. TCF (Sol M. Wurtzel), 1936

Banjo on My Knee. TCF (Nunnally Johnson), 1936

Charlie Chan at the Olympics. 1937

Love Under Fire. TCF (Nunnally Johnson), 1937

Under Suspicion. Produced and released by Columbia Pictures, December 1937

Blockade. Walter Wanger, 1938

In Old Caliente. Produced and distributed by Republic, June 1939

Isle of Destiny. Franklyn Warner Production, released by RKO, April 1940

Ellery Queen, Master Detective. Produced and released by Columbia Pictures, December 1940

Aloma of the South Seas. Paramount (Monte Bell), 1941

Black Gold. Allied Artists Productions, 1947

Unconquered. Released by Paramount Pictures, September 24, 1947. Directed by Cecil B. DeMille

Agnes deMille

BALLET CHOREOGRAPHER

Stagefright. Little Theatre, New York, March 13, 1927. Costumes by Agnes deMille

Jenny Loved a Soldier. Cornell University, University Hall, Ithaca, New York, April 28, 1927. Costumes by Agnes deMille

Two Romantic Waltzes. Cornell University, Ithaca, New York, April 28, 1927. Costumes by Agnes deMille

Ballet Class After Degas. New York, 1928

Harvest Reel. Martin Beck Theatre, New York, February 17, 1929. Costumes by Agnes deMille

May Day. Martin Beck Theatre, New York, February 17, 1929. Costumes by Agnes deMille

Tryout. Martin Beck Theatre, New York, February 17, 1929. Costumes by Agnes deMille

Ouled Naïl. Martin Beck Theatre, New York, May 1929. Costumes by Agnes deMille

Julia Dances. MacDowell Club House, New York, January 26, 1930. Costumes by Agnes deMille

Armistice Day. Craig Theatre, New York, February 1, 1931

Burgomaster's Branle. Craig Theatre, New York, February 5, 1931. Costumes by Agnes deMille

Eighteenth Century Suite. Craig Theatre, New York, February 5, 1931. Costumes by Agnes deMille

Cries of London. Craig Theatre, New York, February 5, 1931. Costumes by Agnes deMille

The Parvenues. Craig Theatre, New York, February 5, 1931. Costumes by Agnes deMille

Themes and Variations. Craig Theatre, New York, February 5, 1931. Costumes by Agnes deMille

Scherzo. Three Arts Club, New York February 27, 1933. Costumes by Agnes deMille

Dance of Excitement. Ballet Club, New York, May 5, 1933. Costumes by Agnes deMille

Hymn No. 2. Mercury Theatre, London, January 4, 1934

Allegro. Mercury Theatre, London, January 4, 1934

Grotesque Héroïque. Mercury Theatre, London, January 4, 1934. Costumes by Agnes deMille

American Suite. Mercury Theatre, London, January 4, 1934

Rehearsal: Symphonic Ballet. Mercury Theatre, London, January 4, 1934. Costumes by Agnes deMille

Incident with the Spanish Ambassador. Guild Theatre, New York, February 3, 1935

Minuet from the Jupiter Symphony. Guild Theatre, New York, February 3, 1935. Costumes by Agnes deMille

Mountain White. Guild Theatre, New York, February 3, 1935. Costumes by Agnes deMille

Dance of Death. Guild Theatre, New York, February 3, 1935. Costumes by Agnes deMille

Witch Spell. Guild Theatre, New York, February 3, 1935. Costumes by Agnes deMille

Plaisir d'Amour. Wilshire Ebell Theatre, Los Angeles, May 5, 1935. Costumes by Agnes deMille

Elizabethan Suite. Playhouse, Oxford, June 18, 1937. Costumes by Agnes deMille

Rehearsal: Modern Dance Group. YMHA, Theresa Kaufmann Concert Hall, New York, January 15, 1939

Strip Tease. YMHA, New York, January 18, 1939. Costumes by Agnes deMille

Conversations Pleasant and Unpleasant. London, 1939–40

Black Ritual. Center Theatre, New York, January 22, 1940

Czech Festival. YMHA, New York, March 17, 1940. Costumes by Agnes deMille

Three Virgins and a Devil. Produced by Ballet Theatre, New York, February 11, 1941

Drums Sound in Hackensack. Maxine Elliott Theatre, New York, October 2, 1941

Night Scene. Memorial Theatre, Chicago, October 30, 1941. Costumes by Agnes deMille

Rodeo (subtitled *The Courting at Burnt Ranch*). Metropolitan Opera House, New York, October 16, 1942. Produced by the Ballet Russe de Monte Carlo, New York

Tally-Ho! (subtitled *The Frail Quarry*). Los Angeles, February 25, 1944. Produced by Ballet Theatre

Fall River Legend. Metropolitan Opera House, New York, April 22, 1948. Produced by Ballet Theatre

The Harvest According. Metropolitan Opera House, New York, October 1, 1952. Produced by Ballet Theatre

Cherry Tree Legend. Municipal Auditorium, Savannah, Ga., October 28, 1953

Grand Fête de Gala. U.S. tour, fall 1953

Agnes deMille Dance Theatre. 1953–54

Gold Rush. June 1954

The Rib of Eve. New York, April 25, 1956. Produced by Ballet Theatre

Sebastian. Phoenix Theatre, New York, May 27, 1957

The Bitter Weird. 1961

The Wind in the Mountains. Presented by American Ballet Theatre at the New York State Theatre, New York, March 17, 1965

The Four Marys. State Theatre, New York, March 23, 1965

The Rehearsal. Hunter College Playhouse, New York, October 26, 1965

Golden Age. 1967

A Rose for Miss Emily. Presented at the North Carolina School of the Arts, Winston-Salem, N.C., October 24, 1970

Agnes deMille Heritage Dance Theater. 1973

Logger's Clog. Winston-Salem, North Carolina School of the Arts, Reynolds Auditorium, April 26, 1973

Matrix. Winston-Salem, North Carolina School of the Arts, Reynolds Auditorium, April 26, 1973

Texas Fourth. Presented by the Agnes deMille Heritage Dance Theater at the North Carolina School of the Arts, 1973

Conversations About the Dance. 1974

Summer. Music Hall, Boston, April 10, 1975

A Bridegroom Called Death. City Center 55th Street Theater, New York, November 1, 1978. Earlier version entitled *Inconsequentials.* Richmond Ballet, November 1981. Earlier version entitled *Bridegroom Called Death*

The Informer. Presented by American Ballet Theatre at the Shrine Auditorium, Los Angeles, March 15, 1988

THEATRE CHOREOGRAPHER

The Black Crook. Hoboken, N.J., 1929, revival

Nymph Errant. Adelphi Theatre, October 6, 1933. Presented by Charles B. Cochran

Tonight at 8:30 (formerly *Tonight at 7:30*). Phoenix Theatre, London, January 1936

Hamlet. A Leslie Howard Production, 1936

Hooray for What? Winter Garden, New York, December 1, 1937

Oklahoma! St. James Theatre, New York, March 31, 1943. Presented by the Theatre Guild

One Touch of Venus. Imperial Theatre, New York, October 7, 1943. Presented by Cheryl Crawford and John Wildberg

Bloomer Girl. Schubert Theatre, New York, October 5, 1944. Presented by John C. Wilson with Nat Goldstone

Carousel. Majestic Theatre, New York, April 19, 1945. Presented by the Theatre Guild

Carousel. Drury Lane Theatre, London, June 7, 1950. Presented by Prince Littler, with the Theatre Guild

Brigadoon. Ziegfeld Theatre, New York, March 13, 1947. Presented by Cheryl Crawford

Gentlemen Prefer Blondes. Ziegfeld Theatre, New York, December 8, 1949. Presented by Herman Levin and Oliver Smith

Paint Your Wagon. Schubert Theatre, New York, November 12, 1951

The Girl in Pink Tights. Mark Hellinger Theatre, New York, March 5, 1954

Goldilocks. Lunt-Fontanne Theatre, New York, October 11, 1958

Juno. Winter Garden Theatre, New York, March 9, 1959

Kwamina. 54th Street Theatre, New York, October 23, 1961

110 in the Shade. Broadhurst Theatre, New York, October 24, 1963

FILM CHOREOGRAPHER

Romeo and Juliet. 1936

London Town. 1945

Oklahoma! 1955

THEATRE DIRECTOR

Allegro. Majestic Theatre, New York, October 10, 1947. Presented by the Theatre Guild. Choreographed by Agnes deMille

The Rape of Lucretia. 1948

Out of This World. 1950

Come Summer. 1970. Choreographed by Agnes deMille

TELEVISION

Omnibus programs:
The Art of Ballet. 1956
The Art of Choreography. 1956
Lizzie Borden. 1957
Bloomer Girl. 1956
Gold Rush. 1958

BOOKS

Dance to the Piper. Atlantic-Little, Brown. 1952
And Promenade Home. Atlantic-Little, Brown. 1958
To a Young Dancer. Atlantic-Little, Brown. 1962
The Book of the Dance. Golden Press. 1963
Lizzie Borden: Dance of Death. Atlantic-Little, Brown. 1968
Dance in America. U.S. Government Printing Office. 1970

Russian Journals. Johnson Reprint. 1971
Speak to Me, Dance with Me. Little, Brown and Company. 1973
Where the Wings Grow. Doubleday & Company, Inc. 1978
America Dances. Macmillan. 1980
Reprieve, A Memoir. Doubleday & Company, Inc. 1981
Articles in *Vogue, Atlantic, Good Housekeeping, McCall's, The New York Times, Esquire, Architectural Digest*

BIBLIOGRAPHY

Atkinson, Brooks, *Broadway*, New York, N.Y.: The Macmillan Company, 1970

Balanchine, George and Francis Mason, *Balanchine's Complete Stories of the Great Ballets*, Garden City, N.Y.: Doubleday & Company, Inc., 1977

Beer, Thomas, *The Mauve Decade*, New York, N.Y.: Vintage Books, 1961

Belasco, David, *The Plays of Henry C. DeMille*, Robert Hamilton Ball, ed., Bloomington, Indiana: Indiana University Press, reissued, 1965

Bickford, Charles, *Bulls, Balls, Bicycles & Actors*, New York, N.Y.: P. S. Eriksson, 1965

Boardman, Gerald, *American Musical Theatre: A Chronicle*, New York, N.Y.: Oxford University Press, 1978

Brahms, Caryl and Ned Sherrin, *Song by Song*, Bolton, England: Ross Anderson Publications, 1984

Brownlow, Kevin, *The Parade's Gone By*, Berkeley, Cal.: University of California Press, 1976 (pb)

Chaplin, Charles, *My Autobiography*, London, England: The Bodley Head; New York, N.Y.: Simon & Schuster, 1964

Chierichetti, David, *Hollywood Director: The Career of Mitchell Leisen*, foreword by Dorothy Lamour, New York, N.Y.: Curtis Books, 1973 (pb)

Cross, Milton and David Ewen, *The Milton Cross New Encyclopedia of the Great Composers and Their Music*, vols. 1 and 2, Garden City, N.Y.: Doubleday & Company, Inc., 1969

deMille, Agnes, *Speak to Me, Dance with Me*, Boston, Mass.: Little, Brown and Company, 1973

———, *Where the Wings Grow*, Garden City, N.Y.: Doubleday & Company, Inc., 1978

———, *Dance to the Piper & And Promenade Home: A Two-Part Autobiography*, New York, N.Y.: DaCapo Press, Inc., 1979 (pb)

———, *Reprieve: A Memoir*, Garden City, N.Y.: Doubleday & Company, Inc., 1981

deMille, Anna George, *Henry George*, Chapel Hill, N.C.: The University of North Carolina Press, 1950

DeMille, Cecil, *The Autobiography of Cecil B. DeMille*, Edited by Donald Hayne, Englewood Cliffs, N.J.: Prentice-Hall, Inc., 1959

———, "How to be a Critic," *Films and Filming*, vol. 4, no. 6 (March 1958)

deMille, Henry C., written with David Belasco, *The Plays of Henry C. DeMille*, New York, N.Y.: Random House, 1965

deMille, William, *Hollywood Saga*, New York, N.Y.: E. P. Dutton & Co., Inc., 1939

Engel, Lehman, *The American Musical Theater*, New York, N.Y.: Collier Books, 1975

Farrar, Geraldine, *Such Sweet Compulsion*, New York, N.Y.: The Greystone Press, 1938

Federal Writers' Project of the Works Progress Administration for the State of California, *California*, New York, N.Y.: Hastings House, 1939

Fordin, Hugh, *Getting to Know Him: A Biography of Oscar Hammerstein II*, New York, N.Y.: Random House, 1977

Frohman, Daniel, *Memories of a Manager*, Garden City, N.Y.: Doubleday, Page & Company, 1911

Gottfried, Martin, *Broadway Musicals*, New York, N.Y.: Harry N. Abrams, Inc., 1979

Green, Stanley, *Encyclopedia of the Musical Theatre*, New York, N.Y.: Da Capo Press, Inc., 1984

Gutterman, Leon, ed., *Wisdom*, vol. 1, no. 10, October 1956

Halliwell, Leslie, *The Filmgoer's Companion*, 7th ed., New York, N.Y.: Charles Scribner's Sons, 1983

———, *Halliwell's Film Guide*, 4th ed., New York, N.Y.: Charles Scribner's Sons, 1985

Hampton, Benjamin B., *History of the American Film Industry From Its Beginnings to 1931* (formerly titled *A History of the Movies*), New York, N.Y.: Dover Publications, Inc., 1970

Head, Edith and Paddy Calistro, *Edith Head's Hollywood*, foreword by Bette Davis, New York, N.Y.: E. P. Dutton, Inc., 1983

Higashi, Sumiko, *Cecil B. DeMille; A Guide to References and Resources*, Boston, Mass.: G. K. Hall & Co., 1985

Higham, Charles, *Cecil B. DeMille*, New York, N.Y.; Charles Scribner's Sons, 1973

———, *Charles Laughton, An Intimate Biography*, Garden City, N.Y.: Doubleday & Company, Inc., 1976

Houseman, John, *Run-Through*, New York, N.Y.: Simon & Schuster, 1972

Johnston, Alva, *The Great Goldwyn*, New York, N.Y.: Random House, Inc., 1937

Katz, Ephraim, *The Film Encyclopedia*, New York, N.Y.: Crowell, 1979

Knight, Arthur, *The Liveliest Art*, New York, N.Y.: The Macmillan Company, 1957

Koury, Phil, *Yes, Mr. DeMille*, New York, N.Y.: Putnam, 1959

Lasky, Jesse L., Jr., *Whatever Happened to Hollywood?*, New York, N.Y.: Funk & Wagnall, 1975

Lasky, Jesse L., *I Blow My Own Horn*, Garden City, N.Y.: Doubleday & Company, Inc., 1957

Lightman, Herb A., ed., *American Cinematographer*, 50th Anniversary Issue, Hollywood, Calif.: ASC Agency, Inc., January 1969

MacGowan, Kenneth, *Behind the Screen, The History and Techniques of the Motion Picture*, New York, N.Y.: Dell Publishing Co., Inc., 1965

Mailer, Norman, *Ancient Evenings*, Boston, Mass.: Little, Brown and Company, 1983

Martin, John, *The Dance: The Story of the Dance Told in Pictures and Text*, New York, N.Y.: Tudor Publishing Company, 1946

Martin, Ralph G., *Jennie, The Life of Lady Randolph Churchill, The Romantic Years 1854–1895*, New York, N.Y., Signet Books, 1970 (pb)

———, *Jennie, The Life of Lady Randolph Churchill, The Dramatic Years 1895–1921*, vol. 2, New York, N.Y.: Signet Books, 1972 (pb)

Marx, Arthur, *Goldwyn: A Biography of the Man Behind the Myth*, New York, N.Y.: Norton, 1976

Morris, Lloyd, *Curtain Time*, New York, N.Y.: Random House, 1953

Mulni, Peter, *Motion Picture Directory*, ch. 5. New York, N.Y.: Falk Publishing Co., 1922

Niven, David, *Bring On the Empty Horses.* New York, N.Y.: Putnam, 1975

Parrish, Robert, *Growing Up In Hollywood*, New York, N.Y.: Harcourt Brace Jovanovich, 1976

Parsons, Louella, *Tell It to Louella.* New York, N.Y.: Putnam, 1961

Pickford, Mary, *Sunshine and Shadow*, foreword

Bibliography

by Cecil B. DeMille, Garden City, N.Y.: Doubleday & Company, Inc., 1955

Pratt, George C., *Spellbound in Darkness, A History of the Silent Film*, Greenwich, Conn.: New York Graphic Society Ltd., revised edition, 1973

Quinn, Anthony, *The Original Sin: A Self-Portrait*, Boston, Mass.: Little, Brown and Company, 1972

Ringgold, Gene and DeWitt Bodeen, *The Films of Cecil B. DeMille*, New York, N.Y.: Citadel Press, 1969

Robinson, David, *Hollywood in the Twenties*, New York, N.Y.: A. S. Barnes & Co., 1968 (pb)

———, *Chaplin, His Life and Art*, New York, N.Y.: McGraw-Hill Book Company, 1985

Rodgers, Richard, *Musical Stages: An Autobiography*, New York, N.Y.: Random House, 1975

Sarris, Andrew, *The American Cinema*, New York, N.Y.: E. P. Dutton & Co., Inc., 1968 (pb)

Schickel, Richard, *D. W. Griffith: An American Life*, New York, N.Y.: A Touchstone Book, Simon & Schuster, Inc., 1984 (pb)

Selznick, David, *Memo from David Selznick*, New York, N.Y.: The Viking Press, 1972

Sight and Sound (London), vol. 27, no. 3, Winter, 1957/58. Review of *The Ten Commandments*

Sobel, Bernard, ed., *The Theatre Handbook and Digest of Plays*, New York, N.Y.: Lothrop, Lee and Shepard Company, 1943

Sperber, A. M., *Murrow: His Life and Times*, New York, N.Y.: Freundlich Books, 1986

Swanson, Gloria, *Swanson on Swanson: An Autobiography*, New York, N.Y.: Pocket Books, 1981 (pb)

Terry, Walter, *Ballet*, New York, N.Y.: Dell, 1959

Webster, Margaret, *Don't Put Your Daughter on the Stage*, New York, N.Y.: Alfred A. Knopf, Inc., 1972

Who's Who in the Theatre, 13th ed., New York, N.Y.: Pitman Publishing Corporation, 1961

Winter, William, *The Life of David Belasco*, 2 vols., New York, N.Y.: Moffat, Yard and Company, 1918

Zierold, Norman, *The Moguls*, New York, N.Y.: Coward-McCann, Inc., 1969

REPOSITORIES FOR DEMILLE MATERIAL

British Film Institute, 127 Charing Cross Road, London WC2H, 0EA, England

Academy of Motion Picture Arts and Sciences, Margaret Herrick Library, 8949 Wilshire Blvd., Beverly Hills, Ca. 90211

University of California at Los Angeles, 405 Hilgard Ave., Los Angeles, Ca. 90024—Film Archive, Melnitz Hall; University Research Library, Special Collections; Theater Arts Library

University of Southern California, University Library, Archives of Performing Arts, Los Angeles, Ca. 90007

Museum of Modern Art, 11 West 53rd St., New York, N.Y. 10019

New York Public Library, Manuscripts and Archives Division, Annex Section, 521 West 43rd St., New York, N.Y. 10018

New York Public Library, Library and Museum of the Performing Arts at Lincoln Center, 111 Amsterdam Ave., New York, N.Y. 10023

Bibliothèque de l'Arsenal, 1 rue de Sully, 75004 Paris, France

Institut des Hautes Etudes Cinématographiques, Palais de Chaillot, 9 Avenue Albert de Mun, 75016 Paris, France

Brigham Young University, Harold B. Lee Library, Arts and Communications Archives, Provo, Utah 84602

George Eastman House, 900 East Avenue, Rochester, N.Y. 14607

Library of Congress, Motion Picture, Broadcasting and Recorded Sound Division, The James Madison Memorial Building, Washington, D.C. 10540

ACKNOWLEDGMENTS

This book could not have been brought to life without the support, assistance, and cooperation of the many surviving members of the DeMille family: Agnes deMille Prude, Richard deMille, Katherine DeMille Quinn, Anthony Quinn, and Cecilia Calvin Presley. Their total honesty, marvelous recall, and intelligent insight added a special dimension to the writing of this family chronicle. My debt to each of them is enormous.

An especial debt of gratitude is owed the very talented Louise Kerz, whose vision, photographic virtuosity, and personal encouragement made this project a unique writing experience.

I would also like to thank Leith Adams, University of Southern California, Archives of Performing Arts; Joyce Aimée, "DeMille Dynasty"; Peter L. Brosnan; Diane Coburn Bruning; Helen Cohen, DeMille Estate; Gilbert Cates, Screen Directors' Guild; Ned Comstock, University of Southern California,

Archives of Performing Arts; Dr. James D'Arc, Brigham Young University; Eleanor M. Gehres, Manager, Denver Public Library; The Henry George School of Social Science, New York; Kristine Krueger, Academy of Motion Picture Arts and Sciences; Mark Locher, Screen Actors Guild; Ronald Marcus, Stamford Historical Society, Connecticut; Meg McSweeny, American Academy of Dramatic Arts, New York; Harry Medved, Screen Actors Guild; Anthony Slide, Academy of Motion Picture Arts and Sciences; Dorothy Swerdlove, Billy Rose Collection, Library of the Performing Arts at Lincoln Center, New York; Roseanne Thesoro, Guadalupe Town Hall; George Turner, American Society of Cinematographers, Los Angeles; Josephine Wyman, Assistant in the Library, The Columbia Historical Society, Washington, D.C.; Melanie Yolles, The New York Public Library.

My appreciation goes as well to Paul Gottlieb, Abrams's enthusiastic publisher, who convinced me to write this book; Phyllis Freeman, my fine editor; John K. Crowley, for his resourceful photographic editing; Dirk Luykx, for his excellent design; Miriam Buhl, editorial assistant; and Barbara Howland, my energetic secretary-assistant.

Once again it comes time to thank my husband, Stephen Citron, whose patient ear and editorial eye can always be relied upon.

But this book could never have been written without the extraordinary lives of all the De-Milles, a family whose contribution to American culture is incalculable and unprecedented. Not only did its members illuminate and elevate the stage, screen, and world of dance, but they represent the capabilities and vision of a family dedicated to the highest levels of art.

INDEX

Index

CREDITS

Photographs and Illustrations

Academy of Motion Picture Arts and Sciences, 8 right, 97 top right, 122; Cecil Beaton, 186; The Bettmann Archive, 87, 102 right, 141 above, 149; Peter Brosnan Collection, 2, 6; Stanley Caiden Collection, 91; Ralph Crane, Life Magazine © Time Inc., 213, 216; The Dance Collection, New York Public Library at Lincoln Center, Astor, Lenox and Tilden Foundations, 104, 119, 124, 161 below, 164, 165, 194 left, 218 below left, 222 right, 223 right; Agnes deMille Collection, 46, 47, 48, 58, 59 below, 62, 68, 78 left, 79, 125, 132 right, 161 above, 162, 171, 187, 191 above, 218 below right, 224 left, 226; Cecil B. DeMille Estate, 12, 18, 20, 30 left, 37, 102 left, 198, 199, 224 right; Cecil B. DeMille Papers, Brigham Young University, 8 left, 29, 30 right, 35 right, 38, 53, 57, 61, 66, 67, 69, 71, 76, 88, 89, 90, 96, 98 right, 100 above and lower right, 101 right, 110, 114 right, 134, 135, 139 above right and left, 141 below, 142, 145, 152, 153, 154, 156, 176, 177, 201, 211 above, 212 below, 217; Cecilia Presley, 157, 218 above; William deMille Collection, Archives of Performing Arts (USC), 60, 78 right, 80; Judith Dowelin, 106; Fred Fehl/The Dance Collection, New York Public Library at Lincoln Center, 164; Phyllis Freeman, 199; Front Row Center, West Hollywood, Ca., 45; Henry George Institute, N.Y., 26; The Henry George School of Social Science, 35; Courtesy of Santo Loquasto, 221; Angus McBean/The Agnes deMille Collection, 150; Gjon Mili, Life Magazine © Time Inc., 168–69; Jack Mitchell, 223, 226; Museum of the City of New York, Theatre Collection, 41 above; Irving Penn/Agnes deMille Collection, 218; Billy Rose Theatre Collection, New York Public Library at Lincoln Center, Astor, Lenox and Tilden Foundations, 19, 41 below, 59 above, 132 left, 138, 144, 179, 182, 184 below right and left, 188, 190, 191 below, 194 right, 203, 211 below, 212 above, 221 above center, 222 left, 223 left; Stanley Simmons Collection, 221 above right, left, below; Soichi Sunami/The Dance Collection, New York Public Library at Lincoln Center, 117–18; Frances Triest Collection, 82; Carl Van Vechten/The Dance Collection, New York Public Library at Lincoln Center, 151; Jerry Vermilye, 121, 173; Marc Wanamaker/Bison Archives, 72, 75, 81, 97 lower right, 100 lower left, 101 left, 108, 114 left, 139 below, 207; Miles White Collection, 168, 184 above right and left, 195; Courtesy of The White House, 224.

Film Copyrights

8, 96–97: *The Ten Commandments*, © 1923 Paramount Pictures Corporation. All rights reserved. Courtesy of Paramount Pictures Corporation. 58: *The Warrens of Virginia*, © 1924 Twentieth Century Fox Film Corporation. 60: *Anton, the Terrible*, © 1916 Paramount Pictures Corporation. All rights reserved. Courtesy of Paramount Pictures Corporation. 66 left: *The Whispering Chorus*, © 1918 Paramount Pictures Corporation. All rights reserved. Courtesy of Paramount Pictures Corporation. 71: *Joan the Woman*, © 1916 Paramount Pictures Corporation. All rights reserved. Courtesy of Paramount Pictures Corporation. 78 right: *The Ragamuffin*, © 1916 Paramount Pictures Corporation. All rights reserved. Courtesy of Paramount Pictures Corporation. 88: *Male and Female*, © 1919 Paramount Pictures Corporation. All rights reserved. Courtesy of Paramount Pictures Corporation. 108: *Ice Bound*, © 1924 Paramount Pictures Corporation. All rights reserved. Courtesy of Paramount Pictures Corporation. 121: *Sign of the Cross*, 1932, Copyright © by Universal Pictures, a Division of Universal City Studios, Inc. All Rights Reserved. Courtesy of MCA Publishing Rights, a Division of MCA, Inc. 132 left: *Four Frightened People*, 1934, Copyright © by Universal Pictures, a Division of Universal City Studios, Inc. All Rights Reserved. Courtesy of MCA Publishing Rights, a Division of MCA, Inc. 134–35: *Cleopatra*, 1934, Copyright © by Universal Pictures, a Division of Universal City Studios, Inc. All Rights Reserved. Courtesy of MCA Publishing Rights, a Division of MCA, Inc. 138: *The Crusades*, 1935, Copyright © by Universal Pictures, a Division of Universal City Studios, Inc. All Rights Reserved. Courtesy of MCA Publishing Rights, a Division of MCA, Inc. 141: *The Plainsman*, 1936, Copyright © by Universal Pictures, a Division of Universal City Studios, Inc. All Rights Reserved. Courtesy of MCA Publishing Rights, a Division of MCA, Inc. 144: *The Buccaneer*, © 1958 Paramount Pictures Corporation. All rights reserved. Courtesy of Paramount Pictures Corporation. 153: *Northwest Mounted Police*, 1940, Copyright © by Universal Pictures, a Division of Universal City Studios, Inc. All Rights Reserved. Courtesy of MCA Publishing Rights, a Division of MCA, Inc. 173: *The Story of Dr. Wassell*, 1944, Copyright © by Universal Pictures, a Division of Universal City Studios, Inc. All Rights Reserved. Courtesy of MCA Publishing Rights, a Division of MCA, Inc. 177: *Unconquered*, 1947, Copyright © by Universal Pictures, a Division of Universal City Studios, Inc. All Rights Reserved. Courtesy of MCA Publishing Rights, a Division of MCA, Inc. 201: *Sunset Boulevard*, © 1950 Paramount Pictures Corporation. All rights reserved. Courtesy of Paramount Pictures Corporation. 198–99 and back jacket: *Samson and Delilah*, © 1949 Paramount Pictures Corporation. All rights reserved. Courtesy of Paramount Pictures Corporation. 203: *The Greatest Show on Earth* © 1952 Paramount Pictures Corporation. All rights reserved. Courtesy of Paramount Pictures Corporation. 211, 212 above, 213: *The Ten Commandments*, © 1956 Paramount Pictures Corporation. All rights reserved. Courtesy of Paramount Pictures Corporation.